OECD SKILLS OUTLOOK 2015

YOUTH, SKILLS AND EMPLOYABILITY

This work is published on the responsibility of the Secretary-General of the OECD. The opinions expressed and arguments employed herein do not necessarily reflect the official views of the OECD member countries.

This document and any map included herein are without prejudice to the status of or sovereignty over any territory, to the delimitation of international frontiers and boundaries and to the name of any territory, city or area.

Please cite this publication as:
OECD (2015), *OECD Skills Outlook 2015: Youth, Skills and Employability*, OECD Publishing.
http://dx.doi.org/10.1787/9789264234178-en

ISBN 978-92-64-21087-5 (print)
ISBN 978-92-64-23417-8 (PDF)

The statistical data for Israel are supplied by and under the responsibility of the relevant Israeli authorities. The use of such data by the OECD is without prejudice to the status of the Golan Heights, East Jerusalem and Israeli settlements in the West Bank under the terms of international law.

Photo credits:
© Jaroslav Machacek/Shutterstock
© Christian Schwier
© goodluz
© Michael Jung /Shutterstock

Corrigenda to OECD publications may be found on line at: *www.oecd.org/publishing/corrigenda*.

Foreword

The transition from school to work has never been particularly easy; but for millions of young people in OECD countries, it has become nearly impossible. Seven years after the 2008 global economic crisis, more than 35 million 16-29 year-olds across OECD countries are neither employed nor in education or training. In fact, young people are twice as likely as prime-age workers to be unemployed. Many of the young people who do manage to find work are not using the skills they acquired during their schooling. And one in four young people who are employed is working on a temporary contract – which limits the opportunities to advance in a career or even to participate in further training. Giving young people a good start to their independent working lives has become a major challenge across OECD countries today.

The inaugural edition of the *OECD Skills Outlook*, published in 2013, reported the results from the first round of the Survey of Adult Skills, a product of the OECD Programme for the International Assessment of Adult Competencies (PIAAC). This edition expands on some of those findings to create a detailed picture of how young people acquire and use their skills – and the potential barriers they face to doing both.

For example, the Survey of Adult Skills shows that 10% of new graduates have poor literacy skills and 14% have poor numeracy skills – not an attractive profile for potential employers. In addition, work and education are too often separate worlds: less than 50% of students in vocational education and training programmes, and less than 40% of students in academic programmes in the 22 OECD countries and regions covered by the Survey of Adult Skills, were participating in any kind of work-based learning at the time of the survey.

The *OECD Skills Outlook 2015: Youth, Skills and Employability* makes clear that where education and the labour market co-exist as two separate worlds, it is very difficult for young people to manage the transition from one to the other. Young people are best integrated into the world of work when education systems are flexible and responsive to the needs of the labour market, when employers are engaged in both designing and providing education programmes, when young people have access to high-quality career guidance and further education that can help them to match their skills to prospective jobs, and when institutionalised obstacles to enter the labour market, even for those with the right skills, are removed.

One of the central messages of this volume is that a concerted effort – by education providers, the labour market, tax and social institutions, employer and employee organisations, and parents and young people themselves – is needed to create these conditions. Youth unemployment and underemployment have adverse and long-lasting consequences for both the individuals and the countries involved. It is in everyone's interest, then, to work together so that young people have a smoother and faster route from the classroom to the workplace.

Acknowledgements

The Skills Outlook is the outcome of close collaboration among several directorates in the OECD. It has been guided by the Skills Strategy Advisory Group and has greatly benefited from feedback and comments from national government delegates. The Outlook was prepared by Stéphanie Jamet and Margarita Kalamova under the oversight of Deborah Roseveare and Andreas Schleicher. It has benefited from comments and contributions from Stjin Broecke, Bert Brys, Simon Field, Francesca Froy, Sylvain Giguere, Paulina Granados Zambrano, Corinne Heckman, Kathrin Hoeckel, Shinyoung Jeon, Mark Keese, David Khoudour, Ineke Litjens, Karen Maguire, Mattias Mano, Guillermo Montt, Laura McDonald, Patricia Mangeol, Fabrice Murtin, Pierce O'Reilly, Marco Paccagnella, Glenda Quintini, Ingrid Teisseire-Lacoste and William Thorn. Marilyn Achiron, Marika Boiron, Célia Braga-Schich, Cassandra Davis, Laura McDonald and Anne-Lise Prigent provided valuable support in the editorial and production process.

Table of Contents

FIGURES

TABLES

This book has...

StatLinkS

A service that delivers Excel® files from the printed page!

Look for the *StatLinks* at the bottom left-hand corner of the tables or graphs in this book. To download the matching Excel® spreadsheet, just type the link into your Internet browser, starting with the *http://dx.doi.org* prefix.
If you're reading the PDF e-book edition, and your PC is connected to the Internet, simply click on the link. You'll find *StatLinks* appearing in more OECD books.

Reader's Guide

Data underlying the figures and country coverage

Data presented in this publication come from various sources including the Survey of Adult Skills (a product of the OECD Programme for the International Assessment of Adult Competencies or PIAAC), the OECD Programme for International Student Assessment (PISA), Education at a Glance, and the OECD Employment and Labour Market Statistics database. Data sources are specified below the tables and figures.

The publication presents results for OECD countries and sub-national entities covered by the Survey of Adult Skills and, when the information is available, for other OECD member countries and some partner countries.

Missing data are denoted with the symbol "m".

Data estimates, including mean scores, proportions, odds ratios and standard errors, are generally rounded to one decimal place.

The statistical data for Israel are supplied by and under the responsibility of the relevant Israeli authorities. The use of such data by the OECD is without prejudice to the status of the Golan Heights, East Jerusalem and Israeli settlements in the West Bank under the terms of international law.

StatLinks

A StatLink URL address is provided under each figure. Readers using the pdf version of the report can simply click on the relevant StatLinks url to either open or download an Excel® worksheet containing the corresponding figure. Readers of the print version can access the Excel® worksheet by typing the StatLink address in their Internet browser.

Calculating international averages (means)

Most figures and tables presented in this report and in the web package include a cross-country average in addition to values for individual countries or sub-national entities. The average in each figure or table corresponds to the arithmetic mean of the respective estimates for each of the OECD member countries included in the figure or table.

Statistical significance

Differences considered to be statistically significant from either zero or between estimates are based on the 5% level of significance, unless otherwise stated.

Education levels

The classification of levels of education is based on the International Standard Classification of Education (ISCED 1997).

Abbreviations

ALMP active labour market policies

EPL employment protection legislation

GDP Gross Domestic Product

ISCED International Standard Classification of Education

ISCO International Standard Classification of Occupations

ICT information and communication technologies

MOOC massive open online courses

NEET neither employed nor in education or training

VET vocational education and training

Executive Summary

In 2013, 39 million 16-29 year-olds across OECD countries were neither employed nor in education or training (NEET) – 5 million more than before the economic crisis of 2008. And estimates for 2014 show little improvement. The numbers are particularly high in southern European countries that were hardest hit by the crisis. In Greece and Spain, for example, more than 25% of young adults were NEET in 2013. More worrying still: around half of all NEETs – some 20 million young people – are out of school and not looking for work. As such, they may have dropped off the radar of their country's education, social, and labour market systems.

These numbers represent not only a personal calamity for those individuals concerned, but a squandered investment, because the skills acquired during education are not being put to productive use, and a potential burden for their countries too: from lower tax revenues, higher welfare payments, and the social instability that may arise when part of the population is out of work and demoralised. Young people should be an asset to the economy, not a potential liability.

What lies at the root of this unacceptable waste of human potential? Among other things, too many young people leave education without having acquired the right skills and so have trouble finding work. According to the Survey of Adult Skills, a product of the OECD Programme for the International Assessment of Adult Competencies (PIAAC), 10% of new graduates have poor literacy skills and 14% have poor numeracy skills. More than 40% of those who left school before completing their upper secondary education have poor numeracy and literacy skills.

In addition, too many young people leave education with little experience of the world of work. Less than 50% of students in vocational education and training (VET) programmes, and less than 40% of students in academic programmes in the 22 OECD countries and regions covered by the Survey of Adult Skills, are participating in any kind of work-based learning.

Even young people with strong skills have trouble finding work. Many firms find it too expensive to hire individuals with no labour market experience. Indeed, young people are twice as likely to be unemployed as prime-age adults.

But even those young people who succeed in entering the labour market often face institutionalised obstacles to developing their skills and advancing their careers. For example, one in four employed young people is on a temporary contract. These workers tend to use their skills less and have fewer training opportunities than workers on permanent contracts. Meanwhile, 12% of employed young people are overqualified for their job. This means that some of their skills are left untapped and unused, and that their employers are not fully benefitting from the investment in these young people.

Given the slow rate of growth predicted for many OECD countries, particularly those in Europe, in the coming few years, the picture is unlikely to brighten anytime soon. What can be done in the meantime?

ENSURE THAT ALL YOUNG PEOPLE LEAVE SCHOOL WITH A RANGE OF RELEVANT SKILLS

Young people need to have a wide range of skills – cognitive, social and emotional – to be successful in all areas of their lives. The OECD Programme for International Student Assessment (PISA) finds a strong association between attendance in pre-primary education and better performance in reading, mathematics and science later on, particularly among socio-economically disadvantaged students. Countries can offer high-quality pre-primary education for all children to help mitigate disparities in education outcomes and to give every child a strong start to their education careers.

Teachers and school leaders can also identify low achievers early on to provide them with the support or special programmes they may need to help them attain sufficient proficiency in reading, mathematics and science, develop their social and emotional skills, and prevent them from dropping out of school entirely.

HELP SCHOOL LEAVERS TO ENTER THE LABOUR MARKET

Educators and employers can work together to ensure that students acquire the kinds of skills in demand and that those skills are used from the beginning of a young person's working life. Work-based learning can be integrated into both VET and academic post-secondary programmes. This kind of learning benefits both students and employers: students become familiar with the world of work and the kinds of skills – including social and emotional skills, such as communication and working with others – that are valued in the workplace; and employers get to know potential new hires – people they have trained to their own standards.

DISMANTLE INSTITUTIONAL BARRIERS TO YOUTH EMPLOYMENT

As many young people enter the labour market on temporary contracts, it is important to ensure that these temporary jobs are "stepping stones" into more stable employment, rather than a series of precarious situations that raise the risk of young people becoming unemployed. The asymmetry between job-protection provisions that make it costly to firms to convert fixed-term contracts into permanent contracts should be reduced. Minimum wages, taxes and social contributions should all be scrutinised and, if necessary, adjusted when trying to reduce the cost to employers of hiring youth with little work experience.

IDENTIFY AND HELP THOSE NEETS NOW "OFF THE RADAR" TO RE-ENGAGE

Governments need to identify the millions of young people who are NEET and who are having trouble entering the labour market or have become disengaged. Public employment services, social institutions and education and training systems can help these youth to find a job or re-enter some form of second-chance education or training. A system of mutual obligations between young people and employment and educational institutions can help to both identify and assist these NEETs. In return for receiving social benefits, young people would be required to register with social institutions or public employment services, and take actions to prepare for the labour market, including by participating in further education and training.

FACILITATE BETTER MATCHES BETWEEN YOUNG PEOPLE'S SKILLS AND JOBS

Anticipating the skills needed in the work force and ensuring that these skills are developed in education and training systems would limit the incidence of mismatch between young people's skills and jobs. And since many employers find it difficult to assess the skills of new young workers, especially in countries with complex education systems, education providers and the business sector can work together to design qualifications frameworks that accurately reflect the actual skills of new graduates.

1

Designing a comprehensive strategy to foster young people's skills and employability

Youth unemployment rates remain high in most OECD countries and, according to the most recent data, more than 15% of youth aged 16-29 were neither in employment nor in education or training in OECD countries in 2013. Countries have already done a lot to raise youth skills and employability. This chapter offers an overview of the whole report, and discusses how countries can continue with reforms by adopting a consistent and comprehensive strategy and engaging all stakeholders.

BETTER YOUTH OUTCOMES FOR INCLUSIVE GROWTH

Young people, those who are aged between 16 and 29 years old, have been strongly hit by the global economic crisis and the scars are still there today. Youth unemployment rates reached high levels at the height of the crisis and since then, have barely changed (Figure 1.1, Panel A). In 2013, 18 million young adults in OECD countries were unemployed. However, youth unemployment encompasses only part of the youth challenge. Some youth leave education and delay their entry into the labour market or become discouraged and withdraw from the labour force. When those who are not in education and not even looking for a job are added to the young unemployed, the number is more than doubled: 39 million young adults in OECD countries were neither in employment nor in education or training in 2013, the so-called NEET group. The NEET rate of the 16-29 year-olds has increased in most OECD countries with the crisis (Figure 1.1, Panel B).

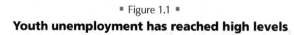

▪ Figure 1.1 ▪

Youth unemployment has reached high levels

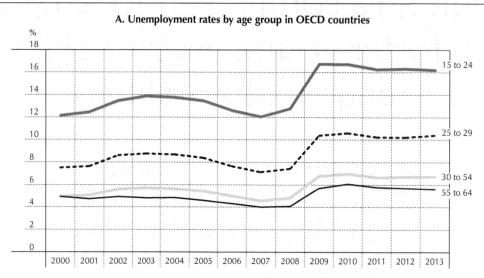

A. Unemployment rates by age group in OECD countries

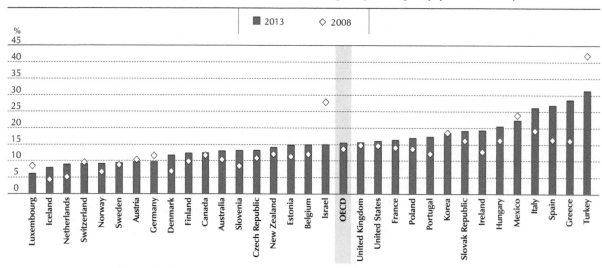

B. Share of youth neither employed nor in education or training as a percentage of population, 15-29 year-olds

Notes: For Korea, data on the NEET rate are from 2012.

Sources: OECD (2015a), *Education at a Glance Interim Report: Update of Employment and Educational Attainment Indicators*, OECD, Paris, *www.oecd.org/edu/EAG-Interim-report.pdf*; *OECD Employment and Labour Market Statistics* (database), *http://dx.doi.org/10.1787/lfs-lms-data-en*.

StatLink ⟐⟐ http://dx.doi.org/10.1787/888933214364

Bad labour market outcomes for youth constitute not only a personal crisis for those who cannot find work and may be permanently scarred by late entry into the labour force; countries also suffer, from wasted investment, lower tax revenues, higher welfare payments, and the social instability that arises when part of the population is out of work and demoralised. Poverty risk for youth is higher than for the whole population in most OECD countries. Between 2007 and 2011, youth have been suffering the most severe income losses and the gap in poverty risk between youth and the whole population has increased in a number of countries, such as Denmark, France, Greece, Norway and New Zealand (OECD, 2015b; Figure 1.2). Ensuring that youth can participate in the economy and society is crucial to securing thriving communities and promoting social cohesion, as well as achieving inclusive growth.

■ Figure 1.2 ■

In most OECD countries, youth are more exposed to the risk of poverty

Relative poverty rate of the 18-25 year-olds; entire population in each year = 100

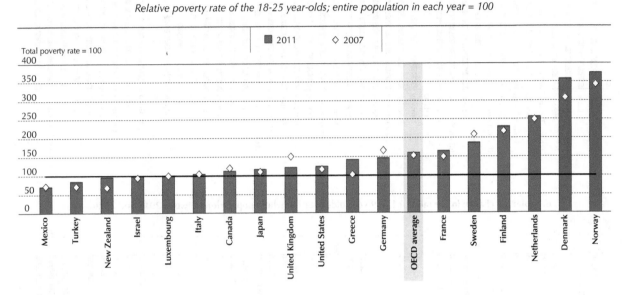

Notes: The relative poverty rate for youth is higher than for the whole population in countries above the black line and lower than for the whole population in countries below the line.

Source: *OECD Income Distribution Database.*

StatLink http://dx.doi.org/10.1787/888933214371

Looking forward, labour markets are expected to slowly but gradually recover in most OECD countries. In the long term, the share of youth in the population will shrink (OECD, 2014a; Figure 1.3). However, as the causes of the problems faced by youth in joining the labour market are partly deeply rooted, these problems will not simply disappear with time. Countries with rapidly ageing populations, and shrinking youth cohorts, will become even more dependent on successful outcomes for youth for future fiscal sustainability, growth and wellbeing.

Improving labour market outcomes for youth in the short and long-term requires raising their employability, which is not only their ability to gain, but also to maintain employment over the course of their working life. Countries have done a lot to raise youth employability. Over the last two years, countries have given priority to education policies and to active labour market policies (ALMPs), in order to invest in skills as a source of growth and to address the persistence of unemployment in a context of weak recovery while the pace of structural reforms has generally slowed down (OECD, 2015b). At the same time, reforms have decelerated in areas such as the wage setting system and employment protection legislation, perhaps due to legitimate concerns that some of these reforms may have contributed to rising inequalities.

These trends raise the question of what else countries can do to strengthen youth employability, or perhaps even more importantly, how they can reform in a better way to achieve better outcomes. At the same time, it should be acknowledged that some reforms take time to fully deliver their effects, as is the case with education, for instance. Many countries also still face deteriorated global economic conditions or a very weak recovery, which makes it difficult to tackle youth employment challenges. Nonetheless, continuing with structural reforms makes the economy more resilient and would help mitigate the impact of future economic shocks on youth. However, reforms could be more consistent over time and more comprehensive, and they could involve stronger co-operation between all stakeholders. Policies could put more focus on skills and individual needs. The impact of reforms and policies could also be assessed more regularly.

▪ Figure 1.3 ▪

The share of youth in the population is projected to fall by 2020

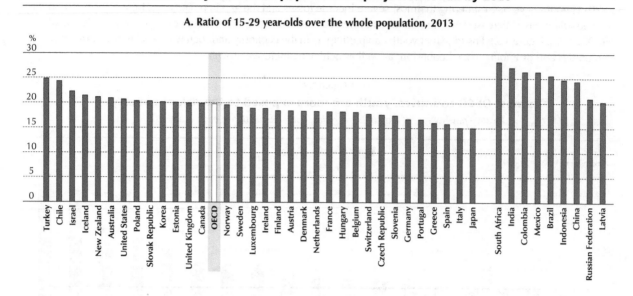

A. Ratio of 15-29 year-olds over the whole population, 2013

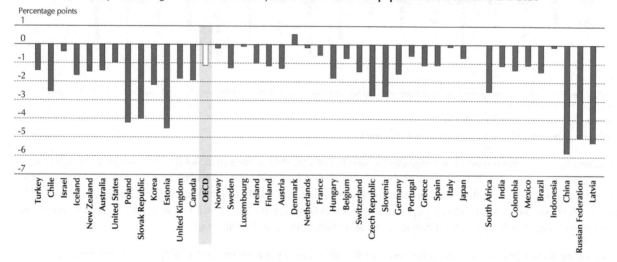

B. Projected change in the ratio of 15-29 year-olds over the whole population between 2013 and 2020

Source: *OECD Historical Population Data and Projections Database.*
StatLink ⇪ http://dx.doi.org/10.1787/888933214389

A COMPREHENSIVE AND CONSISTENT STRATEGY FOR BETTER OUTCOMES

The employability of youth depends on the skills they can bring to the labour market – to get a job today, but also the ability to adapt to future labour market needs, whatever they may be. Youth skills are of little value if youth remain outside or on the margins of the labour market, or if their skills are not used effectively in the workplace. Youth typically face many barriers to get into the labour market, and those with low social capital find it even harder. Furthermore, many employed youth are in precarious jobs and do not use their skills efficiently. Indeed, skills that are not used are likely to atrophy, undermining youth employability, and leading to frustration and potentially social exclusion.

In 2013, the OECD launched its Action Plan for Youth that sets the main principles for actions to cope with today's high youth unemployment and strengthen the long-term employment prospects for young people (Box 1.1). This publication applies the OECD Skills Strategy framework (OECD, 2012) to the challenge of youth employability: it examines how countries can develop relevant skills among youth, bring their skills to the labour market and use their skills effectively to achieve better economic and social outcomes.

20 OECD SKILLS OUTLOOK 2015: YOUTH, SKILLS AND EMPLOYABILITY

Box 1.1 **Key elements of the OECD Action Plan for Youth**

Tackle the current youth unemployment crisis

- Tackle weak aggregate demand and boost job creation.

- Provide adequate income support to unemployed youth until labour market conditions improve, but subject to strict mutual obligations.

- Maintain, and where possible expand, cost-effective active labour market measures.

- Tackle demand-side barriers to the employment of low-skilled youth.

- Encourage employers to continue or expand quality apprenticeship and internship programmes.

Strengthen the long-term employment prospects of youth

- Strengthen the education system and prepare all young people for the world of work.

- Strengthen the role and effectiveness of vocational education and training.

- Assist the transition to the world of work.

- Reshape labour market policy and institutions to facilitate access to employment and tackle social exclusion.

Source: OECD (2013a), "The OECD Action Plan for Youth: Giving Youth a Better Start in the Labour Market", *www.oecd.org/employment/Action-plan-youth.pdf* and *www.oecd.org/employment/action-plan-youth.htm*.

Policies to foster youth employability can go in various directions:

- Countries can, through the education system, develop the skills needed for participation in the labour market. However, this requires developing a broad range of skills that raise youth employability in the short term (and ease their transition to the labour market) as well as in the long term, by giving people the capacity to continue to learn, develop further and adapt their knowledge to labour market needs. Youth often lack certain social and emotional skills such as those involved in working in teams, which can undermine the use of their cognitive skills. Education systems also need to be inclusive and provide equal opportunity to all youth.

- Even though most youth will find a job, more efforts could be made to ease transition from school to the labour market, ensuring that young people do not temporarily end up in situations in which they are neither in the education system nor in employment. Labour market institutions and policies need to be further reformed to ease the transition to the labour market but also to reintegrate those who have disengaged from it.

- Even when young people are employed, their skills are not always used in an efficient manner. Their skills are more frequently underutilised than with prime-age workers and many youth are not "well matched". In addition to possibly undermining youth employability in the longer term, it is also a missed opportunity for the economy and society if a large set of skills is not put to effective use. While the extent and consequences of the underutilisation of the skills of young workers are perhaps more difficult to apprehend, there could be more reflection, discussion and action with regard to making the best use of talent and skills of new graduates and young people.

A comprehensive and consistent approach is needed to raise youth skills and employability in these various dimensions. Countries need to develop a whole-of-government strategy for more coherent policy settings. It requires strengthening education, labour market, tax and social institutions with a greater emphasis on the implications of such reforms on youth skills and employability.

HOW COUNTRIES HAVE PERFORMED IN TERMS OF YOUTH SKILLS AND EMPLOYABILITY IN RECENT YEARS

Young people need the skills to learn throughout life in order to be resilient and able to adapt to the inevitable changes that will occur over their lifetimes. A broad range of skills matters for employability and, more generally, success in society (Box 1.2). Education attainment but also socio-economic background and the use of skills at work influence young people's skills (Box 1.3).

Box 1.2 What skills are needed in the labour market?

Following the conceptual framework developed in OECD (2015c), skills are broadly defined as individual characteristics that drive individual well-being and socio-economic progress. Individuals need a multiplicity of skills to achieve diverse life goals.

Cognitive skills involve the understanding, interpretation, analysis and communication of complex information and the ability to apply this information in situations of everyday life. These skills are general in nature and relevant for all kinds of occupations, considered necessary to provide a foundation for effective and successful participation in the social and economic life of advanced economies. The OECD has developed two major data instruments to assess these skills: the OECD Programme for International Student Assessment (PISA) assessing 15-year-olds in literacy, numeracy and science; and the Survey of Adult Skills, a product of the OECD Programme for the International Assessment of Adult Competencies (PIAAC) assessing adults aged 16-65 in literacy, numeracy and problem solving in technology-rich environments, also called "information-processing skills".

Social and emotional skills are skills involved in working with others (friendliness, respect, caring), in achieving goals (perseverance, self-control, passion for goals) and in managing emotions (calm, optimism, confidence). They are based on recognised taxonomies in personality psychology, particularly the "Big Five" factors (extraversion, agreeableness, conscientiousness, emotional stability, and openness). So far, no comprehensive measures exist, but conceptual work is being carried out to evaluate the potential of developing measurement instruments in the future (OECD, 2015c).

Some skills come from the interaction of cognitive and social and emotional skills. For instance, this is the case of creativity and critical thinking, which are often called "21st-century skills" and are expected to contribute to the capacity to adapt to major changes and to innovate. Creativity involves producing content that is not only novel, original and unexpected but also appropriate, useful and adapted to the task at hand. It has been found to be related to measures of intelligence, as well as social and emotional skills. Critical thinking involves the ability to think strategically and apply the rules to new situations to solve problems. This skill has a strong cognitive component but also incorporates aspects of openness to new experience, such as imagination and unconventionality.

Job and occupation-specific skills – sometimes called technical skills are also demanded by employers. Unlike cognitive and social and emotional skills, they are not relevant for, and portable between, all occupations, but are specific to one occupation. They are typically reflected in the qualification a person holds, but there are currently no measurement instruments available at the international level to assess and compare those skills (OECD, 2010).

All these skills are valued by employers. In surveys, employers mention a combination of some social and emotional skills, job and occupation-specific skills and cognitive skills as the most important when recruiting higher education graduates (Humburg, van der Velden and Verhagen, 2013). Empirical analyses based on employer surveys show that lack of social and emotional skills can create a strong barrier to employment, especially for low-skilled jobs (Heckman and Kautz, 2013).

Box 1.3. Synergies between education, skills and employability

Having the relevant skills increases the chance of succeeding at school and finding a job. However, studying and/or having a job can help to further develop skills. Likewise, young people without a strong skills foundation are more likely to drop out of school and face difficulties finding jobs while those who drop out and are jobless can hardly maintain and enhance their skills. Policies can influence the dynamics between skills, education and employment, and ensure that a larger share of youth follow the virtuous circle of skills which leads to graduation and employment and henceforth to better skills.

Analysis based on the Survey of Adult Skills allows the assessment of the determinants of employment. The *OECD Employment Outlook 2014* shows that educational attainment and skills affect the probability of finding a job and its level of pay (OECD, 2014b). As education attainment is easily observable for employers, it acts as a powerful signalling device for youth trying to enter the labour market. The *OECD Skills Outlook 2013* has also shown the importance of cognitive skills (literacy, numeracy and problem solving in technology-rich environments) on labour market outcomes (OECD, 2013b).

...

The Survey of Adult Skills also allows the assessment of the determinants of skills, in particular certain cognitive skills. As shown in Figure A, having attained at least an upper secondary education reduces the probability of having low literacy skills. However, individuals with a similar level of education may not have the same skills, as skill formation depends on the quality of the education system in addition to other factors. These factors include socio-economic background and the use of skills. Thus having at least one educated parent is associated with lower probability of having low literacy skills. Similarly, being a native speaker or native-born is associated with lower probability of having low literacy skills. Further work is needed to better understand the causality in the relationships between education, skills and jobs.

■ Figure A ■

The relationship between the probability of having low literacy skills, educational attainment, socio-economic background and use of skills

16-29 year-olds, 2012

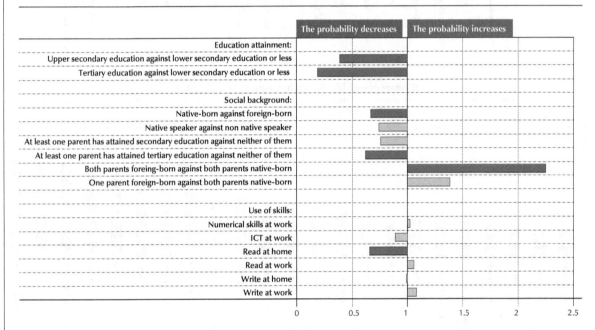

Notes: Youth with low literacy skills are those who score below 226 points in the Survey of Adult Skills (PIAAC). The figure shows the results of a logit regression on all countries accounting for gender, occupation, use of social and emotional skills, number of books at home, health status and country fixed effects. Statistically significant values are shown in darker tones.

Source: OECD calculations based on the *Survey of Adult Skills (PIAAC) (2012)* (database).

StatLink ╦╕╝ http://dx.doi.org/10.1787/888933214391

The Survey of Adult Skills (PIAAC) provides internationally comparable data on a range of cognitive skills (literacy, numeracy and problem solving in technology-rich environments) that are possessed by the adult population in a group of countries (OECD, 2013b). The Survey of Adult Skills reveals a number of key features. First, in many countries, a significant share of youth score at the lowest levels of skills on the literacy and numeracy scales (Figure 1.4). These results are consistent with PISA outcomes, which show that the share of 15-year-old students who fail to reach the basic level of performance in mathematics and reading is still high in many OECD countries, and substantial in most emerging economies covered by the assessment. Second, compared to prime-age adults, on average, youth have higher cognitive skills in most countries partly because of increasing educational enrolment and attainment over time (OECD, 2013a). This raises the question about the specific barriers young people may face to become employed, be it their lack of labour market experience or the effect of labour market institutions.

■ Figure 1.4 ■

Too many youth have low cognitive skills

A. Share of individuals with low literacy skills, 2012

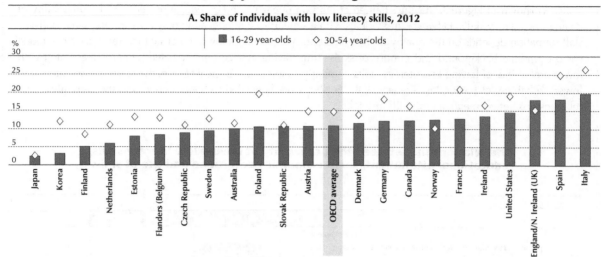

B. Share of individuals with low numeracy skills, 2012

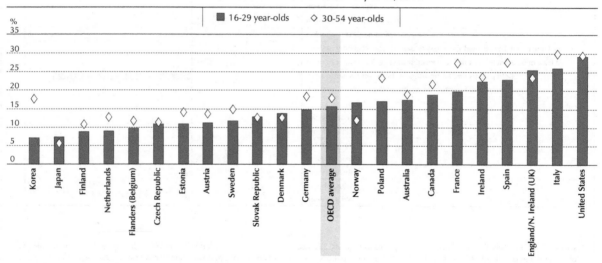

C. Share of individuals with low problem solving skills in technology-rich environments, 2012

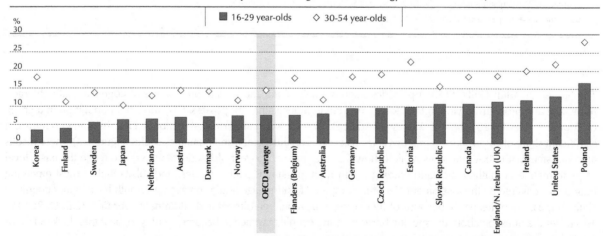

Notes: Results present the share of 16-29 year-olds and of 30-54 year-olds failing to reach Proficiency Level 2 in literacy and numeracy and Proficiency Level 1 in problem solving in technology-rich environment (considered low-skilled adults here). The OECD average result is based on the sample of OECD countries/regions assessed in the Survey of Adult Skills.

Source: OECD calculations based on the *Survey of Adult Skills (PIAAC) (2012)* (database).

StatLink ▄▇▆ http://dx.doi.org/10.1787/888933214406

The Skills Scoreboard on youth employability aims to capture the various dimensions of countries' performance in terms of youth skills and employability over the recent past years (Box 1.4). It assesses:

- How countries develop young people's skills and prepare them for the labour market by looking at the overall levels of youth skills, the inclusiveness of the development of skills and the development of skills among students.

- The extent to which youth are successful in their transitions from school to the labour market by looking at the integration of youth into the labour market as well at the distance of the NEET group to the labour market.

- How youth can develop further their employability through effective use of their skills at work.

Box 1.4 **Skills Scoreboard on youth employability: Methodology**

The Skills Scoreboard on youth employability aims to measure how countries have performed in recent years along the various dimensions of youth employability. The main dimensions that are considered are (six dimensions):

- On the development of young people's skills: 1) the skills of youth; 2) the inclusiveness of the development of skills; and 3) the students' skills and their attachment to the labour market.

- On youth and the labour market: 1) the integration of youth into the labour market; 2) the distance of the NEETs to the labour market.

- On the use of skills at work: the promotion of skill use in the workplace.

The Skills Scoreboard measures countries' outcomes for youth employability and not directly policies or enabling framework conditions. These outcomes are the result of policies in various areas but are also influenced by demographic, social and economic circumstances specific to countries. As structural reforms and policies take time to deliver their effects and due to data availability, outcomes according to the Skills Scoreboard do not reflect the full impact of past policies, especially the most recent ones.

For each of the six dimensions of youth employability, a summary indicator is calculated and presented in Table 1.1. The summary indicator aggregates a set of indicators coming from various OECD databases and the Survey of Adult Skills. The choice of indicators and their link to the dimensions of employability are discussed and presented in the relevant chapters of the publication (Chapter 2 for the three summary indicators on the development of young people's skills, Chapter 4 for the two summary indicators on youth and the labour market and Chapter 6 for the summary indicator on the use of skills at work). Prior to the aggregation, each indicator has been normalised. The summary indicator for each category is calculated as a simple average of indicators.

Countries are ranked according to the summary indicators. The scoreboard shows countries that perform in the bottom 25%, in the top 25% and those around the OECD average (in the remaining part of the distribution). A sharp threshold has been applied and therefore, some countries can be classified in one group (e.g. the bottom 25%) but remain close to the other group (e.g. average).

As with all exercises of this nature, the outcomes of the Skills Scoreboard on Youth Employability should be interpreted carefully:

- The Scoreboard does not reflect the impact of recent policies.

- Due to data availability, indicators can only provide imperfect measures of youth skills and employability in a country and their choice can always been criticised.

- The Scoreboard is based on various dataset including the Survey of Adult Skills and therefore covers only OECD countries which participated in this survey.

- The Scoreboard shows how countries perform relatively to the OECD average, not to an optimal situation.

The Scoreboard reflects countries' performance along these dimensions in 2012-2013 (Table 1.1). It indicates the biggest challenges countries face in improving the skills and raising the employability of their youth, however countries may have already taken action to address the pressing issues and moreover outcomes may improve with better global conditions. Yet, cyclical unemployment for a long period of time can lead to structural unemployment.

■ Table 1.1 ■

Skills Scoreboard on youth employability: Summary indicators

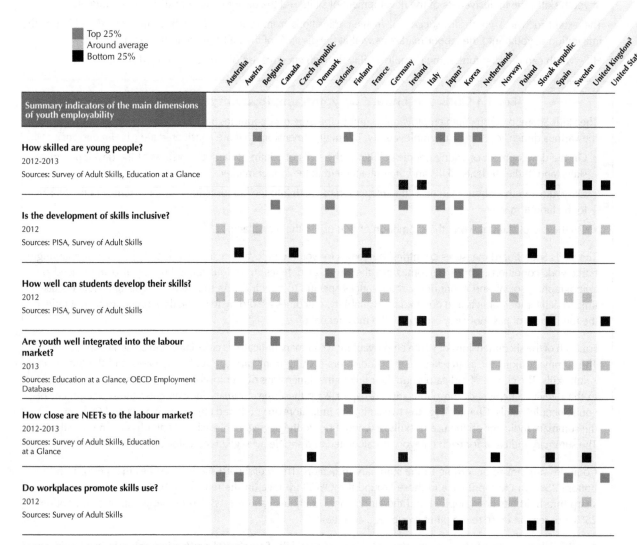

1. All indicators from the Survey of Adult Skills for Belgium refer to Flanders.
2. For Japan, because of data availability: i) the summary indicator "Are youth well integrated into the labour market" is based on two indicators only; ii) the summary indicator for "How close are NEETs to the labour market?" refers to the group aged 15-24 and not to the group aged 15-29 as for other countries.
3. All indicators from the Survey of Adult Skills for the United Kingdom refer to England and Northern Ireland.
Sources: OECD calculations based on OECD (2013c), "PISA: Programme for International Student Assessment", *OECD Education Statistics* (database), *http://dx.doi.org/10.1787/data-00365-en*; OECD (2014c), *Education at a Glance 2014: OECD Indicators*, OECD Publishing, *http://dx.doi.org/10.1787/eag-2014-en*; OECD (2015a), *Education at a Glance Interim Report: Update of Employment and Educational Attainment Indicators*, OECD, Paris, *www.oecd.org/edu/EAG-Interim-report.pdf*; OECD *Employment and Labour Market Statistics* (database), *http://dx.doi.org/ 10.1787/lfs-lms-data-en*; *Survey of Adult Skills (PIAAC) (2012)* (database).

The Skills Scoreboard on youth employability shows that:

■ Most countries do not perform well in one or several dimensions of youth employability, which reinforces the need for a global and consistent approach. Some countries (Italy and Spain) seem to face challenges in most dimensions of youth employability, while others (Finland and the Netherlands) appear to perform well in most of the dimensions.

■ A group of countries appear to have challenges on the side of skills development of their youth, but to a lesser extent concerning the integration of youth into the labour market (Austria, the Czech Republic, Sweden and the United States).

- Some countries that appear to have room to better promote the use of skills at work also face challenges in several other dimensions (Ireland, Italy, the Slovak Republic and Spain).

- Several countries perform relatively well along most of the dimensions of youth employability but the NEETs seem to be relatively far from the labour market (Denmark and Norway), either because a large share of them are inactive or because they have low education attainment or skills.

THE WAY TO MOVE FORWARD

This Skills Outlook looks at how policies can strengthen youth employability along the various dimensions discussed above. It discusses how all young people can be better prepared for the world of work, how they can integrate into the labour market and make better use of their skills at work, in the short and long term. It identifies six main challenges to strengthen youth employability and policy priorities for each of these challenges.

Improving young people's skills and education

All youth should leave education systems with skills that contribute to their employability. It requires taking a more holistic approach to skills. Many skills can be shaped through labour market experience, but during the education phase youth need to develop the capacity to adapt and learn more. In addition, it is important to identify students with the lowest skills and thus the most at risk of failure. These students should benefit from a comprehensive approach with specific support at schools, help from social institutions to address social and behavioural aspects, and the involvement of students and family. Second chance options that propose an alternative type of education with a practical or on-the-job learning component can help youth resume some form of education. A diversity of education programmes with good bridges between them gives students a better opportunity to find the types of programmes that correspond to their expectations and skills, and to continue education further.

Adapting education systems to labour market needs is another crucial challenge to strengthen youth employability. Surveys suggest that both employers and youth find that too many young graduates are not well prepared for the world of work. Employers and other stakeholders could be more engaged in education systems at various stages and through various ways. Developing work-based learning is a crucial way to strengthen the links between the education system and the labour market, enhance youth employability and improve transitions from education to work. Work-based learning can be integrated into vocational education and training (VET) but can also be encouraged in university programmes. VET programmes at both upper secondary and post-secondary levels offer options to develop skills needed in the labour market. They also offer opportunities for employers to engage in the education system. However, these programmes need to be of good quality. Having a strong work-based learning component integrated in VET programmes can act as a quality insurance as employers would be reluctant to provide training places in a programme of poor quality. The funding system can make VET and university programmes more responsive to labour market needs.

Challenge 1: **Ensuring that all youth leave education with adequate skills**

- Take a holistic approach to skills and aim to develop the whole set of skills that raise youth employability.
- Offer high-quality, pre-primary education for all.
- Reach out to students with low skills and those at risk of dropping out.
- Give disengaged youth a second chance to reintegrate into the education system.
- Provide multiple pathways within the education system.

Challenge 2: **Rendering the education system more responsive to labour market needs**

- Develop work-based learning programmes across different types of education, including universities. Engage employers and other stakeholders in the education system at all levels.

- Review vocational education and training (VET) programmes to raise their quality. Ensure that these programmes develop cognitive and social and emotional skills.

- Develop a funding system of universities that better links education to current and future labour market needs, and provides incentives to enhance quality.

- Improve career guidance by ensuring that these services are provided at all education levels and information is based on relevant assessment of the market returns of various career paths.

Integrating youth into the labour market

Smooth transitions from school to work limit the risk of skills depletion and the emergence of "scarring effects" often caused by unemployment spells at the beginning of careers. Labour market institutions influence the labour market outcomes of all groups of workers, but as new entrants to the labour market and thus outsiders, youth are more likely to be affected by institutional arrangements that aim to protect insiders but structurally weaken labour demand. Minimum wages, if they are set at high levels and are associated with high taxes on labour, can have negative effects on the employment of youth who are relatively low skilled and lack work experience. Furthermore, since one in four employed youth are on temporary contracts, it is important to ensure that employment protection legislation does not create barriers to the transition towards permanent employment, in which youth are more likely to fully utilise their skills and raise their employability. Internships after graduation can ease transition to the labour market, but to avoid abusive use, they need to be regulated with a requirement for learning and mentoring, minimum pay and social security coverage.

In most countries, a key challenge is to reach the NEETs and help them re-engage with education or enter the labour market. NEETs are a heterogeneous group. On average accross OECD countries, close to half of NEETs are unemployed, looking for jobs and likely to be in contact with public employment services, and therefore relatively easy to reach. Inactive NEETs are more difficult to reach. Developing a system of mutual obligations can help reconcile the objectives of limiting poverty risks among youth and ensuring that they face financial incentives to enter the labour market. On the side of youth, social benefits need to be accompanied by an obligation to take individualised actions to renew with education or employment and to register with PESs. Effective active labour market policies (ALMPs) can foster NEETs' transitions to jobs. They need to be customised to individual needs and skills. While job-search assistance, counselling and monitoring appear to have positive effects on employment, they can be complemented by training to address skills gaps and by hiring subsidies for youth who face extra hurdles such as low-skilled young immigrants.

Challenge 3: **Smoothing the transition from school to work**

- Develop sound labour market institutions and skills-friendly tax policies to foster employment of low-skilled youth.

- Continue to lower the gap in employment protection legislation between temporary and permanent contracts.

- Encourage end-of-studies internships within a framework that combines flexibility and obligations to firms.

- Develop programmes targeting students at risk of facing difficulties in their school-to-work transitions, but carefully assess their effect.

Challenge 4: **Helping NEETs to (re-) engage with education or the labour market**

- Introduce a system of mutual obligations between youth and institutions. Receiving social benefits should be backed with requirements to register with the public employment services, to take actions and receive help to prepare for the labour market, including through further education.

- Adopt a work-first strategy that encourages employment through efficient job-search assistance and training, monitoring and financial incentives.

Using young people's skills at work

To maintain and develop their employability, youth must use their skills effectively. Furthermore, making good use of youth skills can foster innovation, productivity and economic growth. Measures in various areas can limit skills mismatch and help make better use of skills, but specific measures to address imperfect information and asymmetry of information on youth skills and on the skills required on the job are needed. Education providers can co-operate with social partners on the development of well-designed qualification frameworks, that are based on skills and are continually updated according to the changing needs of the labour market. A formal recognition of skills acquired through non-formal or informal learning, and raising employer awareness of such systems can help young people, in particular immigrants, market their skills. In addition, work organisation and management practices can lead to better use of skills.

Entrepreneurship is a way for individuals to put their skills to effective use and for the economy and society to benefit from these skills but there is evidence that youth face barriers to developing their own firms. Removing barriers to youth entrepreneurship includes both general measures and measures specific to youth. Entrepreneurship education can be integrated at various stages of education including VET and university programmes but needs to be assessed to check quality. Access to finance, which is often identified as the most significant barrier to business start-ups, can be improved through both general policies and better framework conditions for investment and specific support targeted at some groups and limited in time. Finally, various forms of public and private co-operation can develop networks or shared facilities that can help youth in the early phases of their businesses. Strong co-operation between universities and employers can also assist youth at various stages of their business creation.

Challenge 5: **Limit skills mismatch and make better use of skills**

- Remove barriers to geographical mobility to allow for local matching of jobs and skills.
- Take stock of the spread of non-compete clauses and of their impact.
- Develop national and international qualification frameworks to facilitate recruitment processes.
- Develop formal recognition of skills acquired through non-formal and informal learning.
- Promote more effective work organisation and human resource management strategies.
- Develop high-quality systems and tools for assessing and anticipating skills needs.

Challenge 6: **Remove barriers to entrepreneurship**

- Integrate high-quality entrepreneurship education more prominently at all levels of education.
- Make sure that framework conditions are conducive to the creation of dynamic firms.
- Carefully design support for entrepreneurship.
- Encourage the development of various forms of public and private co-operation to develop networks or shared facilities.

Challenges are interconnected

All these challenges are interconnected. For example, measures to improve the development of relevant skills will be ineffective if those better-skilled youth are blocked from moving easily into work due to how the labour markets function, or if their skills are not used effectively once they start a job. Similarly, labour market reforms to improve the school-to-work transition will be undermined if the education system has not provided youth with the skills they need.

Likewise, many policy priorities to address one challenge also help to meet another challenge. For instance, sound employment protection legislation, that allows young workers to move smoothly from temporary to permanent jobs, limits the risk of being trapped in precarious situations with a bigger risk of unemployment but also allows workers to gradually fully use their skills. An internship framework helps develop the right skills when the internship takes place during the course of education but can act as a stepping stone towards employment if undertaken at the end of studies. Strengthening co-operation between universities and employers to ease business creation by youth can also help universities to design programmes that fit labour market needs. Overall, there are various synergies to gain from acting on the various fronts.

Some policy priorities encompass most of the dimensions of youth employability. In particular, high-quality, lifelong guidance can help youth raise their employability during the education phase, transition to the labour market and careers. Lifelong guidance is generally provided by educational institutions and public employment services but youth should be able to access these services at any point in time. However in many countries, there are gaps in the guidance system, with some options not proposed to students or advice not sufficiently based on an assessment of the individuals' skills and demand in the labour market. Consistency and continuity in these services requires strong co-operation between institutions.

Another policy priority is to better anticipate skills needs. This would help to develop the right skills, ease transitions from skills to jobs and mitigate the risk of having skills that are not used in the economy and the society. Most countries have projections of future skills needs from independent or public institutions, and international organisations also undertake these types of analyses, but few countries use this information to adjust their education systems. However, large uncertainties surrounding these estimates, as well as the fact that skills needs will be affected by various shocks, suggest the need to use this information carefully.

Putting it all together to strengthen youth skills and employability

Governments need to make credible commitments to improving youth outcomes that are both convincing to youth, and supported with concrete actions. Action should be concerted across all parts of government and society – social partners, businesses, education providers and civil society. There should also be strong accountability for performance and assessment of actions taken. This requires allocating clear responsibilities to stakeholders accompanied by measurable objectives and indicators of performance.

Social partners (employers and unions) can play an especially important role, building on their existing experience and responsibilities. This can include: tackling the dual labour market in ways that reduce adverse outcomes for youth; engaging in developing effective qualifications systems; supporting training systems and opportunities for youth to develop their skills; more diversified ways of working which do not exploit the vulnerable position of youth in the labour market; and effective career information and career guidance services.

Education providers at all levels can strengthen the employability of their students by focusing their efforts on developing the full range of skills that are needed for employability. Strong gains can be made by fostering closer co-operation between education providers and businesses, which in turn provide work-based learning opportunities for youth and act as stepping stones to good jobs and career paths. At the end of the day, improving youth skills and employability is everyone's responsibility.

References

Heckman, J.J. and **T. Kautz** (2013), "Fostering and measuring skills: Interventions that improve character and cognition", *NBER Working Paper*, No. 19656, National Bureau of Economic Research.

Humburg, M., R. van der Velden and **A. Verhagen** (2013), "The employability of higher education graduates: the employers' perspective", European Commission.

OECD (2015a), *Education at a Glance Interim Report: Update of Employment and Educational Attainment Indicators*, OECD, Paris, *www.oecd.org/edu/EAG-Interim-report.pdf*.

OECD (2015b), *Economic Policy Reforms 2015: Going for Growth*, OECD Publishing, Paris, *http://dx.doi.org/10.1787/growth-2015-en*.

OECD (2015c), *Skills for Social Progress: The Power of Social and Emotional Skills*, OECD Skills Studies, OECD Publishing, Paris. *http://dx.doi.org/10.1787/9789264226159-en*.

OECD (2014a), *OECD Economic Outlook, Volume 2014/2*, OECD Publishing, *http://dx.doi.org/10.1787/eco_outlook-v2014-2-en*.

OECD (2014b), *OECD Employment Outlook 2014*, OECD Publishing, Paris, *http://dx.doi.org/ 10.1787/empl_outlook-2014-en*.

OECD (2014c), *Education at a Glance 2014: OECD Indicators*, OECD Publishing, Paris, *http://dx.doi.org/10.1787/eag-2014-en*.

OECD (2013a), "The OECD Action Plan for Youth: Giving Youth a Better Start in the Labour Market", *www.oecd.org/employment/ Action-plan-youth.pdf* and *www.oecd.org/employment/action-plan-youth.htm*.

OECD (2013b), *OECD Skills Outlook 2013: First Results from the Survey of Adult Skills*, OECD Publishing, Paris, *http://dx.doi. org/10.1787/9789264204256-en*.

OECD (2013c), "PISA: Programme for International Student Assessment", *OECD Education Statistics* (database), *http://dx.doi. org/10.1787/data-00365-en*.

OECD (2012), *Better Skills, Better Jobs, Better Lives: A Strategic Approach to Skills Policies*, OECD Publishing, Paris, *http://dx.doi. org/10.1787/9789264177338-en*.

OECD (2010), *Learning for Jobs*, OECD Reviews of Vocational Education and Training, OECD Publishing, Paris, *http://dx.doi. org/10.1787/9789264087460-en*.

2

Trends in improving young people's education and skills

Education and skills are central to employability. Young people who leave school before they achieve a sufficient level of proficiency in literacy and numeracy find it difficult to enter the labour market. Increasingly, employers are looking for workers who are not only proficient in these cognitive skills, but who can also apply those skills to solve problems, and who are also deft in "soft" skills, such as communicating and working well in a team. This chapter offers an overview of how education today, including compulsory schooling, vocational education and training, and tertiary education, prepares young people for the world of work.

HIGHLIGHTS

- According to the 2012 Survey of Adult Skills, among 16-29 year-olds who had left the education system in the previous two years, 14% had low numeracy skills, on average. The proportion of young people with low numeracy skills ranged from 5% in Korea and Japan to more than 20% in France, Ireland, Italy, the United Kingdom and the United States.

- Those who left school before completing upper secondary education have particularly low cognitive skills. The share of young people scoring low (below proficiency Level 2) in numeracy is twice as high among those who left school before completing upper secondary education, in comparison to those with an upper secondary education as their highest level of qualification.

- Graduates of vocational education and training (VET) have a slightly higher probability of being employed compared to graduates of general programmes at the upper secondary and post-secondary non-tertiary level. However in many countries, students who attended vocational education and training (VET) are 50% more likely to have poor numeracy skills than students in general programmes of a similar education level. Moreover, less than 15% of young people who graduate from upper secondary vocational tracks continue into post-secondary education.

- Less than 50% of VET students and less than 40% of students in general programmes are exposed to work-based learning, on average across OECD countries.

- Tertiary graduates have better labour market outcomes than young adults with less education, but access to tertiary education largely depends on parents' background.

The global economic crisis, with high levels of unemployment, in particular among youth, has stressed the importance of fostering better skills for all. It has put additional pressure on governments to adapt education and training systems to meet changes in the demand for skills, and to improve learning environments in schools and workplaces.

But the role of skills goes well beyond participation in the labour market. Strong skills are important to manage one's finances and life choices, be aware of various risks, adopt healthy behaviour, and more generally, make good and balanced decisions in life (Pallas, 2000). They also help individuals integrate into society, trust and help others, and participate in various activities. Finally, with a strong skills foundation, individuals are likely to transmit healthy behaviours to their children, and help them when needed (OECD, 2013a).

EDUCATION, SKILLS AND EMPLOYABILITY

Educational attainment often determines labour market participation and employment. To employers, education degrees and certificates signal the level of skills a prospective employee, including a recent graduate, will bring to a job. Empirical evidence suggests that workers in OECD countries today need at least an upper secondary diploma to be able to compete in the workforce (see a review in Lyche, 2010). Young people who have not completed school have a difficult time securing stable employment and earn less, on average, than high school graduates (Bradshaw, O'Brennan and McNeely, 2008). In most countries, the share of young people who are neither employed nor in education or training (NEET) is relatively small among those who have completed tertiary education but much larger among those who completed at most lower secondary education (Figure 2.1).

Individuals with similar levels of education do not always have the same level of cognitive skills across countries, as the acquisition of skills depends on the quality of education systems and other factors (Figure 2.2). The main findings from the 2012 Survey of Adult Skills confirm the importance of raising educational attainment to improve labour market outcomes, but also of raising the quality of education systems and ensuring that no young person leaves the education system without a certain level of skills (Figure 2.3; OECD, 2013a). Low cognitive skills, as measured in the Survey of Adult Skills, increase the probability of being NEET (OECD, 2014a).

Today's economy increasingly requires youth to have digital skills as students, job-seekers or workers, consumers, or responsible citizens. Youth with no ICT (information and communication technologies) access and experience will be at a disadvantage, especially in the labour market where today's youth are considered "digital natives". However, basic ICT skills may not add value unless they are well paired with cognitive skills and other skills, such as creativity, communication skills, team work and perseverance.

Lack of social and emotional skills creates barriers to employment (Heckman and Kautz, 2013). Of employers drawn from a national sample in the United States in 1996, 69% reported that they had rejected applicants because they lacked basic social skills, such as showing up every day, arriving to work on time, and having a strong work ethic. This is more than double the percentage of applicants rejected due to inadequate reading and writing skills.

▪ Figure 2.1 ▪

Share of youth neither employed nor in education or training (NEET), by educational attainment

15-29 year-olds, 2013

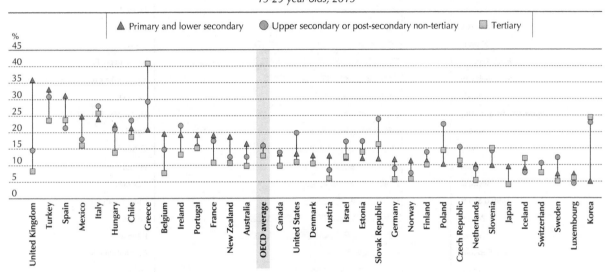

Notes: Data for Japan refer to the 15-24 age group. For Chile, Iceland and Korea, the year of reference is 2012. The OECD average excludes Japan.

Source: OECD (2015), *Education at a Glance Interim Report: Update of Employment and Educational Attainment Indicators*, OECD, Paris, *www.oecd. org/edu/EAG-Interim-report.pdf*.

StatLink ▨▨▨ http://dx.doi.org/10.1787/888933214417

▪ Figure 2.2 ▪

Average numeracy skills of new graduates, by level of education

16-29 year-olds, 2012

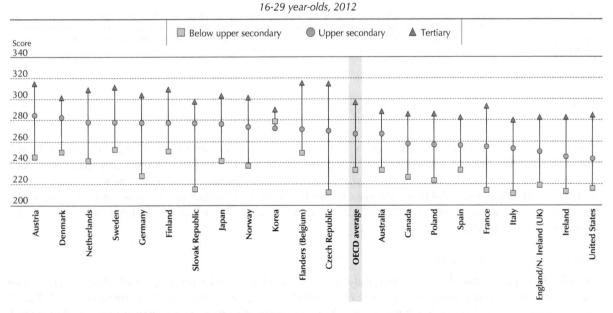

Notes: New graduates are defined as youth who completed their education within two years prior to the survey.

Source: OECD calculations based on the *Survey of Adult Skills (PIAAC) (2012)* (database).

StatLink ▨▨▨ http://dx.doi.org/10.1787/888933214424

▪ Figure 2.3 ▪

The effect of education and literacy proficiency on labour market participation

Adjusted odds ratios showing the effect of education and literacy on the likelihood of participating in the labour market among adults not in formal education, 2012

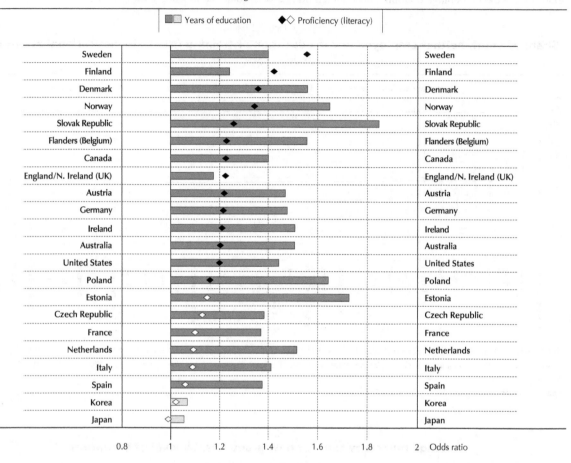

Notes: The figure reads as follows: In Sweden, an adult with three additional years of schooling is 40% more likely to be employed or be looking for work. In addition, the likelihood of labour force participation increases by 56% following a 46-point rise in the literacy score. The odds ratios correspond to a one standard deviation increase in literacy/years of education. Results are adjusted for gender, age, marital and foreign-born status. Statistically significant values for years of education are shown as a dark blue bar and for literacy as a black diamond. Years of education have a standard deviation of 3.05, literacy has a standard deviation of 45.76.

Source: OECD (2013a), *OECD Skills Outlook 2013: First Results from the Survey of Adult Skills*, OECD Publishing, Paris, *http://dx.doi. org/10.1787/9789264204256-en*.

StatLink ⌗⌗⌗ http://dx.doi.org/10.1787/888933214434

The development of skills is a dynamic process and youth with low cognitive and social and emotional skills will also find it harder to further develop and upgrade their skills over their entire lives (Cunha and Heckman, 2007), making them more vulnerable when technological progress leads to changes in job requirements. In general, skills that are important for employability include (see Chapter 1): cognitive skills, such as proficiency in literacy, numeracy and problem solving combined with ICT skills; social and emotional skills, such as self-discipline, perseverance, and teamwork; and occupation-specific skills.

EQUITY IN LEARNING OUTCOMES

Providing high-quality education and training that is accessible to all is crucial for ensuring that all young people acquire the skills needed to participate fully in society and to continue learning throughout their lives. The Survey of Adult Skills shows that low skills and school drop-out go hand-in-hand. Moreover, it identifies a large share of young adults who lack basic cognitive skills despite having attained compulsory education. In addition, Results from the OECD Programme for International Student Assessment (PISA) show that education institutions often tend to reinforce existing patterns of socio-economic advantage, rather than create a more equitable distribution of learning opportunities (OECD, 2013b).

Many countries are working to reduce the share of young people who complete initial education or drop out of the education system with very low skills. PISA results show that the share of 15-year-old students who fail to reach the baseline level of proficiency (Level 2) in reading and mathematics is still large in many OECD countries (Figure 2.4, Panel A). The Survey of Adult Skills shows that among youth who completed education in the two years prior to the survey, in several OECD countries, a large share has low numeracy skills (Figure 2.4, Panel B). Moreover, not all youth possess basic ICT skills despite their universal or at least increasing access to ICT infrastructure (Figure 2.5). The Survey of Adult Skills shows that almost 10% of youth on average (aged 16-29) are not equipped with basic ICT skills.[1]

▪ Figure 2.4 ▪

Low performers in reading and numeracy

A. Reading skills of students at age 15 according to PISA, 2012

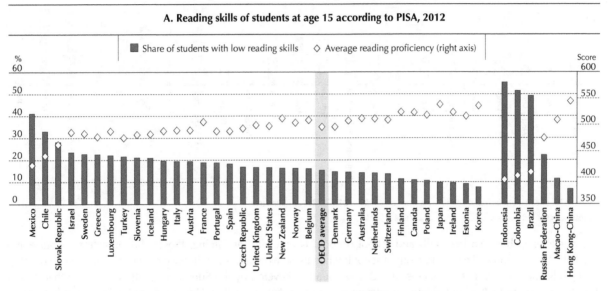

B. Numeracy skills of new graduates aged 16-29 according to the Survey of Adult Skills, 2012

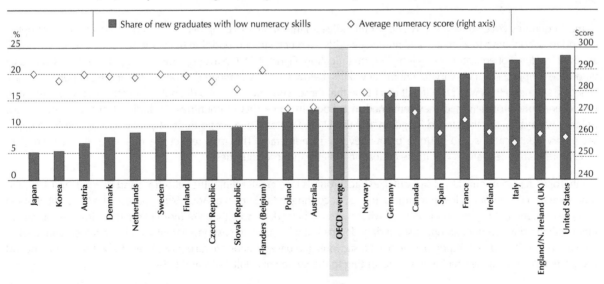

Notes: Panel A shows the share of students who have reading proficiency below Level 2, which is considered the baseline level in PISA. Panel B shows the share of new graduates who completed education during the two years prior to the 2012 Survey of Adult Skills and who perform below Level 2 in numeracy (left axis). The OECD averages for both the results from PISA and the Survey of Adult Skills are based on the sample of OECD countries/regions assessed in the Survey of Adult Skills.

Source: OECD calculations based on the *Survey of Adult Skills (PIAAC) (2012)* (database) and OECD (2013c), "PISA: Programme for International Student Assessment", *OECD Education Statistics* (database), *http://dx.doi.org/10.1787/data-00365-en*.

StatLink ⟨⟩ http://dx.doi.org/10.1787/888933214449

▪ Figure 2.5 ▪

Youth who lack basic ICT skills

Percentage of youth (16-29), 2012

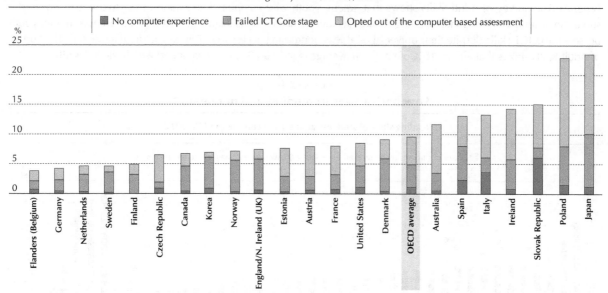

Source: OECD calculations based on the *Survey of Adult Skills (PIAAC) (2012)* (database).

StatLink ⟐⟐ http://dx.doi.org/10.1787/888933214453

The relationship between low skills and school dropout is mutually reinforcing: those who struggle to acquire and develop skills are more likely to drop out of school; while those who drop out will have fewer opportunities to develop their skills later on. On average, across the OECD countries covered by the Survey of Adult Skills, more than 8% of 16-24 year-olds had left school before completing upper secondary education (Figure 2.6). In Spain, one in four young people belongs to this group. By contrast, in Korea nearly every 16-24 year-old has graduated from upper secondary school.

In most countries covered by the Survey of Adult Skills, a large share of young people who have dropped out of upper secondary school have low literacy and numeracy skills – a much larger proportion than among young people who have attained this level of education as their highest qualification (Figure 2.7). On average, more than 40% of 16-24 year-olds who have dropped out have very low numeracy skills (below Level 2), compared to only 17% among upper secondary school graduates. However, it is difficult to assume that those with low skills who did not complete secondary education would be more proficient had they remained in school. In some OECD countries, including Canada, France, Italy, Ireland, Poland, Spain, the United Kingdom and the United States, large proportions of young adults who have upper secondary qualifications also perform below Level 2 in numeracy. This may reflect the quality of upper secondary programmes and inequalities within the education systems in these countries.

Youth from socio-economically disadvantaged backgrounds face greater difficulties at school and beyond, and are over-represented in the groups of low performers. In fact, according to the Survey of Adult Skills, adults who have not attained an upper secondary degree, and neither of whose parents have done so either, are more likely to be low performers in literacy than adults without an upper secondary degree but who have at least one parent who has attained that level of education (OECD, 2013a). Young people from disadvantaged backgrounds are also more likely to be less confident and less proficient at using new technologies according to the Survey of Adult Skills and PISA.

In addition, ensuring equal access to tertiary education remains a challenge, although enrolments have expanded significantly over the past few decades. In most countries, students whose parents have attained tertiary education are more likely to go to university than those whose parents have attained lower levels of education (OECD, 2014b; Causa and Johansson, 2009).

■ Figure 2.6 ■

Youth who left school before completing upper secondary education

Percentage of 16-24 year-olds without an upper secondary degree and who are not in education, 2012

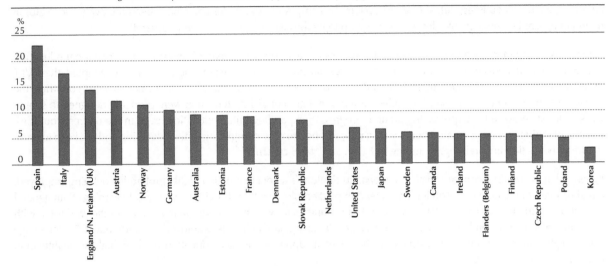

Source: OECD calculations based on the *Survey of Adult Skills (PIAAC) (2012)* (database).
StatLink http://dx.doi.org/10.1787/888933214465

■ Figure 2.7 ■

Numeracy skills among youth who did not complete upper secondary education and those who left education after attaining an upper secondary degree

Percentage scoring below proficiency Level 2, 16-24 year-olds, 2012

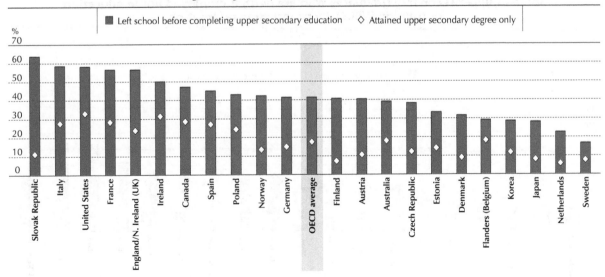

Source: OECD calculations based on the *Survey of Adult Skills (PIAAC) (2012)* (database).
StatLink http://dx.doi.org/10.1787/888933214474

PREPARATION FOR THE WORLD OF WORK

Vocational education and training

Vocational education and training (VET) can directly link young people's skills with the needs of the labour market. There is evidence suggesting that high-quality vocational education pathways, particularly in upper secondary education, can help engage youth who have become disaffected with academic education, improve graduation rates and ensure smooth transitions from school to work (Quintini and Manfredi, 2009). VET can also help to develop a highly skilled and diverse labour force, adding a range of mid-level trade, technical, professional and management skills alongside those high-level skills associated with university education. The global economic crisis has sparked renewed interest in VET in OECD countries, as those countries with strong VET systems, notably Austria and Germany, have been relatively successful in maintaining stable employment rates among young people throughout the crisis (see Chapter 4).

Policy makers in emerging and less-developed countries are also showing greater interest in VET. Vocational education and training is perceived as having driven the industrialisation of East Asian countries, which adapted their VET programmes to respond to changing labour market needs (Fredriksen and Tan, 2008). In former socialist countries, the transition to free-market economies has called for a reorientation of VET systems that were primarily designed to supply workers for state-owned enterprises. In addition, progress in expanding initial education, even in the poorest countries, has meant rapid increase in the number of young people who are now completing initial education and are keen to enrol in further education and training, including VET (Tan and Nam, 2012).

In general at the upper secondary level, vocational curriculum is associated with a higher probability of being employed, a higher share of the potential working time spend in paid employment, and slightly lower hourly earnings than general education (Brunello and Rocco, 2014). Across OECD countries for which data are available, 75% of the workforce with a vocational upper secondary or post-secondary non-tertiary qualification is employed – a rate that is 5 percentage points higher than that among individuals with a general upper secondary education as their highest qualification (OECD, 2014b).

Yet, despite the employment advantge for youth with an upper secondary vocational degree in most countries, the proportion of upper secondary VET graduates who are NEET is larger than the proportion of graduates from upper secondary general programmes who are NEET (Figure 2.8). This is partly because students in general programmes are more likely to continue education after they graduate from secondary school.

■ Figure 2.8 ■

Share of upper secondary graduates who are neither employed nor in education or training (NEET), by programme orientation

16-29 year-olds, 2012

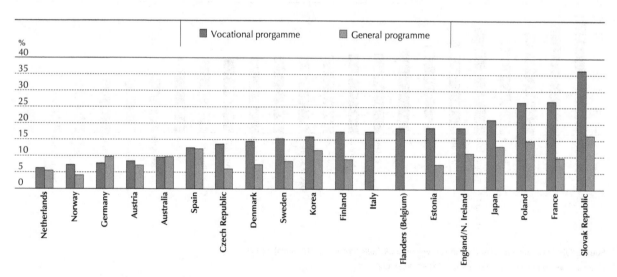

Notes: Upper secondary VET includes programmes classified as ISCED 3C long, ISCED 3B and ISCED 3A identified by countries as vocationally oriented.

Source: OECD calculations based on the *Survey of Adult Skills (PIAAC) (2012)* (database).

StatLink ⬛▨■ http://dx.doi.org/10.1787/888933214481

The gap in earnings between post-secondary and tertiary VET versus academic graduates may also partly explain youth's preference for university education to vocational training (Figure 2.9), although large differences exist between countries and between different programmes and fields of study (OECD, 2014a). This gap is particularly large in countries where the training offered is of poor quality and is badly monitored (OECD, 2014c).

■ Figure 2.9 ■

Relative wages of graduates from post-secondary vocational education and training programmes

16-29 year-olds, 2012

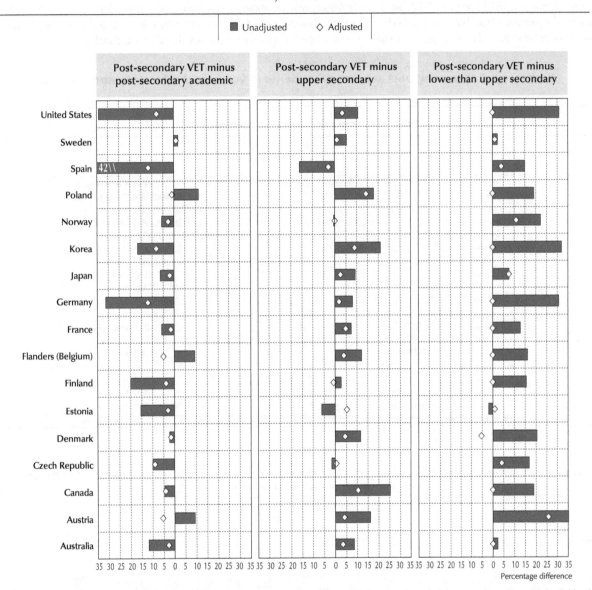

Notes: VET post-secondary programmes include those classified as 4 and 5B in the ISCED framework, excluding "general" studies and the fields of "humanities, languages and arts". Post-secondary academic students are those classified as 5A in the ISCED framework or classified as 4 and 5B with either "general" or "humanities, languages and arts" as their field of study. Hourly earnings with bonuses are considered in purchasing power parity. The wage distribution was trimmed to eliminate the 1st and 99th percentiles. For instance in the United States, graduates of post-secondary vocational programmes earn 30% less than graduates from tertiary education. The difference in earnings is expressed in percentage (no difference = 0%), and those still enrolled in education are excluded. The figure presents results only for countries whose sample size by type of education (i.e. post-secondary VET, post-secondary academic, upper secondary and lower than upper secondary) is larger than 30.

Source: OECD calculations based on the *Survey of Adult Skills (PIAAC) (2012)* (database).

StatLink ⬛⬛⬛ http://dx.doi.org/10.1787/888933214493

VET systems can offer a full range of programmes at different education levels. Many countries have extensive upper secondary vocational programmes while others, particularly English-speaking countries, tend to offer such programmes at the post-secondary level. In Austria, for example, apprentices-to-be choose their target occupation when they are 14 years old. At the opposite extreme, in the United States, occupational specialisation only tends to take place in post-secondary programmes (OECD, 2010). These differences can have a significant impact on students' futures (Lerman, 2013). When occupation-focused education and training is offered relatively late, students may become disengaged from school, particularly those who may thrive with a more practical, hands-on approach to learning. But starting such a programme too early might trap young people in unrewarding fields and limit their adaptability and upward mobility.

A large proportion of VET students, even those in post-secondary programmes, have very low cognitive skills, particularly in numeracy (Figure 2.12, Panel A). In many countries, Australia, Ireland, Norway, Poland, the United Kingdom and the United States, more than 20% of post-secondary VET students aged 16-29 performed below Level 2 in the numeracy assessment in the 2012 Survey of Adult Skills. Furthermore, when compared to academic students who have spent the same number of years in school but have pursued a general programme, a much larger share of VET students perform at Level 1 and below or at Level 2, and a much smaller share perform at Level 3, 4 or 5 in numeracy (Figure 2.10, Panel B).

■ Figure 2.10 ■

Numeracy skills among post-secondary students in vocational education and training

16-29 year-olds, 2012

A. Distribution of numeracy skills among post-secondary VET students

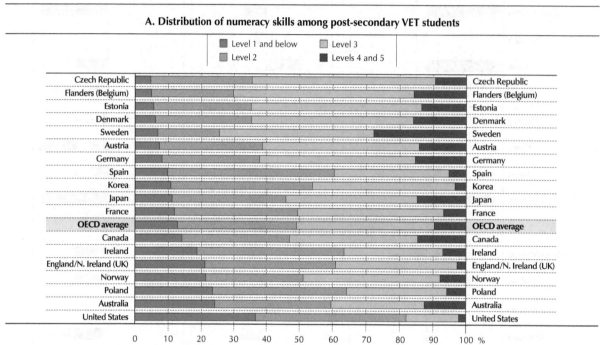

B. Difference in numeracy skills between post-secondary VET students and students in academic programmes who have spent the same number of years in education, by skill level

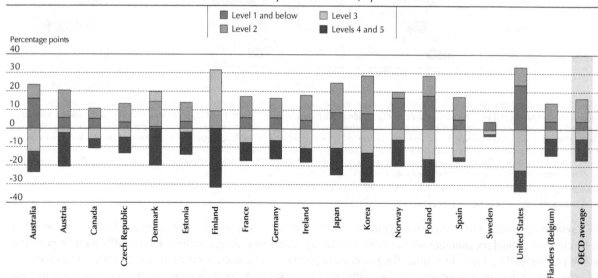

Notes: VET post-secondary programmes include those classified as 4 and 5B in the ISCED framework, excluding "general" and "humanities, languages and arts" fields of study. The figures include only countries with a sample size of post-secondary VET students larger than 30. Panel B reads as follows: for instance, in Australia a smaller share of post-secondary VET students reach Level 3, 4 or 5 than students in academic programmes.

Source: OECD calculations based on the *Survey of Adult Skills (PIAAC) (2012)* (database).

StatLink ᵐˢᵖ http://dx.doi.org/10.1787/888933214501

Although some countries have made substantial progress in linking VET to other parts of the education system (see Chapter 3), on average, less than 15% of young people who graduate from upper secondary vocational tracks continue into post-secondary education (Figure 2.11). In fact, upper secondary VET graduates are nearly five times less likely to enrol in further education than graduates from general secondary schools with similar proficiency in literacy (Figure 2.12).

■ Figure 2.11 ■

Transition from upper secondary vocational education and training to post-secondary education

Share of upper secondary VET graduates enrolled in post-secondary education programmes (ISCED 4, 5A and 5B),
16-29 year-olds, 2012

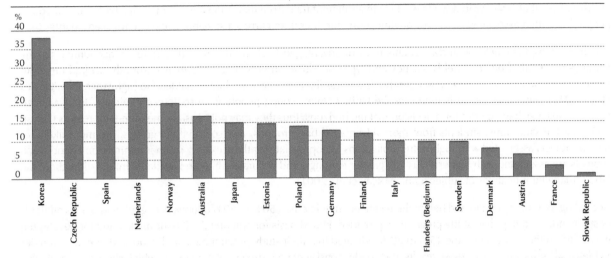

Notes: Upper secondary VET includes programmes classified as ISCED 3C long, ISCED 3B and ISCED 3A identified by countries as vocationally oriented. VET post-secondary programmes include those classified as 4 and 5B in the ISCED framework, excluding "general" and "humanities, languages and arts" fields of study. Post-secondary academic programmes are those classified 5A in the ISCED framework or classified 4 and 5B with either "general" or "humanities, languages and arts" field of study.
Source: OECD calculations based on the *Survey of Adult Skills (PIAAC) (2012)* (database).
StatLink ᴬᵐˢ☞ http://dx.doi.org/10.1787/888933214517

■ Figure 2.12 ■

The effect of upper secondary degrees on participating in further education

Adjusted odds ratios showing the effect of an upper secondary VET degree on the likelihood of pursuing further education,
16-29 year-olds, 2012

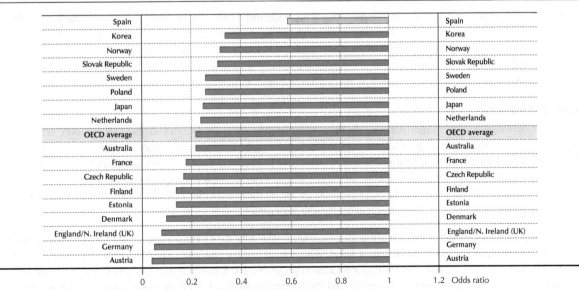

Notes: Upper secondary VET includes programmes classified as ISCED 3C long, ISCED 3B and ISCED 3A identified by countries as vocationally oriented. The odds ratios refer to the probability of pursuing further education after attaining an upper secondary VET degree as compared to attaining a general upper secondary degree. Odds ratios are adjusted for literacy proficiency, gender, health status, parental education and number of books at home. Statistically insignificant results are shown in light blue.
Source: OECD calculations based on the *Survey of Adult Skills (PIAAC) (2012)* (database).
StatLink ᴬᵐˢ☞ http://dx.doi.org/10.1787/888933214523

Tertiary education

In most countries, young adults who complete tertiary education find a job (see Figure 2.1). However, the economic crisis has made the transition to work more difficult for tertiary-educated youth, although the increase in their unemployment rate has been less pronounced than that for graduates with lower levels of education (see Chapter 4).

University-educated youth also enjoy higher wages, on average, but earnings vary, depending on the field of study (e.g. Finnie and Frenette, 2003; Bratti, Naylor and Smith, 2008; Duquet et al., 2010). Recent analysis (OECD, 2014a) using the Survey of Adult Skills confirms that the field of study plays a role in explaining the variation in young people's hourly wages. It also shows that while working in a different field from that studied is not in itself a bad thing for young people, it is often associated with over-qualification, and therefore carries a sizeable wage penalty (see Chapter 6).

When deciding their field of study, students from disadvantaged backgrounds face difficulties in accounting for the earnings potential of different fields of study and types of education programmes. Evidence from the United Kingdom shows that students from low-income households are less likely to choose subjects that lead to high-wage jobs (Davies et al., 2013). Similar evidence is found for the United States: young people from socio-economically disadvantaged backgrounds may have shorter-term decision-making horizons, thus they may not consider medium-term returns (Usher, 2006). At the same time, students from more advantaged backgrounds, and some ethnic groups, are more likely to: regard subjects associated with high-status professions as appropriate for them to study; gather information about which subjects are associated with higher status and greater earnings; and accurately interpret available information about the labour market implications of subject choice (Reay et al., 2001).

According to a survey conducted before the recent economic crisis, 50% to 60% of university graduates across all fields of study indicated that their study programme provided a good basis for entering the labour market and for developing new skills on the job, while some 15% to 20% indicated that their study programme failed to do so (Humburg, van der Velden and Verhagen, 2013). These results are broadly consistent with surveys of employers, which show that employers have a generally positive perception of university graduates, but report that they face skills shortages in some areas and that graduates lack some social and emotional skills (Atfield and Purcell, 2010).

While tertiary-educated students generally have good labour market outcomes, some may graduate only to find that their skills are not required in the labour market. In some countries, the share of tertiary-educated young people who are neither employed nor in education or training is larger than that of young people with upper secondary as their highest level of education (see Figure 2.1). This may be the result of low-quality tertiary programmes and/or a lack of links with the labour market. Over-qualification is rife in many emerging countries, as better-educated youth struggle to find jobs (Quintini and Martin, 2014).

The issue of how tertiary education can better prepare young graduates for the labour market is not new, but has become more prominent as educational institutions face increasing competition and demand for efficiency, new programmes and new modes of delivery. However, universities may be reluctant to teach skills aimed specifically at employability, as that may lower their academic standards and objectives (Lowden et al., 2011). For their part, employers might prefer to train workers on the job rather than investing in institutions of higher education.

Work-based learning

Work-based learning is critical to strengthening the links between the education system and the labour market, enhancing youth employability and improving transitions from education to work. Employer provision of workplace training is an indicator of support for an associated programme. Employers are particularly keen to offer training and internship places in contexts where they have, or expect, labour shortages and where jobs or firms require very specific skills, because trainees may be future recruits (Clark, 2001 and De Rick, 2008). At the same time, workplaces provide a strong learning environment for students because they offer real on-the-job experience.

Many young people in OECD countries work during their studies (Figure 2.13), but only few are in jobs directly related to their studies. Analysis based on the Survey of Adult Skills shows that the share of upper secondary VET students who participate in work-based learning as part of their education programme ("apprenticeship") is very low in most countries – except in Australia, Austria, Denmark, Germany and the Netherlands (Figure 2.14). In these countries, at least 20% of VET students are in apprenticeships thanks to their strong tradition of engaging employers at different educational levels. In other countries, notably England and Norway – with less developed vocational education and training at the upper secondary level, a large share of students has a job unrelated to their field of study. Young students there may be working to finance their education.

■ Figure 2.13 ■

Share of students combining studies and work

16-29 year-olds, 2012

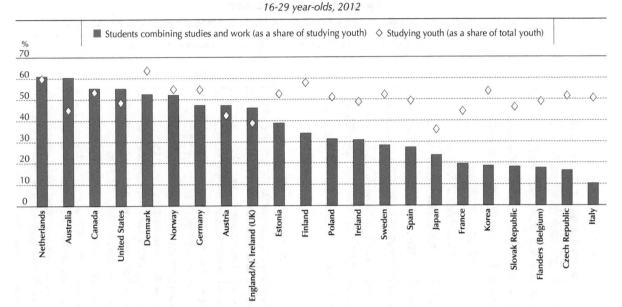

Source: OECD calculations based on the *Survey of Adult Skills (PIAAC) (2012)* (database).
StatLink ᵐᵗᵇ http://dx.doi.org/10.1787/888933214535

■ Figure 2.14 ■

Students in upper secondary vocational education and training, by workplace orientation

16-29 year-olds, 2012

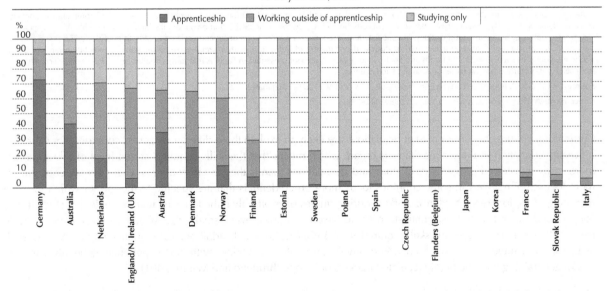

Notes: VET upper secondary programmes include those classified as 3C (long) and 3B in the ISCED framework, excluding "general" and "humanities, languages and arts" fields of study. The figure includes only countries with a sample size of upper secondary VET students larger than 30.

Source: OECD calculations based on the *Survey of Adult Skills (PIAAC) (2012)* (database).

StatLink ᵐᵗᵇ http://dx.doi.org/10.1787/888933214540

At post-secondary VET and university levels, those students who are in work-based learning, working in an area that is close to their field of study (the "matched" students), probably benefit the most from their work experience. Generally, students in post-secondary VET programmes are more involved in work-based learning than students in general programmes (Figure 2.15). Particularly in France and Germany almost all VET students work in occupations directly related to their field of study. In many countries, the share of academic students working outside their field of study is large; in Canada, the Czech Republic, Ireland and the United States, it even represents the majority of students who combine studies and work.

■ Figure 2.15 ■

Post-secondary students combining studies and work in and outside their field of study, by workplace orientation

As a share of all students combining work and study in VET (A) and in general programmes (B), 16-29 year-olds, 2012

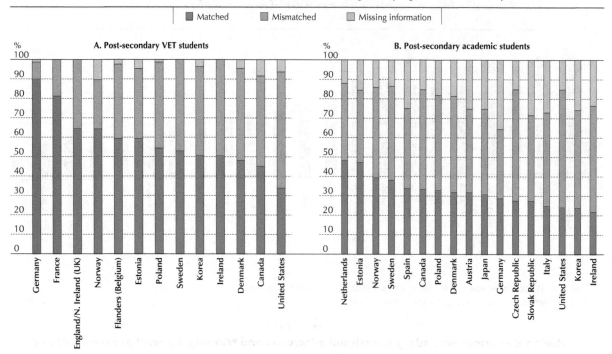

Notes: VET post-secondary programmes include those classified as 4 and 5B in the ISCED framework, excluding "general" and "humanities, languages and arts" fields of study. Post-secondary academic students are those classified 5A in the ISCED framework or classified 4 and 5B with either "general" or "humanities, languages and arts" field of study. Matched students are those who work in an occupation related to their field of study, The figure includes only countries providing information about field of study and occupation classification, with a sample size by programme orientation larger than 30. Therefore, countries such as the Netherlands and Spain, among others, are not presented in Panel A due to the small sample size of post-secondary VET students. Field of study is not available for Australia and Finland.

Source: OECD calculations based on the *Survey of Adult Skills (PIAAC) (2012)* (database).

StatLink ⫶⫶⫶ http://dx.doi.org/10.1787/888933214554

Curriculum, culture and labour market regulations are likely to explain these differences across countries. For example, university education in the United States is broad, which means that the skills acquired at that level of education are more easily transferred across fields of study and occupations than is the case in countries where tertiary education is more focused. Employers in some countries focus more on credentials that are specific to the job for which they are recruiting. Thus, for French students, working during studies pays off only if the job is related to the field of study (Beffy, Fougère and Maurel, 2009). By contrast, in Anglo-Saxon countries, even "small jobs" would be considered valuable because they teach young people skills required at work (OECD, 2014a). In addition, less-regulated labour markets, such as that in the United States, which provide relatively easy entry for workers with little experience, generally offer less workplace training than the highly regulated markets of Europe (Brunello and Medio, 2001).

The Survey of Adult Skills shows how upper secondary VET students use their skills at work, distinguishing between apprentices and those working outside apprenticeships (Figure 2.16). The analysis reveals that apprentices use their cognitive skills (such as problem solving, writing, reading, and using information and communication technologies) more frequently than other working VET students do. Apprentices also learn new things from supervisors or co-workers, learn by doing, and keep up-to-date with new products and services more frequently than their peers working outside apprenticeship (so called "learn at work" category, Figure 2.16).

■ Figure 2.16 ■

Use of skills by upper secondary vocational students who are combining studies and work in and outside of apprenticeships

16-29 year-olds, 2012

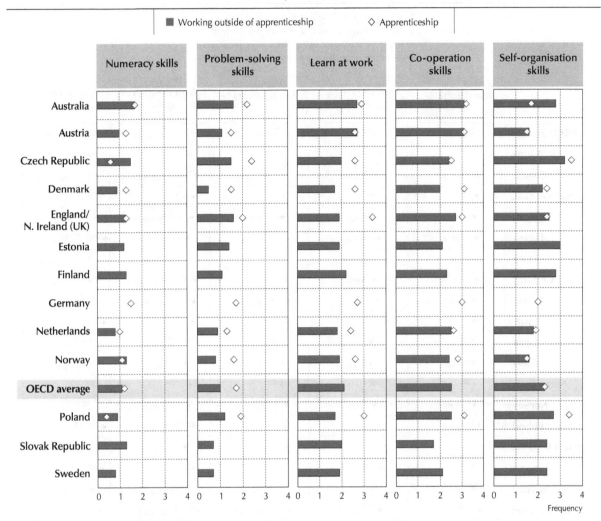

Notes: VET upper secondary programmes include those classified as 3C (long) and 3B in the ISCED framework, excluding "general" and "humanities, languages and arts" fields of study. Except for "learn at work", all skills-use variables are taken directly from questions asked in the background questionnaire of the Survey of Adult Skills. For these variables, frequency values range between 0 (= never used) and 4 (= used daily). "Learn at work" has been derived based on more than one question on supervision and provision of specific training at work using the item response theory (IRT) method, and transformed so that it has a mean of 2 and a standard deviation of 1 across the pooled sample of all participating countries, which allows cross-country comparison. The figure presents results only for countries, whose sample size by workplace orientation (i.e. apprenticeship or working outside apprenticeship) is larger than 15.

Source: OECD calculations based on the *Survey of Adult Skills (PIAAC) (2012)* (database).

StatLink ⫶⫶⫶ http://dx.doi.org/10.1787/888933214565

At post-secondary levels, students also seem to use cognitive and occupation-specific skills more frequently at the workplace when training is related to their field of study (Figure 2.17). For VET students, this is the case for learning at work, problem-solving and self-organising skills. University students who are "matched" to their work also tend to learn at work more frequently than their "mismatched" peers. These results suggest that some skills may be better developed in internships or traineeships related to a student's field of study rather than through other types of working arrangements.

■ Figure 2.17 ■

Use of skills by post-secondary vocational and general students who are combining studies and work in and outside their field of study

16-29 year-olds, 2012

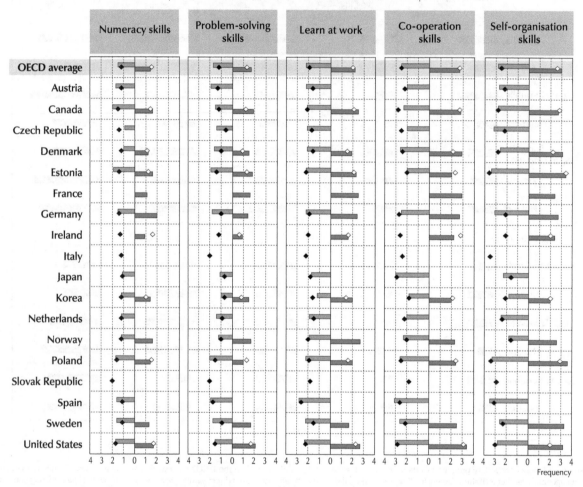

Notes: VET post-secondary programmes include those classified as 4 and 5B in the ISCED framework, excluding "general" and "humanities, languages and arts" fields of study. Post-secondary academic students are those classified 5A in the ISCED framework or classified 4 and 5B with either "general" or "humanities, languages and arts" field of study. Except for "learn at work", all skills-use variables are taken directly from questions asked in the background questionnaire of the Survey of Adult Skills. For these variables, frequency values range between 0 (= never used) and 4 (= used daily). "Learn at work" has been derived based on more than one question on supervision and provision of specific training at work using the item response theory (IRT) method, and transformed so that it has a mean of 2 and a standard deviation of 1 across the pooled sample of all participating countries, which allows cross-country comparison. The figure presents results only for countries, whose sample size by workplace orientation (i.e. matched versus mismatched) is larger than 15. Matched students are those who work in an occupation related to their field of study,

Source: OECD calculations based on the *Survey of Adult Skills (PIAAC) (2012)* (database).

StatLink ⬛⬛⬛ http://dx.doi.org/10.1787/888933214574

Besides developing relevant skills, workplace learning can also provide critical information to students about the line of work they might, or might not, wish to pursue. Students usually choose a field of study before they have any serious work experience; and that can affect their labour market outcomes later on (see Siow, 1984 and Zarkin, 1985, among others). Workplace training, even for short periods, can thus be an important part of career guidance, especially if students have an opportunity to work in several different fields before choosing the next steps in their education and training.

SKILLS SCOREBOARD ON YOUTH EMPLOYABILITY

How skilled are young people?

Educational credentials and strong skills are necessary for fully integrating into and participating in the labour market. Young adults who complete tertiary education generally find a job. However, individuals with similar levels of education do not always have the same level of cognitive skills which affects their labour market outcomes. In particular, low literacy and numeracy skills increase the probability of being neither in employment nor in education and training. To assess these dimensions of employability, the Skills Scoreboard uses five indicators measuring the level of skills and educational attainment among the young population, as well as the share of youth with low skills (Table 2.1).

▪ Table 2.1 ▪

Skills Scoreboard on youth employability: How skilled are young people?

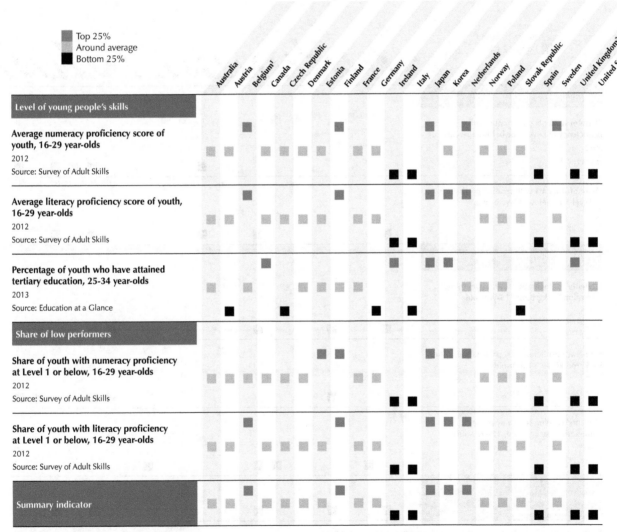

1. All indicators from the Survey of Adult Skills for Belgium refer to Flanders.
2. All indicators from the Survey of Adult Skills for the United Kingdom refer to England and Northern Ireland.

Notes: All indicators have been normalised in a way which implies that a higher value and being among the "top 25%" reflect better performance. The summary indicator is calculated as a simple average of the five indicators.

Sources: OECD calculations based on the *Survey of Adult Skills (PIAAC) (2012)* (database), OECD (2013c), "PISA: Programme for International Student Assessment", *OECD Education Statistics* (database), *http://dx.doi.org/10.1787/data-00365-en* and OECD (2015), *Education at a Glance Interim Report: Update of Employment and Educational Attainment Indicators*, OECD, Paris, *www.oecd.org/edu/EAG-Interim-report.pdf.*

Is the development of skills inclusive?

To participate fully in society and to continue learning throughout their lives, all youth should have access to high-quality education and be given the opportunity to develop their skills. This does not imply that everyone should achieve the same learning outcomes, but that the share of youth who leave education with low skills should be minimised. Furthermore, youth from socio-economically disadvantaged, immigrant and minority backgrounds should have access to quality learning opportunities. An education system is more equitable, the smaller the differences in learning outcomes between youth from different socio-economic backgrounds and the smaller the share of low-skilled youth. To measure these concepts, the Skills Scoreboard uses five indicators showing the share of students with low skills and the impact of parental education and immigration background on learning outcomes (Table 2.2).

■ Table 2.2 ■

Skills Scoreboard on youth employability: Is the development of skills inclusive?

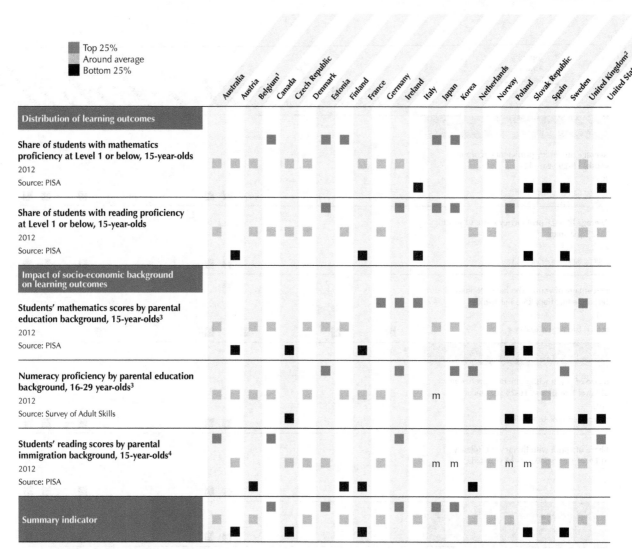

1. All indicators from the Survey of Adult Skills for Belgium refer to Flanders.
2. All indicators from the Survey of Adult Skills for the United Kingdom refer to England and Northern Ireland.
3. The indicators measuring the impact of parental education are calculated as the ratio between the average mathematics (or numeracy) score of youth neither of whose parents has attained upper secondary education and the average mathematics (or numeracy) score of youth who have at least one parent who has attained tertiary education (ISCED 5 and 6).
4. The PISA indicator measuring the impact of parental immigration background is calculated as the ratio between the average reading score of native youth who have both parents of immigrant background and the average reading score of native youth neither of whose parents has an immigrant background.

Notes: All indicators have been normalised in a way which implies that a higher value and being among the "top 25%" reflect better performance. For this purpose, the inverse of the share of low performers is considered in the ranking. Countries which have sample sizes for one of the reference groups smaller than 30 are given a missing value (m). The summary indicator is calculated as a simple average of the five indicators.

Sources: OECD calculations based on the *Survey of Adult Skills (PIAAC) (2012)* (database), OECD (2013c), "PISA: Programme for International Student Assessment", *OECD Education Statistics* (database), *http://dx.doi.org/10.1787/data-00365-en*.

How well can students develop their skills?

Students need to acquire strong skills through education. In addition, to enhance youth employability and improve transition from education to work, multiple education pathways should be available. Work-based learning, if integrated into diverse education programmes beyond compulsory schooling, helps develop relevant skills and guides students in their careers. To measure these aspects of skills development, the Skills Scoreboard uses five indicators presenting the level of skills at age 15 and beyond across different types of education and students' interaction with the labour market (Table 2.3).

■ Table 2.3 ■

Skills Scoreboard on youth employability: How well can students develop their skills?

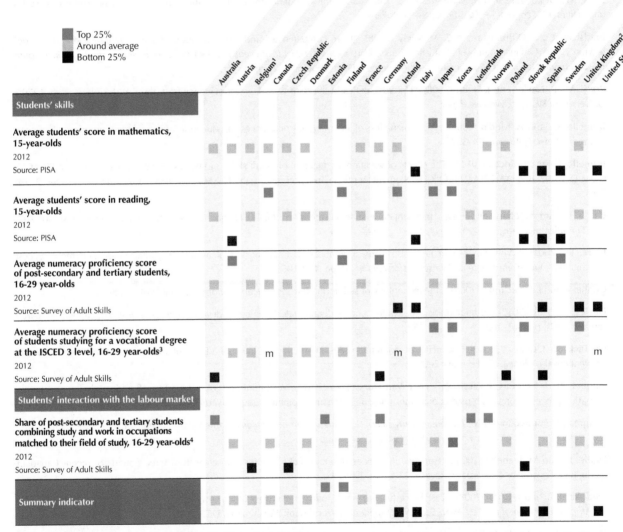

1. All indicators from the Survey of Adult Skills for Belgium refer to Flanders.
2. All indicators from the Survey of Adult Skills for the United Kingdom refer to England and Northern Ireland.
3. Canada, Ireland and the United States which do not offer vocational degrees at the ISCED 3 level have a "missing" value for this indicator. VET upper secondary programmes include those classified as 3C (long) and 3B in the ISCED framework, excluding "general" and "humanities, languages and arts" fields of study.
4. Values for Australia and Finland have been imputed from the overall share of students combining work and study available from the Survey of Adult Skills as they are highly correlated.

Notes: All indicators have been normalised in a way which implies that a higher value and being among the "top 25%" reflect better performance. The summary indicator is calculated as a simple average of the five indicators.

Sources: OECD calculations based on the *Survey of Adult Skills (PIAAC) (2012)* (database), OECD (2013c), "PISA: Programme for International Student Assessment", *OECD Education Statistics* (database), *http://dx.doi.org/10.1787/data-00365-en*.

Note

1. These are youth who did not take computer-based assessment (CBA) either because they have no computer experience, failed the ICT core test, or opted out of the CBA. Although those who opted out of the CBA do not necessarily lack computer experience or the skills to take CBA, they are more similar to the respondents who failed the ICT core test than those who passed and took the CBA (OECD, 2013a).

References

Atfield, G. and K. Purcell (2010), "Graduate labour market supply and demand: Final year students' perceptions of the skills they have to offer and the skills employers seek", *Futuretrack Working Paper 4*.

Beffy, M., D. Fougère and A. Maurel (2009), "L'impact du travail salarié des étudiants sur la réussite et la poursuite des études universitaires", *Economie et Statistique*, No. 422, Paris.

Bradshaw, C., L. O'Brennan and C. McNeely (2008), "Core competencies and the prevention of school failure and early school leaving", in N.G. Guerra and C.P. Bradshaw (eds.), *Core Competencies to Prevent Problem Behaviours and Promote Positive Youth Development*, New Directions for Child and Adolescent Development, 122, pp. 19-32.

Bratti, M., R. Naylor and J. Smith (2008), "Heterogeneities in the returns to degrees: evidence from the British Cohort Study 1970", *University of Warwick Working Paper*.

Brunello, G. and A. Medio (2001), "An explanation of international differences in education and workplace training", *European Economic Review*, 45, pp. 307-322.

Brunello, G. and L. Rocco (2014), "The effects of vocational education on adult skills and wages. What can we learn from PIAAC?", COM/DELSA/EDU/PIAAC(2014)11. OECD document for official use, presented at the 13th Meeting of the PIAAC BPC, 15-16 Dec. 2014, Paris.

Causa, O. and Å. Johansson (2009), "Intergenerational social mobility", *OECD Economics Department Working Papers*, No. 707, OECD Publishing, Paris, *http://dx.doi.org/10.1787/223106258208*.

Clark, D. (2001), "Why do German firms subsidize apprenticeship training? Test of asymmetric information and mobility cost explanation", *Vierteljahreshefte für Wirtschaftsforschung*, 70, pp. 102-106.

Cunha, F. and J. J. Heckman (2007), "The technology of skill formation", *American Economic Review*, Vol. 97, No. 2.

Davies, P., et al. (2013), "Labour market motivation and undergraduates' choice of degree subject", *British Educational Research Journal*, 39(2), pp. 361-382.

De Rick, K. (2008), "Costs and benefits of apprenticeships in the lowest track of VET", International Network on Innovative Apprenticeship, Vienna, 1-2 February 2008.

Duquet, N., I. Glorieux, I. Laurijssen and Y. Van Dorsselaer, (2010), "An unfinished job? The effect of subject choice and family formation processes on labour market outcomes for young men and women", *Journal of Education and Work*, 23(4), pp. 319-338.

European Commission (2013), *Preventing Early School Leaving in Europe: Lessons Learned from Second Chance Education*, http://ec.europa.eu/education/library/study/2013/second-chance_en.pdf.

Finnie, R. and M. Frenette (2003), "Earnings differences by major field of study: Evidence from three cohorts of recent Canadian graduates", *Economics of Education Review*, 22(1), pp. 179-192.

Fredriksen, B. and J.-P. Tan (2008), "East Asia education study tour: An overview of key insights", in B. Fredriksen and J.-P. Tan (eds.), *An Africa Exploration of the East Asian Education Experience*, World Bank, Washington, DC.

Heckman, J.J. and T. Kautz (2013), "Fostering and measuring skills: Interventions that improve character and cognition", *NBER Working Paper*, No. 19656, National Bureau of Economic Research.

Humburg, M., R. van der Velden and A. Verhagen (2013), "The employability of higher education graduates: the employers' perspective", European Commission, http://ec.europa.eu/education/library/study/2013/employability_en.pdf.

Lerman, R.I. (2013), "Skill development in middle level occupations: The role of apprenticeship training", *IZA Policy Paper*, No. 61, Institute for the Study of Labor (IZA).

Lowden, K. et al. (2011), *Employers' perceptions of the employability skills of new graduates*, University of Glasgow SCRE Centre and Edge Foundation.

Lyche, C. (2010), "Taking on the completion challenge: A literature review on policies to prevent dropout and early school leaving", *OECD Education Working Papers*, No. 53, OECD Publishing, Paris, *http://dx.doi.org/10.1787/5km4m2t59cmr-en*.

Mühlemann, S. et al. (2007), "An empirical analysis of the decision to train apprentices", *Labour: Review of Labour Economics and Industrial Relations*, 21(3), pp. 419-42.

OECD (2015), *Education at a Glance Interim Report: Update of Employment and Educational Attainment Indicators*, OECD, Paris, *www.oecd.org/edu/EAG-Interim-report.pdf*.

OECD (2014a), *OECD Employment Outlook 2014*, OECD Publishing, Paris, *http://dx.doi.org/10.1787/empl_outlook-2014-en*.

OECD (2014b), *Education at a Glance 2014: OECD Indicators*, OECD Publishing, Paris, *http://dx.doi.org/10.1787/eag-2014-en*.

OECD (2014c), "Background paper prepared by the OECD", paper prepared for the G20-OECD-EC Conference on Quality Apprenticeships for Giving Youth a Better Start in the Labour Market, *www.oecd.org/els/emp/G20-OECD-EC%20Apprenticeship%20 Conference_Issues%20Paper.pdf*.

OECD (2013a), *OECD Skills Outlook 2013: First Results from the Survey of Adult Skills*, OECD Publishing, Paris, *http://dx.doi. org/10.1787/9789264204256-en*.

OECD (2013b), *PISA 2012 Results: Excellence Through Equity (Volume II): Giving Every Student the Chance to Succeed*, PISA, OECD Publishing, Paris, *http://dx.doi.org/10.1787/9789264201132-en*.

OECD (2013c), "PISA: Programme for International Student Assessment", *OECD Education Statistics (database)*, *http://dx.doi. org/10.1787/data-00365-en* (accessed 8 August 2014).

OECD (2010), *Learning for Jobs,* OECD Reviews of Vocational Education and Training, OECD Publishing, Paris, *http://dx.doi. org/10.1787/9789264087460-en*.

Pallas, A. (2000), "The Effects of Schooling on Individual Lives", in M. T. Hallinan (ed.), *Handbook of the Sociology of Education*, pp. 499-525.

Quintini, G. and **T. Manfredi** (2009), "Going separate ways? School-to-work transitions in the United States and Europe", *OECD Social, Employment and Migration Working Papers*, No. 90, OECD Publishing, Paris, *http://dx.doi.org/10.1787/221717700447*.

Quintini, G. and **S. Martin** (2014), "Same same but different: School-to-work transitions in emerging and advanced economies", *OECD Social, Employment and Migration Working Papers*, No. 154, OECD Publishing, Paris, *http://dx.doi.org/10.1787/5jzbb2t1rcwc-en*.

Reay, D., J. Davies, M. David and **S.J. Ball** (2001), "Choices of degree or degrees of choice? Class, race and the higher education choice process", *Sociology*, 35(4), pp. 855-874.

Siow, A. (1984), "Occupational choice under uncertainty", *Econometrica*, 52, pp. 631-45.

Tan, J.-P. and **Y.-J.J. Nam** (2012), "Pre-employment technical and vocational education and training: Fostering relevance, effectiveness, and efficiency", in Almeida, et al. (eds.), *The Right Skills for the Job?: Rethinking Training Policies for Workers*, World Bank, Washington, DC.

Usher, A. (2006), *Grants for Students: What They Do, Why They Work*, Canadian Education Report Series, Educational Policy Institute, Toronto, Ontario.

Zarkin, G. (1985), "Occupational choice: an application to the market for public school teachers", *Quarterly Journal of Economics*, 100, pp. 409-46.

3

Policies towards improving young people's education and skills

All levels of education – from pre-primary to tertiary – and all modes of education – from learning on the job to massive open online courses – can help to prepare young people for the world of work. This chapter focuses on how governments, policy makers and educators can ensure that all young people leave school well-equipped to enter – and succeed in – the labour market.

Young people need to be better prepared for the world of work. This requires building more responsive education systems. Education systems have to be responsive to children and students' backgrounds, history and specific needs to ensure that nobody is left behind. They should also be responsive to labour market needs and help students acquire strong employability skills. Governments have a leading role to play in reforming their education systems so as to improve young people's skills. However, efforts will be undermined if they are not supported by the whole community. Governments have to work closely with other stakeholders including parents, social institutions and employers.

ENSURING THAT ALL YOUTH LEAVE EDUCATION WITH ADEQUATE SKILLS

A holistic approach to skills

As a wide range of skills is needed to be successful in all facets of life, education systems can develop employability skills through different levels and types of education – schools, vocational programmes and universities. Parents and local communities, including employers, trade unions, voluntary organisations, cultural institutions and social services can also contribute to this goal since these skills are often acquired both inside and outside the education system. Given that the demand for skills is changing rapidly, parents, educators and other stakeholders should help young people build a capacity for lifelong learning so that they can adapt to changing demands.

Empirical evidence based on randomised experiments (mainly in the United States) shows that some intervention programmes, particularly early childhood programmes, have been consistently successful in improving social and emotional skills (Heckman and Kautz, 2013). Programmes targeting adolescents and young adults have been less effective in this respect. This evidence points to the importance of acquiring and developing skills early in life and of the role of parents in the process. Successful programmes typically include pre-school activities and meetings between parents and teachers. Successful intervention programmes for adolescents generally have a mentoring component as part of a work-based activity.

Policy makers in OECD countries are increasingly paying attention to social and emotional skills, after concentrating efforts to increase student achievement in the past decades (OECD, 2015a). Empirical evidence shows that these skills can be developed through both routine education practices and extracurricular activities, such as sports and arts. The skills most often targeted in national curricula include autonomy, responsibility, tolerance, critical thinking and intercultural understanding. Most national curricula include subjects that specifically target students' social and emotional skills, such as physical and health education, civic and citizenship education, and moral or religious education. Some countries also incorporate the development of social and emotional skills in the core curriculum. In addition, many OECD students participate in school governance and classroom management as alternative forms of extracurricular activities. These activities help students to develop the skills necessary for living in democratic societies, such as negotiating, teamwork and taking responsibility.

Most schools may not have the capacity to introduce major innovations to develop different types of social and emotional skills; however, they can adapt existing practices and introduce innovative new ones to foster the development of these skills. Over the past decade, many countries have developed a more holistic approach to education by integrating the development of these skills specifically into school curricula, fostering co-operation between schools and local communities, and introducing major reforms to education (Box 3.1).

Workplaces are learning environments as well. Firms are often better-equipped with the newest technologies – and ideally with the people who know how to use them and guide the learning – than educational institutions, and thus better-suited to provide practical training. At the same time, many cognitive skills, especially problem solving, and social and emotional skills – such as communication and conflict management – may be more effectively taught and learned in workplaces than in classrooms.

Box 3.1 **How some education systems are taking a more holistic approach to skills: Country examples**

In recent years, some countries have adopted a more holistic approach to education. They have made the goal of developing social and emotional skills explicit by including it in their curricula and by introducing concrete actions to achieve it. The OECD publication, Skills for Social Progress, describes some of these actions (OECD, 2015a).

In Korea, school curricula and the ways in which students are tested emphasise learning facts over creative thinking (Jones, 2013). To address this issue, the curriculum was revised in 2009 to include direct and indirect methods for developing creativity and innovation and the academic content of the curriculum was reduced by 20%. The curriculum now includes "creative experiential learning activities" – essentially, extracurricular activities that allow for the learning of the core subjects.

In June 2013, the government of Denmark introduced a comprehensive reform of compulsory education to raise its quality and outcomes. The reform includes the development of a more varied school day to promote curiosity, innovation and entrepreneurship. The national framework sets the number of hours for each discipline, but school leaders have the responsibility of organising school days, including extracurricular activities. Short periods of physical activity have to be included in every school day, and more music lessons are offered. School leaders are asked to be more open to, and to co-operate with, local community organisations, such as sport clubs, cultural centres and other associations.

In addition to including extracurricular activities, the Danish government encourages the development of new forms of teaching to promote social and emotional skills. For example, schools can co-operate with local sports clubs to teach English or maths through physical exercise. In 2014, the government allocated funding to 15 schools, for the academic year 2015/16, to experiment with outdoor education and demonstrate how it could work.

Immigrant students are often unaware that words can have more than one meaning, and have trouble understanding abstract concepts and phrases. In 2014, the Danish government developed a booklet on the "grey zone" of language that can be used by volunteers working in homework cafés, a well-developed system of places, often libraries, where students can go after school to receive help on their homework.

In France, the government introduced in 2014 a new school schedule over four-and-a-half days instead of four days while shortening the school day. The objectives are both to better distribute learning time over the week, with main lessons given in the morning, and to develop extracurricular activities organised by municipalities. These changes aim to develop equal access to extracurricular activities and to move towards a more holistic approach to education.

Sources:

Danish Ministry of Education website, *http://eng.uvm.dk/*.

French Ministry of Education website, *www.education.gouv.fr/pid29074/la-nouvelle-organisation-du-temps-scolaire-a-l-ecole.html*.

Jones, R. S. (2013), "Education Reform in Korea", *OECD Economics Department Working Papers*, No. 1067, OECD Publishing, Paris, *http://dx.doi.org/10.1787/5k43nxs1t9vh-en*.

Korean National Curriculum Information Center website, *http://ncic.kice.re.kr/english.kri.org.inventoryList.do*.

OECD (2015a), *Skills for Social Progress: The Power of Social and Emotional Skills*, OECD Skills Studies, OECD Publishing, Paris, *http://dx.doi.org/10.1787/9789264226159-en*.

High-quality pre-primary education for all

Educational failure can start early in the education process and disparities often emerge early on. PISA shows that students who attended pre-primary school tend to outperform those who did not, at the age of 15, even after accounting for the students' socio-economic status (Figure 3.1). Furthermore, enrolment in high-quality, pre-primary education for all children, regardless of their socio-economic status, can help mitigate inherited disparities (Carneiro and Heckman, 2003; Machin, 2006; d'Addio, 2007; OECD, 2006) and improve cognitive skills in a lasting way (Heckman and Kautz, 2013). The benefits are significant for disadvantaged pupils (e.g. Blau and Currie, 2006). According to PISA, native-born children of immigrants who attended pre-primary school are a full year ahead of their peers who stayed at home, in terms of reading skills. Recognising this, the provision of cost-effective and quality childhood education and care has been on the government's agenda in many OECD countries (Box 3.2). These efforts can be continued.

■ Figure 3.1 ■
Difference in mathematics performance, by attendance at pre-primary school
15-year-olds, 2012

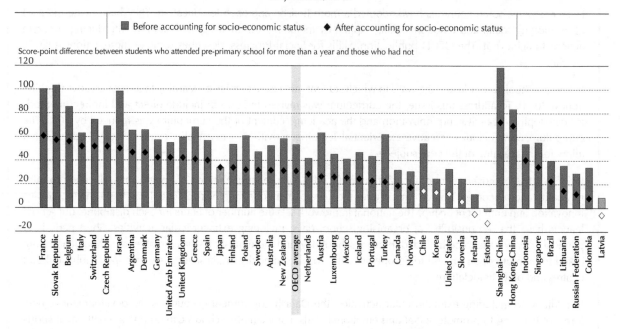

Notes: Score-point differences that are statistically significant are marked in a darker tone. Countries and economies are ranked in descending order of the score-point difference in mathematics performance between students who reported that they had attended pre-primary school (ISCED 0) for more than one year and those who had not attended pre-primary school, after accounting for socio-economic status.

Source: OECD (2013), "PISA: Programme for International Student Assessment", *OECD Education Statistics* (database), *http://dx.doi.org/10.1787/data-00365-en*.

StatLink ⬛⬛ http://dx.doi.org/10.1787/888933214583

Box 3.2 **Enhancing quality in early childhood education and care: Country examples**

Integrating the provision of early childhood education and care (ECEC) from birth to compulsory education is considered a key factor for achieving inclusive education. Only a few OECD countries, notably New Zealand, Norway and Sweden have established such an integrated ECEC system under one lead ministry which provides continuous development for pre-school children.

Prior to 1986 in New Zealand, responsibility for funding and administration of early childhood care and education services was split among the Departments of Education, Social Welfare, and Maori Affairs. The integration of care and education under the Ministry of Education influenced the style of curriculum that was developed. In 1996 the final version of Te Whaariki, the New Zealand national curriculum for children ups to age 5, was launched following a wide consultation process between the curriculum developers, early childhood practitioners, and representatives of the Maori community.

The curriculum includes overall principles and goals for all early childhood education and care programmes putting the child and play at the centre of the curriculum and focusing on experience and meaning rather than mere knowledge acquisition. It has four overall principles: empowerment, holistic development, family and community, and relationships. Five strands shape the outcomes for children: belonging, well-being, exploration, communication and contribution. The curriculum addresses culture and customs in a way that seeks to embrace the diversity of its population. Each curriculum strand is linked with the learning areas and skills in the primary school curriculum. These links clearly describe what children are expected to do in primary school, how this relates to the experiences in ECEC and what activities staff can implement to facilitate transition.

New Zealand uses child assessment practices as a method for reflecting upon curriculum design and implementation. For this purpose, staff and children describe children's experiences in a Learning Story Framework, which focuses on assessment in a narrative form as a story. The desired outcome is that children leave the ECEC setting for further education with the inclination, knowledge and skills to be learners.

...

Similarly, Sweden took a consultative approach to lay the ground for a common organisation of ECEC in the seventies. The Pre-school Act came into force in 1975. In 1996, the goals of early childhood education were re-defined and its responsibility was shifted from the Ministry of Health and Social Affairs to the Ministry of Education and Science. The Curriculum for Pre-school was passed by the Swedish Parliament in 1998. The curriculum explicitly identifies early childhood education as a systemic and integrated approach to children's needs, a family model of pre-school centres and an interest in the holistic development and well-being of children. The curriculum for pre-school education emphasises the importance of learning and play, democratic values, equity and a child-centered pre-school environment based on co-operation between the children's home and the pre-school.

In 2011, Sweden implemented a reform with the aim to further improve quality by making the ECEC more instructive and giving teachers more responsibility. The pedagogical tasks have been strengthened by clarifying the goals for language and communication, mathematics, natural science and technology. The follow up, evaluation and development components were strengthened as well as the responsibility of the head of the pre-school.

ECEC quality in Sweden is regularly and systematically documented, followed up on and evaluated, with the perspective of the child being given an important role. Children and parents can participate in evaluation, and their views are to be given prominence. Additionally, self-evaluation kits have been developed so that professionals can evaluate their knowledge and implementation of the curriculum framework.

Sources:

Meare, M. and V. Podmore (2002), "Early Childhood Education Policy Co-ordination under the Auspices of the Department/Ministry of Education: A Case Study of New Zealand", *UNESCO Early Childhood and Family Policy Series N°1*, March 2002, UNESCO.

O'Dowd, M. (2013), "Early childhood education in Sweden: The market curriculum 2000-2013?", *Revista Española de Educación Comparada*, 21, pp. 85-118.

Taguma, M., I. Litjens and K. Makowiecki (2013), *Quality Matters in Early Childhood Education and Care: Sweden 2013*, OECD Publishing, Paris, *http://dx.doi.org/10.1787/9789264176744-en*.

Taguma, M., I. Litjens and K. Makowiecki (2012), *Quality Matters in Early Childhood Education and Care: New Zealand 2012*, OECD Publishing, Paris, *http://dx.doi.org/10.1787/9789264176690-en*.

Prevention of low skills outcomes and school dropout

Identifying students with the lowest skills and those at risk of dropping out of school is crucial in order to prevent these failures. This requires a comprehensive approach that includes specific support at schools, help from social institutions to address social and behavioural aspects, and the involvement of schools, students and family. Reliable data on the dropout challenge itself and the underlying risk factors should be collected and transferred between school levels to guarantee early preventive measures and selective interventions. Some countries have been successful in identifying students who face difficulties at an early stage (Box 3.3).

Box 3.3 **Identifying youth with low skills and at risk of dropping out: Country examples**

Youth with low skills are more likely to drop out of education and to struggle to integrate into the labour market. Increasingly, OECD countries are making efforts to identify the groups most at risk and reach them quickly.

In the Netherlands, policies to prevent school dropout focus on prevention, keeping students in school, smoothing transition into work, and increasing the provision of work-based learning. As part of this package, the government implemented the so-called qualification requirement for all youth aged 16-23: those youth without a degree from secondary education are obliged to attend school until graduation. Thirty-nine regional report and co-ordination centres (RMCs) have been established to support youth in continuing their education and guiding their school-to-work transition. In addition, the Ministry of Education, Culture and Science allocated funding for better guidance for students in their study and career choice; intensified collaboration between secondary, vocational and adult education schools; and stronger co-operation between a wide range of stakeholders, including local authorities, schools, trade unions and industry, social services and justice departments. The implementation of these policies has coincided with a decline in dropout rates from 5.5% in 2002 to 2.1% in 2013 (although some measurement issues may have contributed, as well).

...

In parallel, a personal identification number (PGN) has been issued to every child in the Netherlands over the age of three and a half. Similar to a social insurance number, the PGN follows students from school to school as they progress through the education system, enabling the system to monitor their school careers, school attendance and dropout risk. These data are linked to socio-economic information (including immigrant background, employment status and entitlement to social benefits). This monitoring process enables the authorities to assess what works, and consequently, to disseminate good practices. The PGN offers complete and reliable figures from national to municipal levels, and all schools in secondary education are expected to register absenteeism, disengagement and dropping out. A monthly report is available to municipalities and schools to allow them to reach those at risk. An RMC contacts the absentees and summons them back to school once these students have missed classes for a number of days.

Similar initiatives have been established in Estonia and Luxembourg, among other countries. The Estonian Educational Information System (EEIS) is a national register that consolidates information on the education system, including information on educational institutions, pupils, teachers, graduation documents and curricula. Local governments can use EEIS to access information on the pupils living in their territory, and on those who have moved to a school located in the territory of another local government. Educational institutions are obliged to enter information into the EEIS and to check and amend the entered information for accuracy. Pupils and teachers can view the education-related information held on them. The register tracks each student's education career. The register also shows if a student has dropped out of school and if he/she has continued in an evening school, vocational school, etc. In Luxembourg, a digital national pupil register and a systematic procedure developed by the Ministry of Education with the services of Local Action for Youth (Action Locale pour Jeunes, ALJ) identifies young people leaving school without a diploma. Monthly lists are produced, which are then used by ALJ to reach early school leavers.

Other programmes worth mentioning are: the URBACT project in several European cities that targets early school leavers with parental involvement; the Glasgow City Education Department Strategy with a comprehensive approach and high commitment on the part of social advisors; and Plug-innovation in Sweden that compiles different strategies to prevent youth from dropping out, one of which is in Gottenburg and has a comprehensive approach including pre-emptive, preventive and remedial interventions.

Sources:

Akkerman, Y. et al. (2011), "Overcoming school failure, policies that work: Background report for the Netherlands", Ministry of Education, Culture and Science, Den Haag.

European Commission (2013), *Preventing Early School Leaving in Europe: Lessons Learned from Second Chance Education*, http://ec.europa.eu/education/library/study/2013/second-chance_en.pdf.

Ministry of Education, Culture and Science (2014), *Kamerbrief nieuwe cijfers over terugdringen voortijdig schoolverlaten 15 Januari 2014*, Ministry of Education, Culture and Science, Den Haag.

Ministry of Education, Culture and Science (2011), *Schooluitval voorkomen in Nederland: Speerpunten huidige aanpak en doorkijk naar vervolgbeleid; Resultaat schooljaar 2009-2010*, (Preventing School Dropout in the Netherlands: Priorities of the Current Approach and Perspective on Follow-up Policy; Results for School Year 2009/10), Ministry of Education, Culture and Science, Den Haag.

http://urbact.eu/urbact-glance.

http://pluginnovation.se.

Preventing students from dropping out of education may, in the short term, limit the difficulties faced by youth in the labour market in times of high unemployment, but also raise their employability in the long term. Institutions would ideally encourage young people to stay in the education system, or to reconnect rapidly with education if they have dropped out, as limiting the duration of disengagement has proven the most effective way of re-engaging early school leavers (Polidano, Tabasso and Tseng, 2012). Countries have developed various strategies to address dropouts in which school leavers are encouraged to resume education immediately, most of the time in work-study programmes (OECD, 2010a gives an overview of initiatives in OECD countries; see Box 3.4). The European Youth Guarantee Framework also goes in this direction (see Chapter 5).

Youth who have left the education system without strong skills for a relatively long period of time should be given a second chance to develop a balanced set of employability skills. A number of factors contribute to the efficiency of second-chance schemes which help youth return to education and potentially integrate into the mainstream education system (European Commission, 2013). Programmes using flexible structures that are not schools and appealing activities such as music or sports, applying innovative curricula and pedagogic approaches, and providing specialised support (e.g. psychological and financial support), counselling and career guidance have been most effective in this respect. Some countries (e.g. European countries) have introduced second-chance schemes (Chapter 5), but the impact of many of these programmes on youth skills and transitions into the labour market still need to be carefully evaluated.

Box 3.4 **Combatting dropout in a preventive way:**
Regent Park "Pathways to Education" Programme in Toronto, Canada

In partnership with parents, community agencies, volunteers, local school boards and secondary schools, the "Pathways to Education Program" in Canada provides four main types of support for students in Regent Park, one of Toronto's most disadvantaged communities: academic tutoring, group and career mentoring, advocacy and financial support. Tutoring sessions focus on homework and study assignments, as well as prepared exercises and other learning activities to help students develop as competent learners, while boosting literacy, numeracy and general knowledge. Group mentoring is provided for Grade 9 and 10 students, while specialty and career mentoring is provided for Grade 11 and 12 students. The overall goal of group mentoring is to provide positive experiences where youth can further develop age-appropriate social skills, including problem solving, team building, communication and negotiation. Career mentoring is designed to support students in pursuing their post-secondary goals, including through formal connections with the high school graduates for two years after high school. Each student is assigned a Student-Parent Support Worker (SPSW), who monitors school attendance, academic progress and programme participation while helping the student build stable relationships with parents, teachers and other students. Pathways' financial aid, such as bus tickets and lunch vouchers, was designed to remove financial barriers that hinder school participation.

Overall, from 2001, when the first cohort of Regent Park students entered Grade 9, until 2010, the programme has helped reduce dropout rates from 56% (which was double the rate for the City of Toronto) to less than 11.7%, for the first five cohorts in Regent Park. Evaluation studies reveal that the programme has been successful in helping participants to achieve their high school credits. As a result, pathways students average more earned credits than the general student population at all three grade levels. In parallel, absenteeism rates continue to decline. Pathways students are consistently more likely to be represented in the academic stream than non-pathways students. Students in the Regent Park Pathways Program in Grades 11 and 12 are continuing to perform well, as both graduation rates and participation rates in post-secondary education remain high.

In 2011-2012, 75% of Ontario's Pathways graduates (approximately 1 170 graduates) had enrolled in post-secondary education compared to the Toronto District School Board's rate of 61% transition. The Canadian Federal Government provided support to expand the Pathways Program in 2013. The programme is now working in 12 additional communities, including with Aboriginal groups in North Winnipeg.

Sources:
Government of Canada, *http://actionplan.gc.ca/en/initiative/pathways-education-canada*.
Pathways to Education (2010), "Pathways to Education: Program Introduction and Overview", *www.pathwaystoeducation.ca/sites/default/files/pdf/Overview%2021_10_10_0.pdf*.
Pathways to Education (2013), "2012 Results Summary: Pathways to Education 2011-2012 Program Results", *www.pathwaystoeducation.ca/sites/default/files/pdf/Results%20summary,%202011%20-%202012%20FINAL.pdf*.

In emerging economies, the high opportunity costs of school education may contribute to early school leaving. When households have difficulties in meeting their basic needs, children can be taken out of school to save on costs and sent to work. Children can work in the labour market, in home-based enterprises, or as substitutes for parents in doing household chores. Children who leave school temporarily may be less likely to return to school. Hence, shocks that induce parents to take their children out of school may have long-term effects on their children's human capital development and future earnings. Conditional cash transfer programmes, such as "Oportunidades" in Mexico, and others around the world (Morley and Coady, 2003) have been used to induce poor parents to send their children to school and care more for their health. These programmes have proven to be effective in raising educational attainment (Schultz, 2004), not only because they get children to school who would not have gone otherwise, but also because the programmes prevent children exposed to shocks from dropping out (De Janvry et al., 2006).

Multiple and flexible pathways to success

An increasing share of the skills needed for the future labour market is likely to be developed beyond upper secondary school, but university is not the only route to pursue further education. In addition, some youth may disengage from education and re-engage at a later stage.

Multiple pathways within the education system provide greater opportunities for all youth to succeed. A diversity of education programmes gives more chances to students to find the types of programmes that correspond to their needs, expectations and skills, and to continue education. But establishing bridges between the different pathways is essential for allowing youth to change career directions while building on their earlier skills investment (Box 3.5). In this respect, it is also important to certify the training component of programmes through a system of nationally or internationally recognised qualifications and competencies, as in the case of some OECD countries (Box 3.6).

Box 3.5 **Providing multiple pathways to enable a smooth transition among learning tracks: Country examples**

Many youth are struggling within education systems because of their inflexibility. Some OECD countries have made efforts to diversify the learning paths for youth, but challenges remain.

In Australia, initial and continuing education are jointly steered and provided with large flexibility to accommodate the specific needs of students of all ages. The system gives second chance opportunities to individuals who did not gain a first qualification or who want to upgrade their skills or change their career pathways (Hoeckel et al., 2008).

The Australian VET system is also flexible and able to satisfy many different needs at many different points in people's lives, whether they are preparing for a first career, seeking additional skills to assist in their work, pursuing learning outside their work needs or catching up on educational attainment. The majority of VET students study part-time and the age range is wide. VET programmes can lead to a single module or unit of competency, or to advanced diplomas. The types of training range from formal classroom learning to workplace-based learning and may include flexible, self-paced learning, or online training. VET takes place in both private and public registered training organisations, in schools, universities or other higher education providers, adult or community education, and various cultural, religious or other bodies providing specific training. However, cross-state differences with regard to skills recognition can reduce the responsiveness of VET to changing needs by impeding labour mobility, since for many occupations a license acquired in one state does not entitle an individual to work in another. Furthermore, there is a lack of streamlined regulatory and governance frameworks between tertiary education institutions (including both VET and higher education), which also creates duplication and inconsistency.

The Austrian VET system aims at providing flexible pathways in and out of the system. Currently, 27% of upper-secondary students enrol in a vocational college, where after five years they can acquire both a vocational diploma and the upper secondary school leaving certificate giving access to university. After several years of professional experience, graduates from technical and agricultural vocational colleges can be granted the title "engineer". The vocational colleges are also accessible for graduates from other upper secondary programmes. Increasingly, vocational colleges provide an important route into tertiary education: one in four university students, and almost one in two students at universities of applied sciences, are now vocational college graduates. However, since the Austrian vocational college programmes combine elements of upper secondary and post-secondary education, they have few international parallels.

In Switzerland, dual diplomas (combining a VET qualification with a university entrance qualification) facilitate access to higher education (Musset et al., 2013).

In Germany, too, access to university for VET graduates was formally enhanced in 2009 and is strongly supported by government campaigns. The new regulations permit those with an advanced vocational qualification general access to academic higher education and holders of other vocational qualifications a subject-specific access to higher education. To support those pursuing this pathway a range of measures have been piloted or rolled out nationally and initiated locally such as advancement scholarships or bilateral credit transfer systems between individual vocational colleges and universities of applied science. Yet, implementation remains a challenge, as it crucially hinges upon the collaboration between individual institutions (Fazekas and Field, 2013).

In the Netherlands, the schooling system is characterised by a high degree of early streaming. However, the different learning routes – including vocational programmes – are structured in such a way that young people have the possibility to go up a step within the track they have chosen, and reach the equivalent of tertiary level education (ISCED 5 level). Possibilities for upstream transfers also exist between vocational and university education (OECD, 2008a).

Sources:

Fazekas, M. and S. Field (2013), *A Skills beyond School Review of Switzerland,* OECD Reviews of Vocational Education and Training, OECD Publishing, Paris, *http://dx.doi.org/10.1787/9789264062665-en.*

Hoeckel, K., et al. (2008), *OECD Reviews of Vocational Education and Training: A Learning for Jobs Review of Australia 2008,* OECD Reviews of Vocational Education and Training, OECD Publishing, Paris, *http://dx.doi.org/10.1787/9789264113596-en.*

Musset, P., et al. (2013), *A Skills beyond School Review of Austria,* OECD Reviews of Vocational Education and Training, OECD Publishing, Paris, *http://dx.doi.org/10.1787/9789264200418-en.*

OECD (2014a), *OECD Economic Surveys Australia,* OECD Publishing, Paris, *http://dx.doi.org/10.1787/eco_surveys-aus-2014-en.*

OECD (2008a), *Jobs for Youth/Des emplois pour les jeunes: Netherlands 2008,* OECD Publishing, Paris, *http://dx.doi.org/10.1787/9789264041295-en.*

Box 3.6 **Towards a better formal recognition of skills through "Skills Passport" systems: Country examples**

In Japan, the Job Card is a document that records the individual's education, training and employment history, and can be used for further training and job searching. The Job Card system, established in 2009, provides on-the-job training in combination with classroom education (officially labelled as a programme to develop vocational ability). At the end of their training, education, and work placements, the skills and knowledge of participants are formally and objectively evaluated and recorded on the Job Cards. Participants in the programme also receive career guidance to facilitate their transition from training to employment.

The European Commission developed the European Skills Passport, an electronic portfolio which documents all the skills and qualifications citizens have acquired, including those learnt during apprenticeships. The idea is to facilitate the validation of employability skills across European countries and fields of work, and to help graduates and students find a job or training.

In Australia, the government has re-introduced legislation to support the introduction of the Unique Student Identifier (USI), which began on 1 January 2015. The USI allows all of an individual's training records, entered in the national VET data collection, to be linked. It will make it easier for students to find, collate and authenticate their VET achievements into a single transcript. It will also ensure that students' VET records are not lost. The USI will stay with the student for life and be recorded with any nationally recognised VET course that is undertaken from when the USI came into effect.

Sources:

Ministry of Health, Labour and Welfare of Japan (2009), *"The 'Job-Card System' in Japan"*, Tokyo.

OECD (2014b), "Background paper prepared by the OECD", paper prepared for the G20-OECD-EC Conference on Quality Apprenticeships for Giving Youth a Better Start in the Labour Market, *www.oecd.org/els/emp/G20-OECD-EC%20Apprenticeship%20Conference_Issues%20Paper.pdf*.

OECD (2010b), *Learning for Jobs*, OECD Reviews of Vocational Education and Training, OECD Publishing, Paris, *http://dx.doi.org/10.1787/9789264087460-en*.

https://europass.cedefop.europa.eu/en/documents/european-skills-passport.

www.innovation.gov.au/SKILLS/NATIONAL/UNIQUESTUDENTIDENTIFIERFORVET/Pages/default.aspx.

Countries that have a school curriculum which is broadly comprehensive with few vocational programmes at the upper secondary level need to offer a wide range of post-secondary programmes with both vocational and academic orientation. Countries with a developed upper secondary VET system should provide options to return to general education and to continue into post-secondary and tertiary programmes. Likewise, students in post-secondary VET should be able to enter university. Raising the quality of VET systems, especially by ensuring that they equip students with strong cognitive skills, would ease transitions into further education.

Above all, admission criteria at all educational levels can become more flexible so that skills and credits acquired through VET programmes and other educational and training paths be better recognised. The learning outcomes from students' professional qualifications would ideally be recognised through access and course exemptions – for example, by permitting students to enter directly into the second or third year of a bachelor programme. Options to gain credits in advance of the next education year, or to retake exams corresponding to the previous year in case of partial failure, can help students with difficulties in given areas to continue their education, while building on their strengths in other areas. Often the problem is a lack of transparency in terms of how different programmes relate to one another, but it may also reflect inadequate incentives for universities, in particular, to offer course exemptions (OECD, 2014c). Some countries have, however, successfully introduced multiple transition pathways (see Box 3.5).

RENDERING THE EDUCATION SYSTEM MORE RESPONSIVE TO LABOUR MARKET NEEDS

Quality work-based learning programmes

Developing work-based learning programmes across different levels and types of education is critical to better integrating students into the labour market. Several countries have made internships compulsory to validate some university qualifications (France, for instance) and many UK universities have integrated work-based training into their curricula along with other initiatives to enhance their graduates' employability (Box 3.7, as well as Chapter 5). Other countries, like Germany and Switzerland, require workplace training to validate an upper secondary or post-secondary VET qualification.

Box 3.7 **Employability skills initiatives in UK universities**

UK universities have been under intense pressure to equip graduates with more than just the academic skills traditionally represented by a subject discipline or a type of degree. A number of reports issued by employers' associations and higher education organisations have urged universities to make more explicit efforts to develop the skills needed to enhance graduate employability (e.g. Council for Industry and Higher Education, 1996).

University responses to this agenda typically include modifications to existing course content (sometimes in response to employer suggestions), the introduction of new courses and teaching methods, and provision of work-based training – all intended to enhance the development of employability skills and/or to ensure that the acquisition of such skills is integrated into the curriculum. In some cases, university departments have sought to embed the desired skills within courses; in other departments, students are offered stand-alone skills courses.

A recent evaluation study suggests that well-integrated work experience has clear positive effects on the ability of graduates to find employment within six months of graduation and to secure employment in graduate-level jobs. The latter job-quality measure is also positively and significantly associated with employer involvement in degree course design and delivery. These results suggest that exposing students to workplace training and decision making during their studies has positive effects on the future matches between graduates and their initial employers following graduation. In contrast, there is no evidence that the emphasis given by university departments to the teaching, learning and assessment of employability skills has a significant effect on either of the labour market outcomes considered.

Sources:

Council for Industry and Higher Education (CIHE) (1996), "Helping students towards success at work: Declaration of intent", CIHE, London.

Mason, G., G. Williams and S. Cranmer (2009), "Employability skills initiatives in higher education: what effects do they have on graduate labour market outcomes?", *Education Economics 17(1)*, pp. 1-30.

The OECD report Skills Beyond School recommends that all vocational education and training programmes should include a strong quality-assured work-based training component, which is well integrated into the curriculum and not too narrowly focused as a condition of receiving government funding (OECD, 2014c). Introducing such requirements would more strongly engage employers in the education system and could streamline many programmes, as those which are of little interest to employers may not be able to fulfil the requirement (Box 3.8).

Box 3.8 **Fostering co-operation between education providers, employers and other stakeholders to align VET with labour market needs: Country examples**

Social partners can engage with the various levels of the VET system, from secondary to higher education, to improve the quality of the VET system by ensuring the system's alignment with market requirements.

In Switzerland, the involvement of professional organisations (trade and employer organisations and trade unions) in VET policy making is required by law. Professional organisations draft the core curricula and have the leading role in the examination process of both secondary and post-secondary programmes. The role of Swiss authorities (at Confederation level) is to approve the curricula and examination rules, supervise examinations and issue federal diplomas. When new federal diploma qualifications are approved, they are industry-led, but the federal authorities check that the proposed qualification has the support of the whole industry sector, not just some enterprises. This ensures that the whole industry sector can be engaged in the updating of the qualification in response to changes in technology or industry organisation.

In Germany, social partners are closely engaged in the development and updating of training plans for each qualification, which are formally issued by the thematically involved federal ministry (e.g. economy, health) in accordance with the Ministry of Education. Such training plans regulate the duration of the workplace training, describe the profile of the profession, and set out final exam requirements. Apprenticeship salaries are determined through collective wage negotiations. The chambers of commerce advise participating companies, register apprenticeship contracts, examine the suitability of training firms and trainers, and set up and grade final exams.

...

Similarly, in Denmark social partners are strongly involved at the secondary and post-secondary levels of the VET system. With school associations and other institutions, they are part of advisory bodies that monitor labour market needs and make recommendations on the need to create new VET qualifications and to adapt existing ones, or to merge or re-organise programmes. In addition, they fund the trade committees that advise on the content, structure and evaluation of VET programmes at the sector level. Social partners also sit on the boards of vocational schools and post-secondary VET colleges and academies. When new needs emerge in areas not covered by trade committees, the Ministry of Education can appoint development committees to investigate whether new programmes are required.

As far as post-secondary VET is concerned, the United Kingdom government recently implemented a drastic reform to reduce qualification numbers for higher VET programmes from thousands to hundreds, following recommendations from OECD reviews and Whitehead (2013). Now each course/programme needs to provide five support letters from diverse employers. This gives employers more influence over the mix of training provisions and can ensure better alignment of these programmes with labour market needs.

While social partners in Sweden have had limited influence over secondary VET programmes so far, they play a prominent role at the post-secondary level. Each post-secondary VET programme in each institution has a steering group including employers, who provide training to students and advise on provision and programme content. To launch a programme, an education provider has to show that there is a demand among employers for skills associated with a specific qualification and that it has a framework to engage employers. The National Agency for Higher VET is responsible for the sector, and the social partners are part of a council that advises the agency on the future demand for skills and on how this might be met.

Sources:

Field, S., et al. (2012), *A Skills beyond School Review of Denmark,* OECD Reviews of Vocational Education and Training, OECD Publishing, Paris, *http://dx.doi.org/10.1787/9789264173668-en*.

Kuczera, M. (2013), "A skills beyond school commentary on Scotland", *www.oecd.org/edu/skills-beyond-school/ASkillsBeyondSchoolCommentary OnScotland.pdf*.

OECD (2014c), *Skills beyond School: Synthesis Report,* OECD Reviews of Vocational Education and Training, OECD Publishing, Paris, *http://dx.doi.org/10.1787/9789264214682-en*.

OECD (2010b), *Learning for Jobs,* OECD Reviews of Vocational Education and Training, OECD Publishing, Paris, *http://dx.doi.org/10.1787/9789264087460-en*.

Whitehead, N. (2013), "Review of adult vocational qualifications in the UK", UK Commission for Employment and Skills.

The portability of occupation-specific skills to various firms or sectors is a common concern about any occupation-specific training in VET. Firm-based apprenticeship training, as opposed to school-based systems, can limit mobility and adaptability at older ages, as occupation and job-specific skills can become obsolete at a faster rate than cognitive and social and emotional skills (Hanushek, Woessmann and Zhang, 2011).[1] However, research using German data shows that the skills taught in German apprenticeship training are often general (Geel and Gelner, 2009; Geel, Mure and Backes-Gellner, 2011; Clark and Fahr, 2001; Goggel and Zwick, 2012). Furthermore, countries with a long tradition of apprenticeships and stakeholder engagement exhibit a smoother transition from school to work, lower NEET rates and youth unemployment, and below average repeated unemployment spells than countries with a school-based system (Quintini and Manfredi, 2009).

While building occupation-specific skills, VET schemes, in particular, need to ensure that solid cognitive and social and emotional skills are enhanced, so that human capital acquired in these schemes is neither too general nor too specific or narrow. Students need both a set of practical occupation-specific skills that will make them immediately employable and productive, and thus facilitate their entry into the labour market, as well as a set of broader transferable skills, including numeracy, literacy, problem solving, teamwork, communication skills, flexibility and the capacity to learn new skills (OECD, 2014c). These skills are important as many VET graduates working as professionals and technicians are likely to be confronted with complex job tasks.

Weak cognitive skills among some VET students suggest that some programmes may not be selective enough, possibly because they have been maintained despite a lack of interest on the side of employers. Concerning entrance into apprenticeship programmes, many OECD countries do not specify any educational and skills requirements, while others aim to ensure high skill levels among participants (OECD, 2014b). However, the issue of selection criteria in VET programmes cannot be disconnected from the question of raising the quality of these programmes. When programmes have proved to lead to positive labour market outcomes and a work-based element is included, they automatically become selective, due to higher demand and the difficulties finding training places.

Support for work-based learning

The funding of training places influences the number of workplaces provided by employers, and thereby, the development of VET systems and other education programmes with a well-integrated work-based learning component. The workplace training salary should not be a barrier for employers but at the same time it should not generate risks of abuse (see also Chapter 5). In countries that have successfully developed apprenticeship systems, the workplace training salary is often negotiated through collective bargaining and depends on the experience of students. In these countries, employers know the benefits of providing training places and do not need financial incentives. However, employers will be less likely to provide work-based training in times of low labour demand or for some specific groups of youth. Hence temporary measures to foster the provision of workplaces or to acquire work-based learning outside the business sector might be needed in times of prolonged economic downturns. In countries with co-ordination problems in the labour market and poaching externalities (Pischke, 2005; Stevens, 1994), as well as no history of stakeholder engagement, government incentives may also be necessary (Box 3.9). These financial incentives have to be well targeted in time and on students and firms.

Box 3.9 **Encouraging the development and provision of work-based training through the funding system: Country examples**

Varying mixes of tax breaks, direct subsidies, student grants and levies are often available to encourage the participation of employers and students in work-based training.

Corporate tax deductibility of training costs is widespread across OECD countries, some (e.g. Austria) even allowing deductions greater than the costs incurred (OECD, 2014d). Such schemes help to shift the incentive balance towards training rather than recruiting skills externally. Small and young firms generally benefit little from tax breaks, but careful design of the tax arrangements can also create incentives for this group of companies. The Netherlands, for example, recently experimented with an extra deduction from taxable profits on training expenditures, plus an additional deduction for firms spending less than a specified amount. In targeting firms with low absolute levels of training expenditure, the incentive automatically targeted small firms while minimising deadweight losses (Stone, 2010). However, although targeting can lower deadweight expenditure, it may exacerbate bureaucracy or lead to unintended substitutions.

Direct subsidies, in the form of grants or training vouchers may facilitate targeting specific groups of enterprises and thereby may be more effective than tax incentives. That way, it might be easier to reduce deadweight effects. In general, subsidies need to be subject to comprehensive eligibility criteria and approval processes in order to alleviate potential moral hazard and adverse selection problems. Evidence from Switzerland suggests that subsidies can be an effective support mechanism for firms not yet involved in workplace training (Mühlemann et al., 2007), but they have limited effect on those firms that already provide training (Wacker, 2007). In addition to grants for enterprises, in many countries young trainees also qualify for grants complementing their wage income.

Many countries, especially in Europe, use levies – a compulsory form of collective assistance and cost sharing. Such schemes can result in higher levels of employer-based training, while addressing poaching, by requiring all firms to contribute to training expenditures. They also offer considerable scope for facilitating training among small employers through earmarking funds. Some schemes are criticised, however, for encouraging inefficient and inappropriate training, and favouring larger employers. Therefore, levies should ideally be set in a larger context beyond their function as a financial instrument (Iller and Moraal, 2013).

In Germany, the responsibility for funding vocational schools lies with the Länder and local authorities, while companies bear the costs of training in the workplace. In some sectors, there is a general fund to which all companies pay contributions and through which the costs for the apprenticing institutions are covered, while in other sectors each company bears its own costs.

Sources:

Iller, C. and D. Moraal (2013), "Kollektive Vereinbarungen in der Steuerung betrieblicher Weiterbildung. Beispiele aus den Niederlanden und Deutschland", *Magazin erwachsenenbildung.at Das, Fachmedium für Forschung, Praxis und Diskurs*, No. 18, Vienna.

Mühlemann, S. et al. (2007), "An empirical analysis of the decision to train apprentices", *Labour: Review of Labour Economics and Industrial Relations*, Vol. 21, No. 3, pp. 419-42.

OECD (2014b), "Background paper prepared by the OECD", paper prepared for the G20-OECD-EC Conference on Quality Apprenticeships for Giving Youth a Better Start in the Labour Market, *www.oecd.org/els/emp/G20-OECD-EC%20Apprenticeship%20Conference_Issues%20Paper.pdf*.

OECD (2014d), "Designing skill-friendly tax policies", *OECD Skills Strategy Spotlight*, No. 6, *http://skills.oecd.org/developskills/documents/designing-skill-friendly-tax-policies.html*.

Stone, I. (2010), *Encouraging Small Firms to Invest in Training: Learning from Overseas*, UK Commission for Employment and Skills, No. 5, June.

Wacker, J. (2007), *Teure neue Lehrstelle : Eine Untersuchung zur Effizienz des BlumBonus*, NÖ Arbeiterkammer (NOAK), Vienna.

Additional arrangements might be necessary to encourage the provision of workplace training among small and medium-sized enterprises (SMEs), as they are less likely to invest in skills development than large companies for several reasons (e.g. Black and Lynch, 2001; Leuven and Oosterbeek, 1999; Bassanini et al., 2005; Lillard and Tan, 1986; and Almeida and Aterido, 2010, for developing countries). First, SMEs are more likely to lack the financial resources to invest, in spite of the possibly large expected returns on investment. Second, in spite of possibly large average returns, SMEs have worse access to information, face greater uncertainty regarding the returns on investment or have larger co-ordination problems with their workers than larger firms. Last but not least, many small firms tend to have limited or no corporate tax liability to benefit from tax subsidies.

Encouraging co-operation between SMEs to organise workplace training, to share expenses for training and its administration, and to take advantage of economies of scale can enable them to overcome the barriers their limited scale implies. Time and resources spent by one employer, e.g. on engaging with education institutions to develop curricula and test design, or to consult the local authorities, can thus be made available to other employers in the same sector. Big employers possessing very advanced training facilities and well-established contacts with education providers can also facilitate training in smaller companies that are part of their supply chain since they should have an interest in the quality of the products they receive from suppliers.

Some evidence, though not conclusive, suggests that employers might be more likely to engage in training if they are supported by an external intermediary (OECD, 2010b). Such intermediaries offering brokerage services can help employers establish the skills and related training needs, figure out which providers offer adequate education programmes that respond to their needs and engage them in the design of the training programme. Online platforms pooling information sources can also help decrease the burden of identifying the right training to employers. This may make training more accessible and affordable for employers. It can also ensure that investments are worthwhile, because the impact of training on the development of necessary skills is high.

The role of funding in higher education

The funding system can also play an important role in linking post-compulsory education to current and future labour market needs and more generally improving its quality. To achieve these objectives, direct public transfers to higher education institutions (HEIs) can be linked to their performance. Experiences in countries suggest that, to minimise unintended impacts, such as the narrowing of universities' missions, in particular, performance funding programmes need to use broad and good performance indicators (Dougherty and Reddy, 2011). These indicators can include both intermediate achievement (such as for instance retention rate and the share of students who reach certain credit thresholds) and final outcome (such as the number of students graduating and their labour market performance). As labour market needs are volatile and difficult to anticipate, there are limits to the extent to which tertiary education should respond to changes in labour market needs. For short professional programmes, the link between funding and labour outcomes can be relatively narrow while other types of performance indicators should play a bigger role for longer programmes with uncertainty on their future demand.

However, if public funding to HEIs is increasingly based on performance, there could be disincentives for them to enrol socio-economically disadvantaged students. This can be addressed by making performance targets vary with the characteristics of students (Dougherty and Reddy, 2011). There could also be direct incentives to admit students from disadvantaged backgrounds. More generally, co-operation between HEIs and the government can help define indicators of performance that minimise the unintended consequences of performance based funding.

Tuition fees may improve quality by intensifying competition between HEIs for attracting students; they may also prompt youth to choose programmes on the basis of expected labour market outcomes, especially in a system in which students have to borrow to finance education. For socio-economically disadvantaged youth, cost sharing of higher education provision needs to be accompanied by measures which remove financial barriers to undertaking higher education in the first place (Johnstone, 2004; Johnstone and Marcucci, 2010). For instance, there is evidence that the growing imbalance in access to higher education by family background, as higher education expanded in the United Kingdom, is partly driving the decline in intergenerational mobility in the country (Blanden, Gregg and Macmillan, 2007). To counteract such trends, tuition fees have to be accompanied with mean-tested student grants and income-contingent loans to finance tuition fees (Dearden, Fitzsimons and Wyness, 2011 for the United Kingdom; Box 3.10). Open education can also help to expand access to tertiary education while saving costs without compromising quality (Mangeol, 2014 and Box. 3.11).

Box 3.10 Designing a funding system for universities that ensures equal access and strong labour market outcomes: Country examples

In all countries, providing sufficient and stable resources to tertiary education while ensuring equal access and stong outcomes is a central objective. Countries differ widely in terms of funding systems for tertiary education but many have made substantial reforms to move towards this objective.

In the United States, states have a large experience with public performance-based funding. In the first wave of funding, grants were mainly allocated according to indicators of final outcomes with labour market outcomes playing a large role (Dougherty and Reddy, 2011). The role of labour market outcomes in funding has been downplayed in the second wave of funding systems due to the impact of the economic downturn. In Ohio for instance, public funding is now only allocated according to the number of courses and degrees completed by students. The allocation of grants also attempts to ease access of students from disadvantaged backgrounds. In Tennessee for instance, institutions are eligible to a 40% bonus for completion of low-income and adult students.

Around half of US university funding comes from tuition fees. Tuitions fees have been increasing since 1990 to reach the current high levels. Overall public and private expenditure per student in tertiary education was in 2012 the highest in the OECD, which may have contributed to the high quality of some US universities. Government-sponsored student loans have enabled students from disadvantaged backgrounds to finance tertiary education (Becker, 2012). However, this funding system has led to increasing, and now substantial, student debt as well as to loan defaults with the economic downturn. These trends have had consequences for public finances as the government provides guarantees and in some cases pays interest for less advantaged students. Furthermore, contrary to other loans, student loans are not dischargeable through personal bankruptcy, which leads to the long-lasting effects of student indebtedness. Government guarantees of student loans may have encouraged universities to raise tuition fees, which, in turn, have exacerbated public and private debt. To limit the impact of student debt on public debt, the government introduced income-contingent loans in 1993 but the intake of these loans has been low so far. The government has also developed a College Scorecard, which provides information on study costs, graduation rates, loan default rates, median borrowing and employment outcomes by college.

In France, two *Grandes Écoles*, Sciences-Po Paris and Université Paris Dauphine, have introduced tuition fees tied to the student's parental income or the student's own income, if he/she is independent from his/her parents (Mangeol, 2014). The purpose of the approach is to increase resources and ensure social equity. For example, in Sciences-Po, the 2014/15 fees for an undergraduate degree range from zero for students from lower socio-economic backgrounds to EUR 9 940 for those from upper socio-economic families, with 11 different brackets. This approach remains highly contentious in France. It could lead to the polarisation of universities between affluent and constrained institutions, since the resources generated highly depend on the socio-economic composition of the student body).

In 2012-2013, the United Kingdom implemented reforms to deregulate the university sector. The government removed student number caps, allowed universities to increase tuition fees and developed access to publically funded loans. The government also improved the website that gathers information on programmes and institutions in terms of various outcomes. The objective of these reforms was to face increasing demand for tertiary education and deliver a high-quality university sector that is more responsive to the needs of students. It is too early to apprehend all the results of the reforms. According to the first round of assessments, the number of undergraduate applications fell in 2012/13 but increased in 2013/14 (Higher Education Funding Council for England, 2013). However, there has been a decline in part-time students. At this stage, evidence suggests that the reforms have not made young people from disadvantaged backgrounds less likely to study full-time. Indeed, the Government has developed financial support for these students. There are signs that some universities are building employability more firmly into their strategies as a response to the change in the funding system. The impacts of the reforms will have to be monitored closely.

In the second half of 2014, Australia introduced a reform to improve the quality and competitiveness of its HEIs by deregulating tuition fees while at the same time reducing government funding to Australian universities by as much as 20%. The expectation is that universities will then increase tuition fees to whatever levels domestic and international education markets can bear in order to offset the shortfall in government funding. At the same time, student grants can be received for most higher education programmes while they used to be available for only a group of them. It is too early to tell what the implications of this reform will be, but it has raised concerns that higher tuition fees may limit access to higher education.

...

In Denmark, higher education (as other levels of education) is mostly publically funded through grants determined by the so-called "taximeter" system and there is no tuition fee. In addition, students receive student grants to cover their living costs. Taximeter "rates" are applied to the activity of institutions, with activity being measured by the number of students who have completed the programme. Taximeter rates are set by the government according to various criteria, including the field of education, political priorities, teachers' salaries and building and administrative costs. Ex post however, institutions are free to allocate the grant as they wish and can move funds from one area to another. The system gives institutions incentives to adjust their capacity to demand and to raise efficiency, and it ensures that resources are automatically transferred from programmes with declining activity to those with rising activity. However, this funding system can also lead universities to lower the standards and manipulate outcomes in order to achieve the expected performance. In addition, the system does not provide incentives to students to choose an education programme or a field of study according to its labour market outcomes.

In order to strengthen the quality of higher education, the Danish government set up an independent expert committee that published a first set of recommendations in April 2014. Following these recommendations, in September 2014, the government decided to try to limit the intake of education programmes that have led to relatively bad labour market outcomes. If, over the last 10 years, a group of related education programmes has had an unemployment rate for graduates (after two years) that is more than 2 percentage points above the average unemployment rate for graduates in at least seven of the years, the student intake of programmes in the group will be adjusted. The number of places in this group of programmes will be lowered by 10 to 30% depending on the size of the unemployment gap for graduates. Universities are then free to allocate the reduction in places among programmes.

Sources:

Australian Government, Department of Education, *www.education.gov.au/public-universities*.

Becker G. (2012), "Is student debt too great?", 28 May 2012, *www.becker-posner-blog.com/2012/05/is-student-debt-too-great-becker.html*.

Dougherty, K. and V. Reddy (2011), "The impacts of state performance funding systems on higher education institutions: Research literature review and policy recommendations", *CCRC Working Paper No. 37*, Community College Research Center, Teachers College, Columbia University, New York, December.

Higher Education Funding Council for England (2013), *Financial Health of the Higher Education Sector: 2012-13 to 2015-16 Forecasts*, Issues Paper, 29 October 2013, *www.hefce.ac.uk/media/hefce/content/pubs/2013/201329/HEFCE_2013_29.pdf*.

Mangeol, P. (2014), "Chapter 2 : Strengthening business models in higher education institutions: An overview of innovative concepts and practices", in OECD (2014), *The State of Higher Education 2014*, OECD, Paris, www.oecd.org/fr/sites/eduimhe/stateofhighereducation2014.htm.

OECD (2015b), *Education Policy Outlook 2015: Making Reforms Happen*, OECD Publishing, Paris, *http://dx.doi.org/10.1787/9789264225442-en*.

Box 3.11 **Ensuring equal access and responding to labour market needs through open education**

Massive open online courses (MOOCs) have developed in recent years. They offer opportunities to anyone at any age willing to take a course via the web. The MOOCs can help young people deepen their skills or acquire new ones through online courses from top universities, the business sector and independent experts at little to no cost. They can shorten programme completion by allowing secondary school students to start attending introductory-level higher education courses while still in high school (Bowen 2013).

MOOCs can make the education sector more responsive to the labour market demands of employers. The American telecommunication firm AT&T, for instance, has recently launched the first MOOC Master's degree in Computer Science in a joint initiative with Georgia Tech and Udacity. Not only has the firm co-designed the curriculum of the course, but it also envisages offering up to 100 paid internships to excelling students of this degree. Such initiatives serve multiple goals. First, employers determine to a large extent the learning contents of the course with respect to their immediate and future skills requirements and train future workers to use and engage in problem-solving with new technologies. Second, by making the course available to students worldwide, employers enlarge their pool of potential recruits. Third, education providers experiment with new learning and teaching practices which can trigger improvements in pedagogical models and bring learning contents closer to the industry also in traditional education programmes. Fourth, learners can access, update and upgrade knowledge and skills throughout their working lives and expand intellectual, professional and personal networks around the world.

...

MOOCs can improve access to higher education across socio-economic groups and reduce inequalities. In principle, most MOOCs are offered for free or at a very low cost. For instance, the degree of AT&T and Georgia Tech, discussed above, can be obtained for USD 7 000, while the average tuition fees for undergraduates amount to USD 19 339. New technologies also enable people from rural and isolated areas, as well as disadvantaged groups, to enrol and participate in higher education. Finally, MOOCs introduce more flexibility in teaching and learning practices, thus facilitating participation of different segments of the population (e.g. part-time workers and elderly persons).

Despite the potential virtues of MOOCs, they face various challenges. First, students need to have a computer with Internet access in order to participate in a MOOC, which means that students from disadvantaged backgrounds may be penalised. Second, students need to possess the skills to learn on their own and to find the time to follow the class. HarvardX and MITx released an analysis after one year of edX, which provides some socio-demographic information about the learners. This analysis covers seventeen MOOCs from Harvard and MIT and 841 687 registrants (with 292 852 (35%) registrants who never engaged with the online content). Knowing that the median age is 26 years old and that 66% have a bachelor's degree or above, for now, it is mainly the highly educated and motivated who benefit from MOOCs. Third, most MOOCs do not grant credits or degrees and as result, may have little signalling power on the labour market. Finally, MOOCs are not able to successfully recreate a number of aspects of the face-to-face, on-campus university experience that are very relevant to the educational experience.

Sources:

Bowen, W.G. (2013), *Higher Education in the Digital Age*, Princeton University Press;.

Ho, A.D. et al. (2014), "HarvardX and MITx: The first year of open online courses", *HarvardX and MITx Working Paper No. 1*.

OECD (2014e), *E-Learning in Higher Education in Latin America*, Development Centre Studies, OECD Publishing, Paris, *http://dx.doi.org/10.1787/9789264209992-en*.

In systems that combine high tuition fees and high student indebtedness, student loan default has become a problem with consequences for public finances if some of these loans are guaranteed by the government (Mangeol, 2014). This partly reflects the effect of the economic downturn but also illustrate that students choose their education pathways according to a range of factors, with labour market outcome being only one of them. To help students make better education choices in a system with tuition fees, allocating grants and income contingent repayment loans can be made conditional on the outcomes of the particular programme and HEI.

Career guidance

Better career guidance and improved information about likely job prospects can help youth make informed decisions about the field of study they might like to specialise in, and the best education institution for them to attend. The high level of non-completion of tertiary programmes (Figure 3.2) reflects failures in the guidance process from compulsory to higher education, as well as poor programme quality and financial cost of education (OECD, 2008b).

To reach all youth, career guidance services need to be provided at all educational levels and types of institutions (European Lifelong Guidance Policy Network, 2014). In schools, good-quality guidance can contribute to increasing students' engagement and success in school, and support their transition from school to further education or work, as well as the acquisition of career management skills. Career guidance should provide a full picture of the various pathways in the education system, covering notably the vocational education option. Guidance in vocational education and training has an important role to play in supporting individuals to identify how they can best use the skills they have developed through their course of education and training in order to build fulfilling careers. Career guidance in universities can support effective transitions to the workplace by involving employers (including through career fairs and employer workshops) to provide work-related learning opportunities, and can help to ensure that graduates' skills are well used.

More efforts can be dedicated to providing individuals and families with timely, relevant information on the market returns of various career paths, and on appropriate education and training programmes that have been monitored to ensure quality. Some countries are raising the relevancy of career guidance services by developing indicators of labour market outcomes of alumni by institutions and programmes (Box 3.12). These indicators have to be of good quality and easy to understand. To ensure transparency, they should exist at institution and programme levels. Furthermore, they need to account for labour outcome over a sufficiently long period of time. These indicators have to be disseminated to students but with other types of information such as major trends in labour market needs and the risk of bottleneck to help students make informed choices. Other countries, notably Scotland, are enhancing the quality of advisors by recognising career guidance as a "distinct, defined and specialist profession" and providing a comprehensive view (OECD, 2014c).

■ Figure 3.2 ■

Proportion of students that start tertiary education and leave without a degree

2008

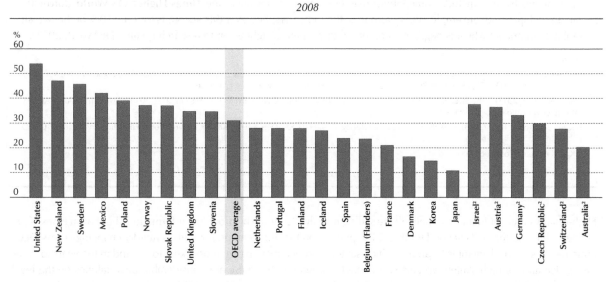

1. Includes students entering single courses who may never intend to study all courses needed for a degree.
2. Tertiary-type A only.

Notes: Countries are ranked in descending order of the proportion of students who leave tertiary education without obtaining a degree. Some of the students who have not graduated may still be enrolled, or may have finished their education at a different institution, as in the United States.

Source: OECD (2010c), *Education at a Glance 2010: OECD Indicators*, OECD Publishing, Paris, *http://dx.doi.org/10.1787/eag-2010-en*.

StatLink ⧉ http://dx.doi.org/10.1787/888933214592

Box 3.12 **Developing labour market information as a tool for career guidance: Country examples**

One of the major characteristics of good quality career guidance is the timely and accurate provision of labour market information about different education paths, programmes and institutions. Many OECD countries have made efforts recently to start a systematic and comprehensive data collection process.

In Italy, since 1994, Universities have joined together in a Consortium – the Almalaurea Consortium – which has developed a student and graduate tracking survey aiming to collect information on the profile of graduates and on their performance when entering the labour market. After 20 years, the Consortium now tracks 80% of the graduates from Italian institutions and the results (published and accessible online at *www.almalaurea.it*) are returned to higher education institutions to help them further develop and fine-tune their provision of programmes.

Since September 2012 in the United Kingdom, would-be students have had access to information on the universities they are considering. For the first time, students can get additional help choosing a university as they can access detailed sets of information and make comparisons between institutions using Key Information Sets (KIS) published on the Unistats site. The KIS cover 17 aspects of full- and part-time undergraduate courses, including student satisfaction, employment and earnings outcomes/salary data, learning and teaching activities, assessment methods, tuition fees and student finance, accommodation, and professional accreditation. The data are regularly updated (*www. thecompleteuniversityguide.co.uk*). Moreover, higher education institutions publish their employability statements. These statements set out what universities and colleges offer to their students to support their employability and transition into employment and beyond (*http://www.hefce.ac.uk/*).

In 2010, the Swedish Government tasked the National Agency for Higher Education to develop a new quality evaluation system for first and second-cycle courses based on government directives. The evaluation system essentially focuses on measuring the extent to which intended learning outcomes are achieved in terms of three major concepts: i) knowledge and comprehension; ii) competency and skills; and iii) judgment. The description of learning outcomes and professional qualifications emerge in close co-operation with professional associations. In the new quality evaluation system, labour market aspects are quite prominent, which is manifested in the increasing importance of alumni surveys and the composition of (external) assessment panels (*Högskoleverket*, 2011).

...

In addition, international benchmarking of academic institutions could be a valuable tool for career guidance if the rankings were to include some labour market criteria. For instance, the **Times Higher-QS World University** ranking adopts graduate employability as one of the indicators; however this accounts for only 10% of the overall ranking, an impact which is negligible compared to the high weight given to research quality (De Weert, 2011).

Sources:

De Weert, E. (2011), "Perspectives on higher education and the labour market: Review of international policy developments", IHEM/CHEPS Thematic report C11EW158, December 2011, Centre for Higher Education Policy Studies, Enschede.

Högskoleverket (2011), "The Swedish National Agency for Higher Education's Quality Evaluation System 2011-2014", Swedish National Agency for Higher Education (Högskoleverket).

Kuczera, M. and S. Field (2013), *A Skills beyond School Review of the United States*, OECD Reviews of Vocational Education and Training, OECD Publishing, Paris, *http://dx.doi.org/10.1787/9789264202153-en*.

UK government information accessed at *http://www.hefce.ac.uk/*.

www.almalaurea.it.

High-quality career guidance can help fill the skills gap in the economy by providing information about what types of jobs are available and the skills needed for them. The perception that the demand for skills is rapidly changing across OECD countries has spurred attempts to predict which sectors and occupations are most likely to expand in the years to come. Rising demand for high-skilled workers is expected to continue, but there are considerable uncertainties on the levels and kinds of skills in future demand (Handel, 2012). Current projections from the OECD suggest a continuing increase in employer demand for a highly skilled workforce, with a shift from manufacturing to service-based economies. Although the demand for low-skilled jobs may globally decrease, it may still continue to grow in some sectors. For instance, with the ageing of populations, demand for long-term care services will increase as well as other types of personal services (Ono, Lafortune and Schoenstein, 2013). The demand for non-routine occupation-specific skills will remain high in many sectors and countries. In addition, local labour markets can differ in their skill requirements.

Better anticipating skills needs will help make better use of youth skills in the future. Most countries have projections of future skills needs from independent or public institutions. International organisations also undertake these types of analyses, but few countries use this information to evolve their education systems. Large uncertainties surrounding these estimates, as well as the fact that skills needs may be affected by various shocks, suggest prudence in using such information. Still, trying to better anticipate skills needs and to use this information to adapt education systems are areas in which more work is needed.

KEY POINTS FOR POLICY

High-quality education institutions and strong co-operation with employers and other stakeholders are needed to ensure that youth are well prepared for the labour market and life. When leaving the education system, young people should have developed a broad range of skills and ideally acquired initial labour market experience.

Ensuring that all youth leave education systems with sufficient skills

- Take a holistic approach to skills and aim to develop the whole set of skills for employability.
- Offer high-quality, pre-primary education for all to mitigate inherited disparities between children.
- Reach out to students with low skills and those at risk of dropping out. Develop a system to monitor and validate the development of students' skills along the various tracks of education and training.
- Give disengaged youth a second chance to reintegrate into the education system. Carefully evaluate the impact of second chance schemes on education attainment and labour market outcomes and allocate funding to the most effective ones.
- Provide multiple pathways within the education system to enable smooth transitions into further education or the labour market.

Rendering the education system more responsive to labour market needs

- Develop work-based learning programmes across different types of education, including universities. Engage employers and other stakeholders in the education system at all levels.

- Review vocational education and training (VET) programmes to raise their quality. Integrate high-quality work-based learning components into these programmes. In parallel, ensure that these programmes also well develop cognitive and social and emotional skills.

- Develop a funding system of universities that better links education to current and future labour market needs, and provides incentives to enhance quality.

- Improve career guidance by ensuring that these services are provided at all education levels and information is based on relevant assessment of the market returns of various career paths.

Note

1. Lerman (2013) confronts the argument of Hanushek, Woessmann and Zhang (2011) that the erosion of gain at older ages is most pronounced in countries that emphasise apprenticeship, such as Denmark, Germany and Switzerland. The author claims that according to several estimates in Hanushek's paper, the advantage in employment rates linked to VET in the apprenticeship countries remains through approximately age 60. Moreover, in the apprenticeship countries, the advantage in employment rates is sizeable, providing men with VET a 9 percentage point higher employment rate at age 40 and a 4-point advantage at age 50.

References

Akkerman, Y. et al. (2011), "Overcoming School Failure, Policies that Work: Background Report for the Netherlands", Ministry of Education, Culture and Science, Den Haag.

Almeida, R. and **R. Aterido** (2010), "The investment in job training: Why are SMEs lagging so much behind?", *IZA Discussion Papers*, No. 4981, Institute for the Study of Labor (IZA).

Bassanini, A. et al. (2005), "Workplace training in Europe", *IZA Discussion Papers*, No. 1640, Institute for the Study of Labor (IZA).

Becker, G. (2012), "Is student debt too great?", 28 May 2012, *www.becker-posner-blog.com/2012/05/is-student-debt-too-great-becker.html*.

Black, S. and **L. Lynch** (2001), "How to compete: The impact of workplace practices and information technology on productivity", *Review of Economics and Statistics*, 83(3), pp. 434-445.

Blanden, J., P. Gregg and **L. Macmillan** (2007), "Accounting for intergenerational income persistence: Noncognitive skills, ability and education", *Economic Journal*, 117(519), C43-C60, 03.

Blau, D. and **J. Currie** (2006), "Chapter 20: Pre-school, day care, and after-school care: Who's minding the kids?", *in Handbook of the Economics of Education*, Volume 2, North-Holland, Amsterdam, pp. 1163-1278.

Bowen, W.G. (2013), *Higher Education in the Digital Age*, Princeton University Press.

Carneiro, P. and **J. Heckman** (2003), "Human capital policy", *IZA Discussion Papers*, No. 821, Institute for the Study of Labor (IZA).

Clark, D. and **R. Fahr** (2001), "The promise of workplace training for non-college-bound youth: Theory and evidence from German apprenticeship", *IZA Discussion Papers*, No. 378, Institute for the Study of Labor (IZA).

Council for Industry and Higher Education (CIHE) (1996), "Helping students towards success at work: Declaration of intent", CIHE, London.

D'Addio, A.C. (2007), "Intergenerational Transmission of Disadvantage: Mobility or Immobility Across Generations?", *OECD Social, Employment and Migration Working Papers*, No. 52, OECD Publishing, Paris, *http://dx.doi.org/10.1787/217730505550*.

Dearden, L., E. Fitzsimons and **G. Wyness** (2011), "The impact of tuition fees and support on university participation in the UK", *Centre for the Economics of Education Discussion Paper*, 126, London School of Economics.

De Janvry, A. et al. (2006), "Can conditional cash transfer programs serve as safety nets in keeping children at school and from working when exposed to shocks?", *Journal of Development Economics*, 79 (2), pp. 349-373.

De Weert, E. (2011), "Perspectives on higher education and the labour market: Review of international policy developments", IHEM/CHEPS Thematic report C11EW158, December 2011, Centre for Higher Education Policy Studies, Enschede.

Dougherty, K. and **V. Reddy** (2011), "The impacts of state performance funding systems on higher education institutions: Research literature review and policy recommendations", *CCRC Working Paper No. 37*, Community College Research Center, Teachers College, Columbia University, New York, December.

European Commission (2013), *Preventing Early School Leaving in Europe: Lessons Learned from Second Chance Education*, *http:// ec.europa.eu/education/library/study/2013/second-chance_en.pdf*.

European Lifelong Guidance Policy Network (2014), "The evidence base on lifelong guidance: A guide to key findings for effective policy and practice", European Lifelong Guidance Policy Network.

Fazekas, M. and **S. Field** (2013), *A Skills beyond School Review of Switzerland*, OECD Reviews of Vocational Education and Training, OECD Publishing, Paris, *http://dx.doi.org/10.1787/9789264062665-en*.

Field, S., et al. (2012), *A Skills beyond School Review of Denmark*, OECD Reviews of Vocational Education and Training, OECD Publishing, Paris, *http://dx.doi.org/10.1787/9789264173668-en*.

Geel, R. and **U. Backes-Gellner** (2009), "Occupational mobility within and between skill clusters: An empirical analysis based on the skill-weights approach", *Economics of Education Working Paper Series*, 0047, University of Zurich, Institute for Strategy and Business Economics (ISU).

Geel, R., J. Mure and **U. Backes-Gellner** (2011), "Specificity of occupational training and occupational mobility: An empirical study based on Lazear's skill-weights approach", *Education Economics*, 19(5), pp. 519-535.

Goggel, K. and **T. Zwick** (2012), "Heterogenous wage effects of apprenticeship training", *Scandinavian Journal of Economics*, 114(3), pp. 756-779.

Handel, M. (2012), "Trends in job skill demands in OECD countries", *OECD Social, Employment and Migration Working Papers*, No. 143, OECD Publishing, Paris, *http://dx.doi.org/10.1787/5k8zk8pcq6td-en*.

Hanuschek, E.A., L. Woessmann and **L. Zhang** (2011), "General education, vocational education, and labor-market outcomes over the life-cycle", *NBER Working Paper*, No. 17504, National Bureau of Economic Research.

Heckman, J.J. and **T. Kautz** (2013), "Fostering and measuring skills: Interventions that improve character and cognition", *NBER Working Paper*, No. 19656, National Bureau of Economic Research.

Higher Education Funding Council for England (2013), *Financial Health of the Higher Education Sector: 2012-13 to 2015-16 forecasts*, Issues Paper, 29 October 2013, *www.hefce.ac.uk/media/hefce/content/pubs/2013/201329/HEFCE_2013_29.pdf*.

Ho, A. D. et al. (2014), "HarvardX and MITx: The first year of open online courses", *HarvardX and MITx Working Paper* No. 1.

Hoeckel, K. et al. (2008), *OECD Reviews of Vocational Education and Training: A Learning for Jobs Review of Australia 2008*, OECD Reviews of Vocational Education and Training, OECD Publishing, Paris, *http://dx.doi.org/10.1787/9789264113596-en*.

Högskoleverket (2011), "The Swedish National Agency for Higher Education's Quality Evaluation System 2011-2014", Swedish National Agency for Higher Education (Högskoleverket).

Iller, C. and **D. Moraal** (2013), "Kollektive Vereinbarungen in der Steuerung betrieblicher Weiterbildung. Beispiele aus den Niederlanden und Deutschland", *Magazin erwachsenenbildung.at, Das Fachmedium für Forschung, Praxis und Diskurs*, No. 18, Vienna.

Johnstone, D.B. (2004), "The economics and politics of cost sharing in higher education: Comparative perspectives", *Economics of Education Review*, 23.

Johnstone, D.B. and **P. Marcucci** (2010), *Financing Higher Education Worldwide: Who Pays? Who Should Pay?*, Johns Hopkins University Press, Baltimore.

Jones, R. (2013), "Education Reform in Korea", *OECD Economics Department Working Papers*, No. 1067, OECD Publishing, Paris, *http://dx.doi.org/10.1787/5k43nxs1t9vh-en*.

Kuczera, M. (2013), "A skills beyond school commentary on Scotland", *www.oecd.org/edu/skills-beyond-school/ ASkillsBeyondSchoolCommentaryOnScotland.pdf*.

Kuczera, M. and **S. Field** (2013), *A Skills beyond School Review of the United States*, OECD Reviews of Vocational Education and Training, OECD Publishing, Paris, *http://dx.doi.org/10.1787/9789264202153-en*.

Lerman, R.I. (2013), "Skill development in middle level occupations: The role of apprenticeship training", *IZA Policy Paper*, No. 61, Institute for the Study of Labor (IZA).

Leuven, E. and **H. Oosterbeek** (1999), "Demand and supply of work-related training: Evidence from four countries", *Research in Labor Economics*, 18, pp. 303-330.

Lillard, L.A. and **H. Tan** (1986), "Private sector training: Who gets it and what are its effects?", *Research in Labor Economics*, Vol. 13, pp. 1-62.

Machin, S. (2006), "Social disadvantage and education experiences", *OECD Social, Employment and Migration Working Papers*, No. 32, OECD Publishing, Paris, *http://dx.doi.org/10.1787/715165322333*.

Mangeol, P. (2014), "Chapter 2: Strengthening business models in higher education institutions: An overview of innovative concepts and practices", in OECD (2014), *The State of Higher Education 2014*, OECD, Paris, *www.oecd.org/fr/sites/eduimhe/ stateofhighereducation2014.htm*.

Mason, G., G. Williams and **S. Cranmer** (2009), "Employability skills initiatives in higher education: What effects do they have on graduate labour market outcomes?", *Education Economics*, 17(1), pp.1-30.

Meare, M. and **V. Podmore** (2002), "Early Childhood Education Policy Co-ordination under the Auspices of the Department/Ministry of Education: A Case Study of New Zealand", *UNESCO Early Childhood and Family Policy Series* N°1, March 2002, UNESCO.

Ministry of Education, Culture and Science (2014), *Kamerbrief nieuwe cijfers over terugdringen voortijdig schoolverlaten 15 Januari 2014*, Ministry of Education, Culture and Science, Den Haag.

Ministry of Education, Culture and Science (2011), *Schooluitval voorkomen in Nederland: Speerpunten huidige aanpak en doorkijk naar vervolgbeleid; Resultaat schooljaar 2009-2010*, (Preventing School Dropout in the Netherlands: Priorities of the Current Approach and Perspective on Follow-up Policy; Results for School Year 2009/10), Ministry of Education, Culture and Science, Den Haag.

Ministry of Health, Labour and Welfare of Japan (2009), "The 'Job-Card System' in Japan", Tokyo.

Morley, S. and **D. Coady** (2003), *From Social Assistance to Social Development: Targeted Education Subsidies in Developing Countries*, Center for Global Development and IFPRI.

Mühlemann, S. et al. (2007), "An empirical analysis of the decision to train apprentices", *Labour: Review of Labour Economics and Industrial Relations*, 21(3), pp. 419-42.

Musset, P. et al. (2013), *A Skills beyond School Review of Austria*, OECD Reviews of Vocational Education and Training, OECD Publishing, Paris, *http://dx.doi.org/10.1787/9789264200418-en*.

O'Dowd, M. (2013), "Early childhood education in Sweden: The market curriculum 2000-2013?", *Revista Española de Educación Comparada*, 21, pp. 85-118.

OECD (2015a), *Skills for Social Progress: The Power of Social and Emotional Skills,* OECD Skills Studies, OECD Publishing, Paris, *http:// dx.doi.org/10.1787/9789264226159-en*.

OECD (2015b), *Education Policy Outlook 2015: Making Reforms Happen*, OECD Publishing, Paris, *http://dx.doi. org/10.1787/9789264225442-en*.

OECD (2014a), *OECD Economic Surveys: Australia 2014*, OECD Publishing, Paris, *http://dx.doi.org/10.1787/eco_surveys-aus-2014-en*.

OECD (2014b), "Background paper prepared by the OECD", paper prepared for the G20-OECD-EC Conference on Quality Apprenticeships for Giving Youth a Better Start in the Labour Market, *www.oecd.org/els/emp/G20-OECD-EC%20Apprenticeship%20 Conference_Issues%20Paper.pdf*.

OECD (2014c), *Skills beyond School: Synthesis Report*, OECD Reviews of Vocational Education and Training, OECD Publishing, Paris, *http://dx.doi.org/10.1787/9789264214682-en*.

OECD (2014d), "Designing skill-friendly tax policies", *OECD Skills Strategy Spotlight*, No. 6, *http://skills.oecd.org/developskills/ documents/designing-skill-friendly-tax-policies.html*.

OECD (2014e), *E-Learning in Higher Education in Latin America*, Development Centre Studies, OECD Publishing, Paris, *http://dx.doi. org/10.1787/9789264209992-en*.

OECD (2013), "PISA: Programme for International Student Assessment", *OECD Education Statistics* (database), *http://dx.doi. org/10.1787/data-00365-en* (accessed 8 August 2014).

OECD (2010a), *Off to a Good Start? Jobs for Youth*, OECD Publishing, Paris, *http://dx.doi.org/10.1787/9789264096127-en*.

OECD (2010b), *Learning for Jobs,* OECD Reviews of Vocational Education and Training, OECD Publishing, Paris, *http://dx.doi. org/10.1787/9789264087460-en*.

OECD (2010c), *Education at a Glance 2010: OECD Indicators*, OECD Publishing, Paris, *http://dx.doi.org/10.1787/eag-2010-en*.

OECD (2008a), *Jobs for Youth/Des emplois pour les jeunes: Netherlands 2008*, OECD Publishing, Paris, *http://dx.doi. org/10.1787/9789264041295-en*.

OECD (2008b), *Tertiary Education for the Knowledge Society: Volume 1 and Volume 2*, OECD Publishing, Paris, *http://dx.doi. org/10.1787/9789264046535-en*.

OECD (2006), *Starting Strong II: Early Childhood Education and Care*, OECD Publishing, Paris, *http://dx.doi. org/10.1787/9789264035461-en*.

Ono, T., G. Lafortune and **M. Schoenstein** (2013), "Health workforce planning in OECD countries: A review of 26 projection models from 18 countries", *OECD Health Working Papers*, No. 62, OECD Publishing, Paris, *http://dx.doi.org/10.1787/5k44t787zcwb-en*.

Pathways to Education (2013), "2012 Result Summary: Pathways to Education 2011-2012 Program Results", *www.pathwaystoeducation. ca/sites/default/files/pdf/Results%20summary%2C%202011%20%202012%20FINAL.pdf*.

Pathways to Education (2010), "Pathways to Education: Program introduction and overview", *www.pathwaystoeducation.ca/sites/ default/files/pdf/Overview%2021_10_10_0.pdf*.

Pischke, J. (2005), "Comments on 'Workplace training in Europe' by Bassanini et al.", *Working Paper*, London School of Economics.

Polidano, C., D. Tabasso and **Y.-P. Tseng** (2012), "A second chance at education for early school leavers", *IZA Discussion Papers*, No. 6769, Institute for the Study of Labor (IZA).

Quintini, G. and **T. Manfredi** (2009), "Going separate ways? School-to-work transitions in the United States and Europe", *OECD Social, Employment and Migration Working Papers*, No. 90, OECD Publishing, Paris, *http://dx.doi.org/10.1787/221717700447*.

Schultz, T.P. (2004), "School subsidies for the poor: Evaluating the Mexican Progresa Poverty Program", *Journal of Development Economics*, 74(1), pp. 199-250.

Stevens, M. (1994), "A theoretical model of on-the-job training with imperfect competition", *Oxford Economics Papers*, 46, pp. 537-562.

Stone, I. (2010), "Encouraging small firms to invest in training: Learning from overseas", UK Commission for Employment and Skills.

Taguma, M., I. Litjens and **K. Makowiecki** (2013), *Quality Matters in Early Childhood Education and Care: Sweden 2013*, OECD Publishing, Paris, *http://dx.doi.org/10.1787/9789264176744-en*.

Taguma, M., I. Litjens and **K. Makowiecki** (2012), *Quality Matters in Early Childhood Education and Care: New Zealand 2012*, OECD Publishing, Paris, *http://dx.doi.org/10.1787/9789264176690-en*.

Wacker, J. (2007), *Teure neue Lehrstelle : Eine Untersuchung zur Effizienz des BlumBonus*, NÖ Arbeiterkammer (NOAK), Vienna.

Whitehead, N. (2013), "Review of adult vocational qualifications in the UK", UK Commission for Employment and Skills.

4

Trends in integrating youth into the labour market

Many young people face difficulties integrating into the labour market. Transitions from school-to-work can take time and include spells of unemployment and short-term contracts. In addition, some youth disengage from education and the labour market; they are not in employment, education or training, often referred to as NEETs. The economic crisis has exacerbated the challenges faced by youth to find a job and maintain employment. This chapter offers an overview of how youth are integrated into the labour market. It also looks at those who have disengaged from education and the labour market and attempts to assess their distance from the labour market in terms of educational attainment, skills and additional barriers they may face.

HIGHLIGHTS

- In 2013, among all 16-29 year-olds in OECD countries: 7% were unemployed and not in education, 8% were inactive in the labour market (i.e. they were not looking for a job) and not in education, and overall, 15% were neither in employment, nor in education or training (NEET). This means that 39 million young people in OECD countries were exposed to the risk of exclusion from the economy and society, 5 million more than in 2008.

- Youth are two times more exposed to the risk of unemployment than prime-age workers.

- One in four young people who are employed has a temporary contract.

- Barriers to youth labour market integration go beyond skills. According to the Survey of Adult Skills, young NEETs, on average, have completed upper secondary education and have an intermediate level of numeracy, literacy and problem solving skills. In most OECD countries, more than 10% of the NEETs have attained tertiary education. In countries covered by the Survey of Adult Skills, only 20% of NEETs have low literacy skills and 29% of them have low numeracy skills.

In order to maintain and enhance their employability, youth need to successfully integrate into the labour market by finding jobs that allow them to use and strengthen their skills. Most youth do find jobs and successfully integrate into the labour market, but some encounter trouble in the school-to-work transition, at least temporarily. These young people face a significant lasting economic and social penalty. They may not only become discouraged, but also enter a vicious cycle where their unused skills are likely to atrophy over time, while employers become less willing to consider employing them. This is not only a poor outcome for the individual: society's investment in developing their skills is wasted and social cohesion is undermined.

YOUNG PEOPLE'S INTEGRATION INTO THE LABOUR MARKET

Transitions from school to work

The majority of young people do find jobs. Among youth, the employment rate increases with age, and the youth employment rate of 25-29 year-olds is very close to that of prime-age workers (Figure 4.1, Panel A). Youth enter the labour market later than they did 15 years ago. In 2000, 11% of 15-19 year-olds were employed, and no longer in education, while 80% were in education. By 2012, the share of those in education had risen to 87% and the share of those working had fallen to only 6%. This reflects both the long-term increasing trends in educational attainment rates and the consequences of the global crisis (Figure 4.1, Panel B). More significant shifts have taken place among the 20-24 year-olds, where the share of those in employment and not in education has fallen gradually over the last 15 years, while the share in education has risen. The transition to the labour market has become more gradual: the share of youth who combine work and study has increased for the 25-29 year-olds (Figure 4.1, Panel C).

■ Figure 4.1 ■
The evolution of the share of youth, by employment and education status
OECD average, 1997-2013

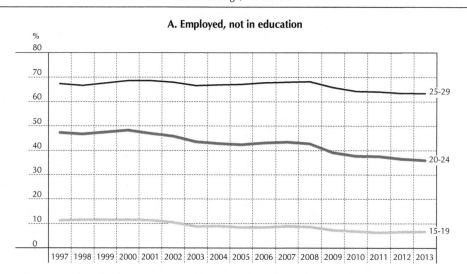

■ Figure 4.1 (continued) ■

The evolution of the share of youth, by employment and education status

OECD average, 1997-2013

B. In education, not employed

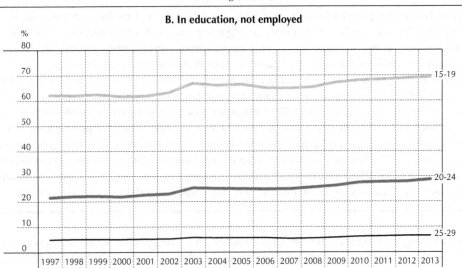

C. In education, employed, or in work-study programmes

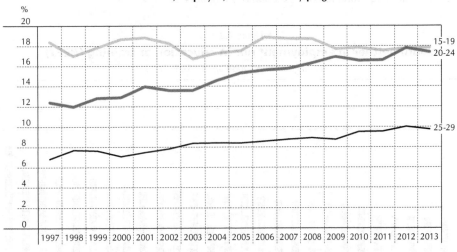

D. Neither in employment nor in education or training

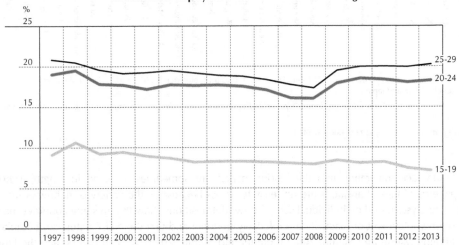

Source: OECD (2014a), *Education at a Glance 2014: OECD Indicators*, OECD Publishing, Paris, *http://dx.doi.org/10.1787/eag-2014-en*.

StatLink ⬛ http://dx.doi.org/10.1787/888933214600

> ## Box 4.1 **Measuring the share of youth who are neither in employment, nor in education or training (NEET)**
>
> NEET data published in the OECD Education at a Glance publication and by Eurostat are collected through labour force surveys. The data are based on a question regarding one's status "in employment or in any form of education and/or training at the time of the survey or in the four weeks preceding the survey". This same question is expressed in a slightly different manner in the Survey of Adult Skills (PIAAC) as individuals are asked if "they are in employment or studying for any kind of formal qualification" at the time of the survey, but not in the four weeks prior to it. As a result, the NEET rate computed with the Survey of Adult Skills on the basis of this question (as in this publication) is not directly comparable to the NEET rate based on labour force surveys. Another indicator available in the Survey of Adult Skills is the share of the population neither in employment nor in education at the time of the survey and who has not participated in training in the 12 months prior to the survey. This indicator is not used as the primary measure of NEETs in this publication since it is relatively restrictive, as some respondents may have participated in training in the 12 months prior to the survey but have been inactive for a number of months before the survey. However, as it conveys useful information, it is also presented and discussed in this chapter.

Too many youth still struggle to integrate into the labour market. The young people whose skills need to be activated for employability are those who are neither in employment, nor in education or training (Box 4.1). With the economic crisis, this group has increased up to 15% for 15-29 year-olds, on average, accross OECD countries in 2013 (Figure 4.1, Panel D). However, there are large variations across countries (Figure 4.2).

▪ Figure 4.2 ▪

Youth neither in employment nor in education or training (NEET)

Percentage of population aged 15-29, 2013

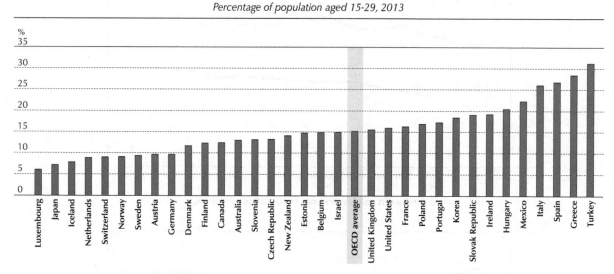

Notes: Countries are shown in ascending order of the NEET rate. For Chile, the year of reference is 2011 and for Japan, the age group is 15-24 year-olds. The OECD average excludes Chile and Japan.

Source: OECD (2015), *Education at a Glance Interim Report: Update of Employment and Educational Attainment Indicators*, OECD, Paris, *www.oecd. org/edu/EAG-Interim-report.pdf*.

StatLink ⬛⬛⬛ http://dx.doi.org/10.1787/888933214610

The difficulties youth face integrating into the labour market are sometimes reflected in lengthy school-to-work transitions. The patterns of these transitions are not easy to assess because of the variety of pathways from school to work. Nonetheless, analyses based on individual school-to-work transitions show that in some countries, pathways that include periods of unemployment or inactivity are relatively frequent and that the NEET status can be quite persistent (OECD, 2010; Quintini, Martin and Martin, 2007; Quintini and Martin, 2014). In both Europe and the United States, more than 10% of youth have experienced around 15 months of unemployment over a four-year period (Carcillo et al., 2015). Lengthy school-to-work transitions are more likely to lead to disengagement and scarring effects.

The role of macroeconomic conditions, education and labour market institutions

Difficulties faced by youth in entering the labour market are caused by general factors affecting all workers, as well as those specific to youth. Unfavourable macroeconomic conditions in many countries are associated with low labour demand for all workers. Likewise, labour market institutions influence labour market outcomes for all age groups. However, when labour market institutions protect incumbent workers, negative shocks on the labour demand tend to have a stronger impact on youth. In times of strong labour demand, most youth find jobs, but when labour demand falls, youth struggle, in particular the least-skilled. The quality of education systems and educational attainment primarily affect youth employment outcomes, but they can also play a role for older population groups.

The ratio of youth to prime-age adult unemployment rates is an indicator of the hurdles youth face integrating into the labour market. The employment rate by age group can also give some indication on youth's labour market integration but is influenced by the duration of study. Based on these indicators, it is possible to distinguish between four groups of countries (Figure 4.3):

- Several countries have a relatively large gap between youth and prime-age unemployment rates and low employment rates for both young and prime-age workers, and hence, a specific youth employment problem in addition to a more general one (Greece and Italy). These countries face unfavourable conditions and weaknesses in their labour markets, social and education institutions, interacting in a way that leads to a specific youth employment problem, and overall low employment rates.

- Some countries have specific problems integrating youth into the labour market, and relatively high employment rates for prime-age workers (France, New Zealand, Norway, Sweden and the United Kingdom). This could indicate the prevalence of several factors in labour market and education systems that negatively affect youth labour market outcomes, but to a lesser extent other groups of workers.

- A few countries have a small gap between youth and prime-age unemployment rates combined with low youth and prime-age employment rates (Spain and Turkey). These countries may not necessarily have a specific youth employment problem and are more likely to be affected by unfavourable macroeconomic conditions or weaknesses in labour market institutions that affect all workers.

- Finally, some countries have high youth and prime-age employment rates and a small gap between youth and prime-age unemployment rates (Austria, Canada, Germany, the Netherlands and Switzerland), which can be attributed to relatively favourable macroeconomic conditions as well as sound education, social and labour market institutions.

■ Figure 4.3 ■

Employment and unemployment rates of youth and prime-age workers

2007-2013

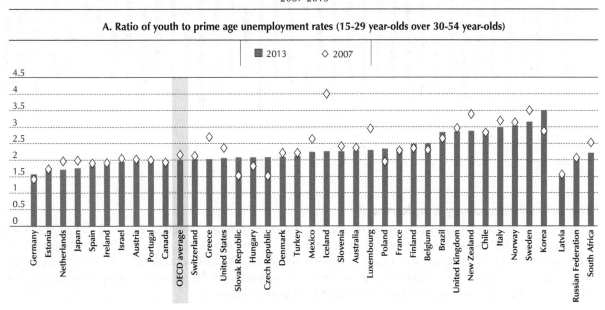

▪ Figure 4.3 (continued) ▪

Employment and unemployment rates of youth and prime-age workers

2007-2013

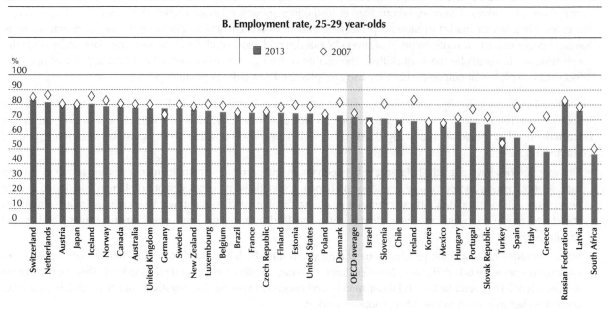

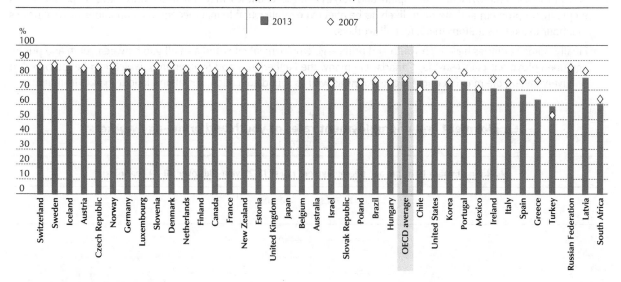

Source: OECD *Employment and Labour Market Statistics* (database), *http://dx.doi.org/ 10.1787/lfs-lms-data-en*.

StatLink ⯈ http://dx.doi.org/10.1787/888933214624

The role of temporary employment

When youth enter the labour market, many do so on a temporary contract. In almost all OECD countries, 25% of employees aged between 15 and 24 years old had a fixed-term contract in 2013 (Figure 4.4). When self-employment is excluded, this proportion reaches 50% in many countries and up to 73% in Slovenia (OECD, 2014b). Some countries appear to have a relatively low share of youth on temporary contracts, but this sometimes hides other forms of non-regular work, such as casual work in Australia[1] and informal work in Turkey.

Temporary contracts are far more prevalent among youth than among prime-age workers in most OECD countries. This suggests that many young entrants in the labour market procure initial temporary contracts, but then manage to transition into more stable positions. This is confirmed by the recent empirical literature, which suggests that accepting a temporary job offer does not reduce – and sometimes slightly increases – the chances of securing a permanent position later in one's career (OECD, 2014b). However, these findings do not mean that temporary jobs are stepping stones towards stable employment, but simply that on average, youth manage the transition even if they started with a temporary contract. Studies that try to assess the impact of being in temporary contracts on longer term labour market outcomes lead to mixed results (Bassanini and Garnero, 2012).

▪ Figure 4.4 ▪

Youth in temporary employment

As a share of total employment in each age group, 2013

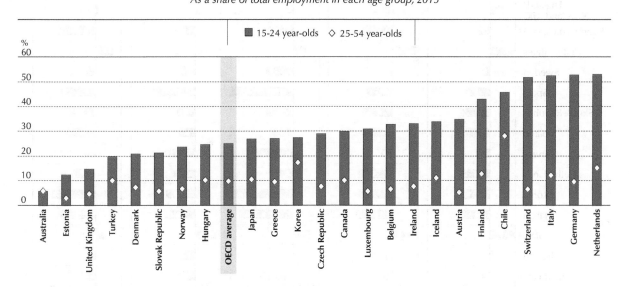

Notes: For Australia and Japan, the year of reference is 2012.

Source: *OECD Employment and Labour Market Statistics* (database), *http://dx.doi.org/ 10.1787/lfs-lms-data-en*.

StatLink ᴍᴤ🔗 http://dx.doi.org/10.1787/888933214639

Temporary jobs might simultaneously be a stepping-stone for some workers and a trap for others. A study found that fixed-term contracts lead to permanent positions only in the case of the highly educated, but not for youth, women and low-educated workers (Casquel and Cunyat, 2008). Recent estimates suggest that in almost all European countries, less than half of the workers that were on temporary contracts in a given year are employed on full-time permanent contracts three years later (OECD, 2014b). The type of temporary contract may matter. For instance, experience in the United States shows that temporary jobs with direct hire by employers, and thereby higher employer commitment, improve low-skilled employment while it is not the case for temporary-help jobs provided by agencies where the agency is the employer (Autor and Houseman, 2010). A number of studies have also pointed out that, while one spell of temporary employment might be beneficial for obtaining a permanent job, this is not necessarily the case when spells of temporary jobs are repeated (OECD, 2014b).

The Survey of Adult Skills suggests that workers on temporary contracts use their cognitive skills less intensively than workers in permanent employment, which can expose them to the risk of skills depreciation (Figure 4.5). The results are less clear-cut for social and emotional or job-specific skills: workers on temporary contracts learn more at work than those on permanent contracts, but use their influencing and task discretion skills less intensively (OECD, 2013a).

Less access to training for workers on temporary contracts could lead to an increase in the skills gap between workers on different employment contracts; this may be another reason why some workers cannot escape precarious jobs (OECD, 2006). The causal effect of the type of contract on the likelihood of benefiting from employer-sponsored training is however difficult to assess, as workers endowed with less productive abilities are both less likely to secure a permanent contract and to receive employer-sponsored training. Tentative analysis based on PIAAC data[2] shows that on average, being on a temporary contract reduces the probability of receiving employer-sponsored training by 14% (OECD, 2014b).

■ Figure 4.5 ■
Use of skills at work, by type of employment contract
16-29 year-olds, 2012

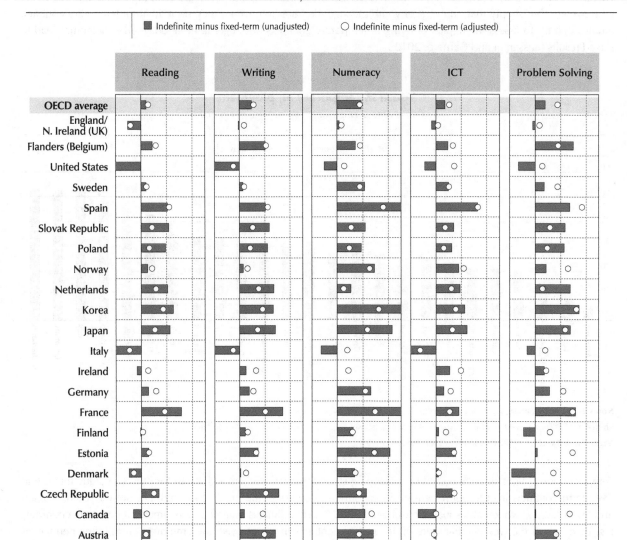

Notes: Adjusted estimates are based on OLS regressions including controls for literacy and numeracy proficiency scores, hours worked, and occupation dummies (ISCO 1 digit).

Source: OECD calculations based on the *Survey of Adult Skills (PIAAC) (2012)* (database).

StatLink ⊞ http://dx.doi.org/10.1787/888933214647

As youth are more likely to be on temporary contracts than on permanent ones, they have been disproportionally hit by the crisis. Temporary contracts are primarily used by firms to adjust to a lower demand. Furthermore, even when youth are on permanent contracts, they are more exposed to dismissal as employment protection legislation (EPL) generally favours older workers, for instance through last-in-first-out rules. More generally, a large share of temporary employment in the economy tends to lower labour market resilience due to large increases in the unemployment response to output shocks, and shifts the cost of the crisis on youth (OECD, 2014b). For example, the dramatic upsurge in unemployment in Spain during the recent crisis was essentially due to the destruction of temporary jobs (OECD, 2013b). Overall in the OECD, youth employment, both permanent and temporary, has fallen substantially with the crisis and has not yet fully recovered (Figure 4.6).

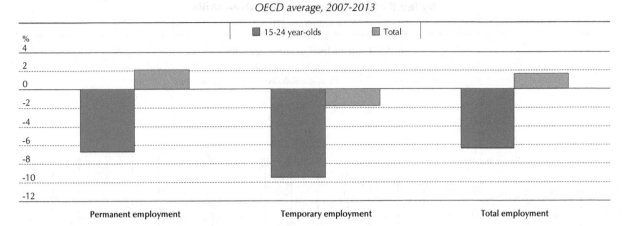

- Figure 4.6 -
The evolution of youth employment, by labour market contract
OECD average, 2007-2013

Source: OECD *Employment and Labour Market Statistics* (database), *http://dx.doi.org/ 10.1787/lfs-lms-data-en*.

StatLink http://dx.doi.org/10.1787/888933214653

Youth who are more likely to become NEET

Education attainment and cognitive skills influence the likelihood of becoming NEET (OECD, 2014b). In most countries, the NEET rate for youth having completed tertiary education is relatively small (Chapter 2). Young people with low literacy and numeracy skills are more likely to belong to the NEET group. In all countries covered by the Survey of Adult Skills, except Japan and to some extent Italy, those with the lowest levels of cognitive skills have the highest NEET rate (Figure 4.7). There is large variability between countries in the NEET rates for youth with low cognitive skills, with this rate reaching high levels in some countries (e.g. Ireland, the Slovak Republic, and Spain). By contrast, the NEET rate for those with the highest numeracy and literacy skills remains contained, even in countries with a relatively high average NEET rate.

- Figure 4.7 -
The share of youth neither in employment nor in education or training, by level of proficiency in cognitive skills
16-29 year-olds, 2012

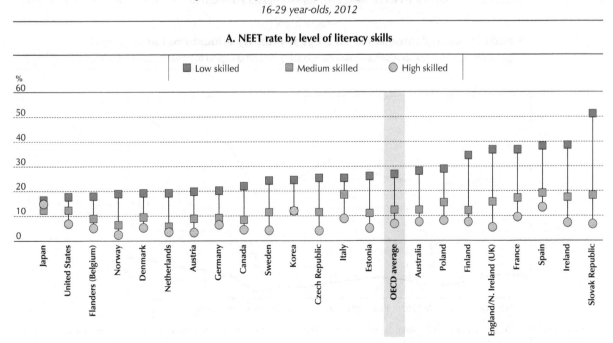

A. NEET rate by level of literacy skills

■ Figure 4.7 (continued) ■

The share of youth neither in employment nor in education or training, by level of proficiency in cognitive skills

16-29 year-olds, 2012

B. NEET rate by level of numeracy skills

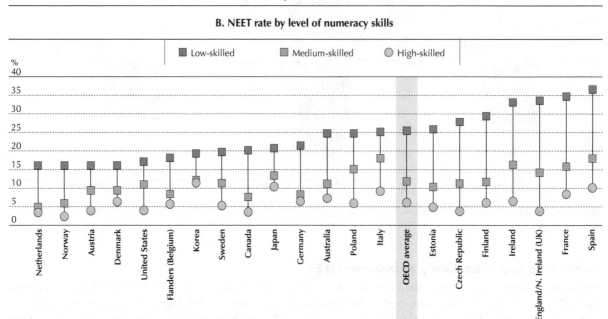

Notes: The figure shows the NEET rate for three levels of proficiency in literacy and numeracy skills. "Low-skilled" corresponds to Level 1 or below; "Medium-skilled" to Levels 2 and 3; and "High-skilled" to Levels 4 and 5. The NEET rate is the share of individuals who were neither in employment nor in education or training at the time of the survey.

Source: OECD calculations based on the *Survey of Adult Skills (PIAAC) (2012)* (database).

StatLink ◤◢◤ http://dx.doi.org/10.1787/888933214665

The economic crisis has exacerbated the difficulties for lower-educated youth to find jobs. Between 2008 and 2011, the unemployment rate for youth, who have not attained upper secondary education has increased substantially while youth with higher levels of education have been less affected (Figure 4.8). Youth with relatively low levels of education and skills may have been crowded out of the labour market by tertiary-qualified youth as competition for jobs has increased.

■ Figure 4.8 ■

Trends in unemployment for 25-34 year-olds, by educational attainment

Average in OECD countries, as a percentage of the corresponding group in the labour force, 1997-2013

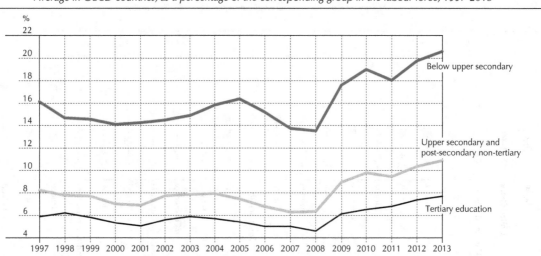

Source: OECD (2015), *Education at a Glance Interim Report: Update of Employment and Educational Attainment Indicators*, OECD, Paris, *www.oecd. org/edu/EAG-Interim-report.pdf*.

StatLink ◤◢◤ http://dx.doi.org/10.1787/888933214679

Larger enrolment in education has to some extent mitigated the impact of the crisis on youth, by limiting the increase in NEET rates (see Figure 4.1; OECD, 2013c). This has been the case particularly for the youngest cohort. On average accross OECD countries, for those aged 15-19, increased or prolonged enrolment in education has at least temporarily offset the negative impact of the crisis on employment, and the NEET rate has remained broadly stable. For those aged above 19, enrolment in education has only partly offset the decrease in employment, and the NEET rate has increased. These evolutions, for OECD countries as a whole, hide differences between countries. In Denmark, Poland, Portugal and Slovenia, the NEET rate has increased with the crisis, even for the youngest NEETs. While the increase in the share of youth continuing education may improve the employability of the current generation in the long term, today's generation will one day have to compete with a younger generation in the labour market, making it even more important to develop the right skills (see Chapter 3).

In emerging economies, as in other countries, youth with lower levels of education face greater difficulties to find a job (Quintini and Martin, 2014). At the same time, there are still large dropout rates from secondary education in these countries, such as in Latin America (OECD/ECLAC, 2012). This is partly due to the cost of continuing education, especially for those who live in rural areas, as there is generally no educational grant whereas taking a job provides an immediate return (Chapter 3). Low-skilled youth are more likely to be pushed into the informal sector. One of the main concerns with informal employment is the inherent difficulties in identifying those who need help to escape precarious employment situations in which they run the risk of being trapped. In addition, informality exposes youth to the risk of poverty, as they are not protected by labour market and social institutions.

NEETS AND THE LONG ROAD TO THE LABOUR MARKET

The skills of young NEETs

Educational attainment and skills are not the only barriers to youth employment. The educational attainment of young NEETs varies widely across countries (Figure 4.9). In some countries (the Czech Republic, Israel, Poland, the Slovak Republic, Sweden, Switzerland and the United States,) young NEETs generally have an upper secondary degree while in others (Denmark, Iceland, Mexico, Spain and Turkey), the majority have not attained upper secondary education. Yet, in most countries, NEETs have attained at least upper secondary education.

▪ Figure 4.9 ▪

Educational attainment of youth neither in employment nor in education or training

15-29 year-olds, 2013

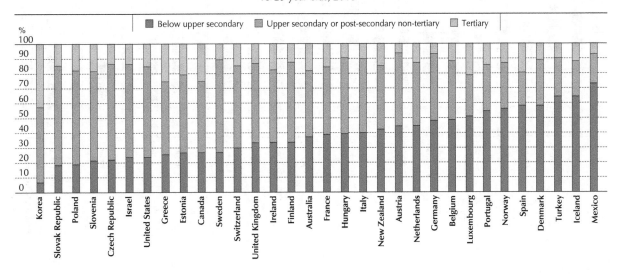

Source: OECD (2015), *Education at a Glance Interim Report: Update of Employment and Educational Attainment Indicators*, OECD, Paris, *www.oecd.org/edu/EAG-Interim-report.pdf*.

StatLink ᴴᵗᵗ http://dx.doi.org/10.1787/888933214685

Most young NEETs have relatively good cognitive skills as measured in the Survey of Adult Skills (Figure 4.10). Moreover, in many countries, a significant share of NEETs have high literacy, numeracy and problem-solving skills. On average, in OECD countries, only 20% of NEETs have low literacy skills (Level 1 and below) and 29% have low numeracy skills.

▪ Figure 4.10 ▪

Cognitive skills of youth neither in employment nor in education or training

16-29 year-olds, 2012

A. Literacy skills

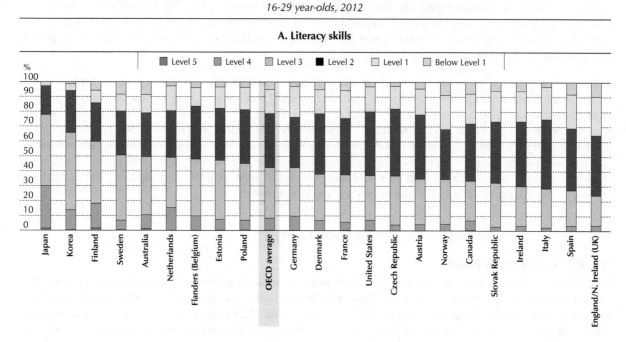

B. Numeracy skills

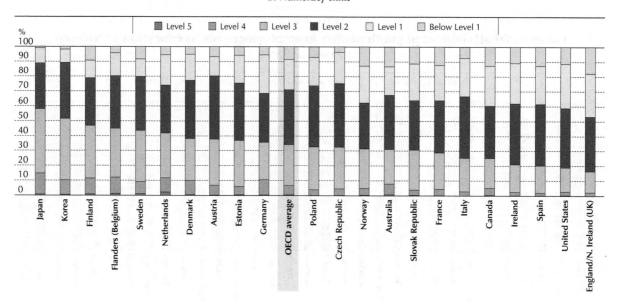

▪ Figure 4.10 (continued) ▪

Cognitive skills of youth neither in employment nor in education or training

16-29 year-olds, 2012

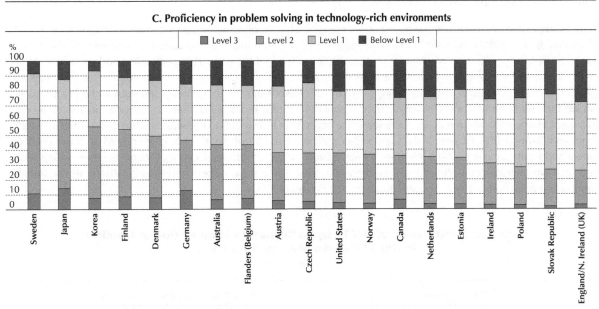

C. Proficiency in problem solving in technology-rich environments

Source: OECD calculations based on the *Survey of Adult Skills (PIAAC) (2012)* (database).

StatLink ᴍ🔗 http://dx.doi.org/10.1787/888933214698

Unemployed and inactive NEETs

Some NEETs are unemployed and looking for jobs, while others are inactive and not seeking employment. Those who are not looking for a job may not be registered with public employment services or social institutions, especially in countries with no welfare benefits for youth and no requirement to prepare for the labour market. These inactive NEETs may be particularly hard to reach by education providers and labour market, and social services. The share of inactive NEETs is large in countries sush as Australia, Israel, Korea, Mexico, Norway, Turkey, and the United States (Figure 4.11).

▪ Figure 4.11 ▪

Youth neither in employment nor in education or training, by labour force status

15-29 year-olds, 2013

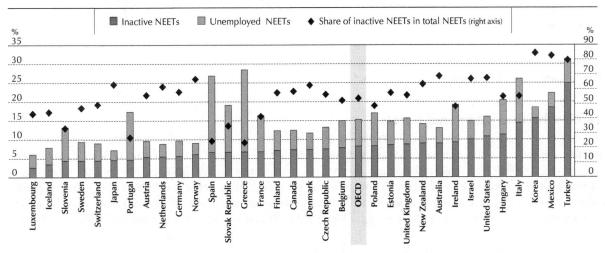

Notes: The left scale shows unemployed NEETs and inactive NEETs as a share of population aged 15-29 and the right scale shows the share of young inactive NEETs as a share of total young NEETs. For Chile, the year of reference is 2011 and for Japan, the age group is 15-24 year-olds. The OECD average excludes Chile and Japan.

Source: OECD (2015), *Education at a Glance Interim Report: Update of Employment and Educational Attainment Indicators*, OECD, Paris, *www.oecd.org/edu/EAG-Interim-report.pdf*.

StatLink ᴍ🔗 http://dx.doi.org/10.1787/888933214703

Being NEET for a long period of time is associated with lower skills. Youth who are NEET and have not participated in education or training in the 12 months prior to the survey have lower literacy and numeracy[3] skills than those who have participated in education or training (Figure 4.12). This result may be attributed to individual characteristics or reflect that skills erode with time spent out of education and work.

There is ample evidence that youth who experience a spell of unemployment following graduation are more likely to be affected by unemployment later in their careers, and by lower earnings – the so-called "scarring effect" (Nordström Skans, 2004; Oreopoulos, Von Wachter and Heisz, 2006; Doiron and Gørgens, 2008; Schmillen and Umkehrer, 2013). Since it is harder for employers to assess the skills of workers with little experience in the labour market, they may take spells of unemployment and inactivity to signal youth with lower skills. Furthermore, youth outside the labour market can see their skills atrophy over a relatively short period of time (Pissarides, 1992). Self-confidence can also erode with time spent in inactivity, which may also deteriorate the capacity of individuals to mobilise and use their skills (Goldsmith, Veum and Darity, 1997). Erosion of skills and self-confidence also contribute to scarring effects. When scarring effects appear and youth struggle to find a job, they are more likely to face poverty, especially in countries where young adults tend to leave their parental homes early. Furthermore, they run the risk of becoming marginalised, and potentially slipping into addiction or crime (Fougère, Kramarz and Pouget, 2009).

■ Figure 4.12 ■

Average literacy skills of NEETs, by participation in education or training in the 12 months prior to the survey

16-29 year-olds, 2012

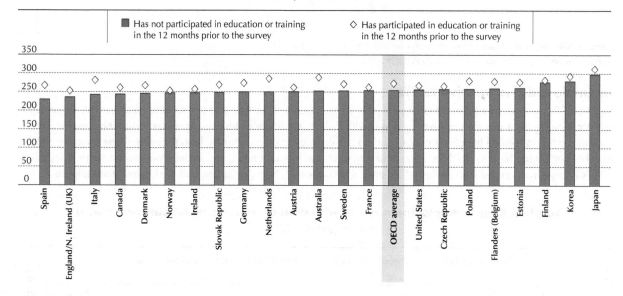

Source: OECD calculations based on the *Survey of Adult Skills (PIAAC) (2012)* (database).
StatLink ⬛🔗 http://dx.doi.org/10.1787/888933214718

Youth who face additional hurdles

In many countries, women face extra hurdles to integrate into the labour market, very often because they face low incentives to do so as a consequence of limited or costly childcare facilities and of parental leave policies, or because of social norms. The NEET rate is higher for young women than for young men in most OECD countries (Figure 4.13). This is particularly the case in Mexico and Turkey, but it is also so in many developing economies, where a large share of young women leave the education system to raise families, rather than taking jobs. Yet, in most countries covered by the Survey of Adult Skills, the average score on the literacy scale of female NEETs is similar to that of male NEETs (Figure 4.14).

▪ Figure 4.13 ▪

Youth neither in employment nor in education or training, by gender

Percentage of population aged 15-29, 2013

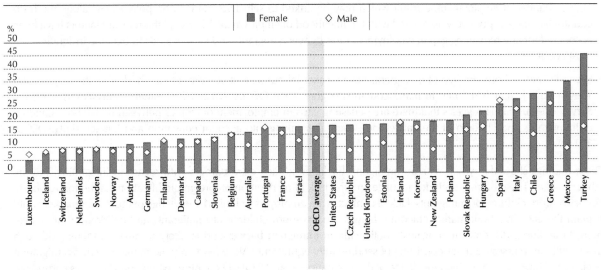

Notes: The year of reference is 2011 for Chile and 2012 for Korea.

Source: OECD (2015), *Education at a Glance Interim Report: Update of Employment and Educational Attainment Indicators*, OECD, Paris, *www.oecd. org/edu/EAG-Interim-report.pdf*.

StatLink 🔗 http://dx.doi.org/10.1787/888933214724

▪ Figure 4.14 ▪

Mean literacy scores of youth neither in employment nor in education or training, by gender

16-29 year-olds, 2012

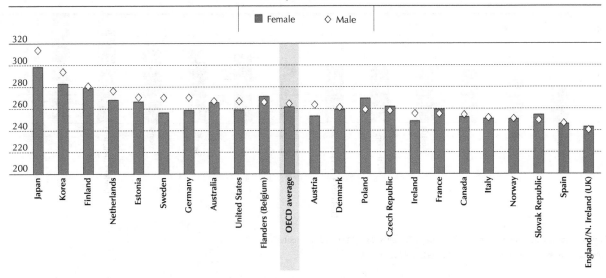

Source: OECD calculations based on the *Survey of Adult Skills (PIAAC) (2012)* (database).

StatLink 🔗 http://dx.doi.org/10.1787/888933214736

Youth with immigrant backgrounds have lower employment outcomes than children of the native-born:

▪ Firstly, foreign-born adults have lower employment rates than native-born persons in all countries except Italy and the United States (Bonfanti and Xenogiani, 2014). The gap is especially large for those with high education attainment. Low-qualified foreign-born adults are often as likely, if not more likely, to work than low-qualified native-born. An analysis based on the Survey of Adult Skills, but not specific to youth, shows that foreign-born labour market outcomes depend on education levels and literacy skills, as for natives. However, for the same education level and literacy skills, having a foreign qualification is associated with a lower probability of employment in some countries (e.g. Finland and the Netherlands). This suggests imperfect transferability and recognition of the skills of those with foreign credentials. In contrast, in the United States and to some extent in Estonia, migrants with a foreign qualification have, on average, higher chances of employment, a result which may be linked to selective immigration policies. Speaking the host-country language is positively associated with the likelihood of employment.[4] Once all the relevant factors have been accounted for, the remaining gap in employment rates between migrants and natives tends to become insignificant in most countries.

- Secondly, native-born children of immigrants have weaker labour market outcomes than children of the native-born. They have a higher NEET rate in many countries (Figure 4.15; OECD, 2012a). Preliminary analysis based on the Survey of Adult Skills suggests that there are persisting gaps in employment outcomes between native-born children of immigrants and children of the native-born, even after taking into account education and literacy skills (OECD, 2014c).

These findings show that youth with an immigrant background face extra barriers with regard to integrating into the labour market. These barriers include language and the lack of recognition of foreign qualifications of the foreign-born. For native-born children of immigrants, lack of contacts with employers or limited knowledge of the labour market could explain the gaps in labour market outcomes between native-born children of immigrants and children of the native-born. In addition, discrimination against youth with an immigrant background is likely to also contribute, although this is difficult to assess. Studies consisting of sending fully equivalent CVs, where only the name indicates a migration background have revealed a high incidence of discrimination in all 18 OECD countries where the study was carried out (OECD, 2013d).

▪ Figure 4.15 ▪

Share of youth neither in employment nor in education or training, by parents' place of birth

16-29 year-olds, 2012

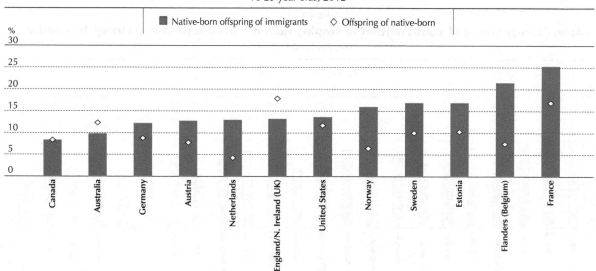

Source: OECD calculations based on the *Survey of Adult Skills (PIAAC) (2012)* (database).
StatLink 🔗 http://dx.doi.org/10.1787/888933214749

Other groups of youth face extra hurdles. Youth living in rural or remote areas (in developing economies but also in OECD countries like Ireland, for instance) lack access to the same range of information, advice, infrastructure and opportunities found in urban areas, and are more likely to work in the informal sector. Young people from low socio-economic backgrounds may also face difficulties in building networks, which can be crucial to getting jobs (Kramarz and Nordström Skans,2013).

Youth with mental disorders also face greater difficulties finding jobs and activating their skills (OECD, 2012b). In addition, the type of assistance and benefits they may receive can lower their incentives to take jobs, especially if they cannot be cumulated with revenues from work. In the recent past, the number of youth with mental disorders has increased in several countries, although this may partly reflect better recognition of disorders (Figure 4.16).

▪ Figure 4.16 ▪

Percentage of youth with mental disorders

People aged 15-24 with mental disorders as a percentage of the total youth population, mid-1990s to late 2000s

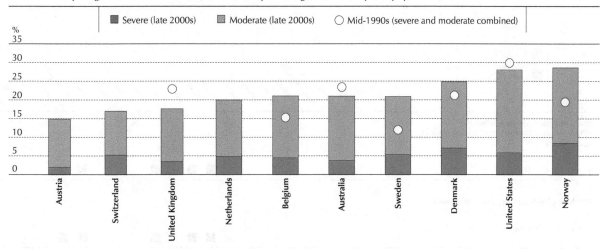

Source: OECD (2013e), *Mental Health and Work: Norway*, Mental Health and Work, OECD Publishing, *http://dx.doi.org/10.1787/9789264178984-en*.

StatLink 🔗 http://dx.doi.org/10.1787/888933214755

Very often, disadvantages cumulate in the labour market, leading to vicious circles. Low-skilled youth living in rural areas cannot afford to leave their parents' homes to look for jobs and become discouraged, possibly leading to mental disorders, which further harms their employment chances. Tight housing markets and high house prices in some cities and regions have reinforced the difficulties for youth to make successful school-to-work transitions, especially when doing so involves geographical relocation, lengthening the period of transition and increasing the risks of skills loss and possibly mental disorders. By contrast, youth who are not financially constrained can afford a sequence of unpaid jobs as "interns" in the hope of gaining relevant work experience and access to permanent, paid employment. Youth from high socio-economic backgrounds can rely on their social capital (including networks) to find the right jobs.

SKILLS SCOREBOARD ON YOUTH EMPLOYABILITY

Are youth well integrated into the labour market?

To enhance employability, youth need to find a job upon graduation and remain employed. However, youth face particularly higher risks of working on a temporary contract, remaining unemployed, or even fully withdrawing from the labour market. These risks are even stronger in times of high unemployment and low labour demand. The Skills Scoreboard uses four employment indicators to measure the integration of youth into the labour market and the vulnerability of youth compared to prime-age workers to the unemployment risk (Table 4.1).

How close are NEETs to the labour market?

Youth who are NEETs should be helped to reintegrate into the labour market or the education system in a timely manner; however, some NEET groups are more at risk of permanent detachment from the labour market than others. Education attainment and cognitive skills as well as the duration of unemployment and engagement with the labour market influence the likelihood of becoming and remaining a NEET. The Skills Scoreboard uses four indicators to measure the share of the NEETs who are more at risk of persistent detachment from the labour market (Table 4.2).

■ Table 4.1 ■

Skills Scoreboard on youth employability: Are youth well integrated into the labour market?

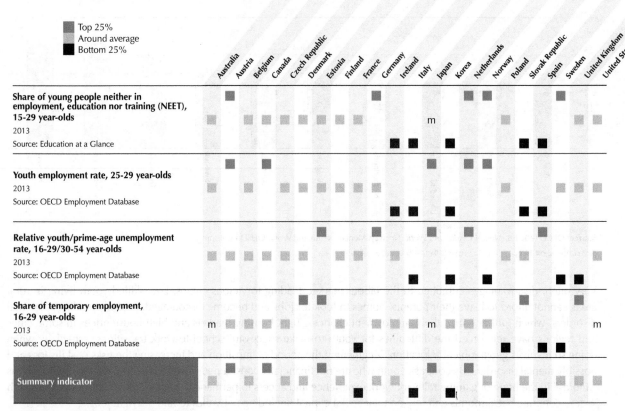

Top 25%
Around average
Bottom 25%

Share of young people neither in employment, education nor training (NEET), 15-29 year-olds
2013
Source: Education at a Glance

Youth employment rate, 25-29 year-olds
2013
Source: OECD Employment Database

Relative youth/prime-age unemployment rate, 16-29/30-54 year-olds
2013
Source: OECD Employment Database

Share of temporary employment, 16-29 year-olds
2013
Source: OECD Employment Database

Summary indicator

Notes: All indicators have been normalised in a way which implies that a higher value and being among the "top 25%" reflect better performance. For this purpose, the inverse of all indicators except "Youth employment rate" is considered in the ranking. For the NEET indicator, data for Korea is from 2012 and Japan has a missing value, as data are available only for the 15-24 age group. The summary indicator is calculated as a simple average of the four indicators.

Sources: OECD calculations based on: OECD (2015), *Education at a Glance Interim Report: Update of Employment and Educational Attainment Indicators*, OECD, Paris, *www.oecd.org/edu/EAG-Interim-report.pdf*;

OECD *Employment and Labour Market Statistics* (database), *http://dx.doi.org/ 10.1787/lfs-lms-data-en*.

■ Table 4.2 ■

Skills Scoreboard on youth employability: How close are NEETs to the labour market?

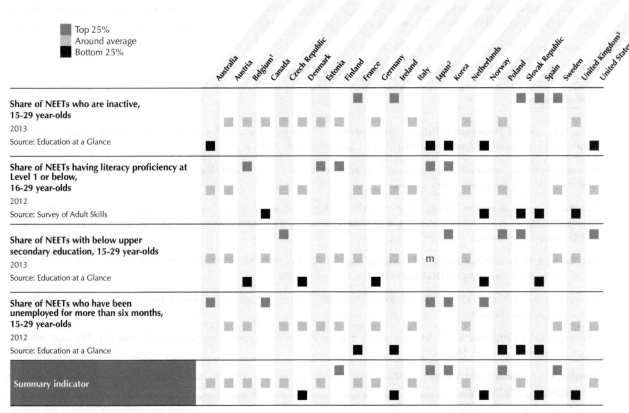

Top 25%
Around average
Bottom 25%

1. All indicators from the Survey of Adult Skills for Belgium refer to Flanders.
2. Data for Japan refer to the NEETs group aged 15-24 except for the indicator based on the "Share of the NEETs having literacy proficiency at Level 1 or below" from the Survey of Adult Skills.
3. All indicators from the Survey of Adult Skills for the United Kingdom refer to England and Northern Ireland.

Notes: All indicators have been normalised in a way which implies that a higher value and being among the "top 25%" reflect better performance. For this purpose, the inverse of all indicators is considered in the ranking. For Korea, all data refer to 2012. For the indicators calculated based on Education at a Glance, Japan reports results for the 15-24 age group. Japan has a missing value for the indicator "Share of the NEETs with below upper secondary education", as data are not reported at that education level. The summary indicator is calculated as a simple average of the four indicators.

Sources: OECD calculations based on: OECD (2014a), *Education at a Glance 2014: OECD Indicators*, OECD Publishing, *http://dx.doi.org/10.1787/eag-2014-en*; OECD (2015), *Education at a Glance Interim Report: Update of Employment and Educational Attainment Indicators*, OECD, Paris, *www.oecd.org/edu/EAG-Interim-report.pdf*;
Survey of Adult Skills (PIAAC) (2012) (database).

Notes

1. Casual employees in Australia can be dismissed without notice or severance pay. Their hours can also be varied from week to week, or day to day.

2. Cognitive skills from the Survey of Adult Skills (PIAAC) can be used as a measure of workers' general abilities acquired prior to starting jobs, and are not affected by training. This helps to identify the causal effect of the type of contract on employer-sponsored training.

3. Similar results are found for numeracy skills, but are not shown.

4. This may be because literacy proficiency takes such language skills into account.

References

Autor, D.H. and **S.N. Houseman** (2010), "Do temporary-help jobs improve labor market outcomes for low-skilled workers? Evidence from Work First", *American Economic Journal: Applied Economics*, Vol. 2, No. 3.

Bassanini, A. and **A. Garnero** (2012), "Dismissal Protection and Worker Flows in OECD Countries: Evidence from Cross-Country/Cross-Industry Data", *IZA Discussion Papers*, No. 6535.

Bonfanti, S. and **T. Xenogiani** (2014), "Migrants' skills: Use, mismatch and labour market outcomes – A first exploration of the International Survey of Adult Skills (PIAAC)", in OECD and European Union, *Matching Economic Migration with Labour Market Needs*, OECD Publishing, Paris, *http://dx.doi.org/10.1787/9789264216501-11-en*.

Carcillo, S., R. Fernandez, S. Königs and **A. Minea** (2015), "NEET Youth in the Aftermath of the Crisis: Challenges and Policies", *OECD Social, Employment and Migration Working Papers*, No. 164, *http://dx.doi.org/10.1787/5js6363503f6-en*.

Casquel, E. and **A. Cunyat** (2008), "Temporary contracts, employment protection and skill: A simple model", *Economics Letters*, Vol. 100, No. 3, pp. 333-336.

Doiron, D. and **T. Gørgens** (2008), "State dependence in youth labor market experiences, and the evaluation of policy interventions", *Journal of Econometrics*, Vol. 145.

Fougère, D., F. Kramarz and **J. Pouget** (2009), "Youth unemployment and crime in France", *Journal of the European Economic Association*, 7 (5): pp.909–938.

Goldsmith, A., J. Veum and **W. Darity** (1997), "Unemployment, joblessness, psychological well-being and self-esteem: Theory and evidence", *The Journal of Socio-Economics*, Vol. 26, No. 2.

Kramarz, F. and **O. Nordström Skans** (2013), "When strong ties are strong: networks and youth labor market entry", *CEPR Discussion Papers*, No. 9620.

Nordström Skans, O. (2004), "Scarring effects of the first labour market experience: A sibling based analysis", *IFAU Working Paper Series*, 2004:14, IFAU, Uppsala.

OECD (2015), *Education at a Glance Interim Report: Update of Employment and Educational Attainment Indicators*, OECD, Paris, *www.oecd.org/edu/EAG-Interim-report.pdf*.

OECD (2014a), *Education at a Glance 2014: OECD Indicators*, OECD Publishing, Paris, *http://dx.doi.org/10.1787/eag-2014-en*.

OECD (2014b), *OECD Employment Outlook 2014*, OECD Publishing, Paris, *http://dx.doi.org/10.1787/empl_outlook-2014-en*.

OECD (2014c), "Labour market integration of immigrants and their children: Developing, activating and using skills", in OECD, *International Migration Outlook 2014*, OECD Publishing, Paris, *http://dx.doi.org/10.1787/migr_outlook-2014-5-en*.

OECD (2013a), *OECD Skills Outlook 2013: First Results from the Survey of Adult Skills*, OECD Publishing, Paris, *http://dx.doi.org/10.1787/9789264204256-en*.

OECD (2013b), *The 2012 Labour Market Reform in Spain: A Preliminary Assessment*, OECD Publishing, Paris, *http://dx.doi.org/10.1787/9789264213586-en*.

OECD (2013c), *OECD Employment Outlook 2013*, OECD Publishing, Paris, *http://dx.doi.org/10.1787/empl_outlook-2013-en*.

OECD (2013d), "Discrimination against immigrants – measurement, incidence and policy instruments", in *International Migration Outlook 2013*, OECD Publishing, Paris, *http://dx.doi.org/10.1787/migr_outlook-2013-7-en*.

OECD (2013e), *Mental Health and Work: Norway*, Mental Health and Work, OECD Publishing, Paris, *http://dx.doi.org/10.1787/9789264178984-en*.

OECD (2012a), *Settling In: OECD Indicators of Immigrant Integration 2012*, OECD Publishing, Paris, *http://dx.doi.org/10.1787/9789264171534-en*.

OECD (2012b), *Sick on the Job?: Myths and Realities about Mental Health and Work,* Mental Health and Work, OECD Publishing, Paris, *http://dx.doi.org/10.1787/9789264124523-en*.

OECD/ECLAC (2012), *Latin American Economic Outlook 2013: SME Policies for Structural Change*, OECD Publishing, Paris, *http://dx.doi.org/10.1787/leo-2013-en*.

OECD (2010), *Off a Good Start? Jobs for Youth*, OECD Publishing, Paris, *http://dx.doi.org/10.1787/9789264096127-en*.

OECD (2006), *OECD Employment Outlook 2006: Boosting Jobs and Incomes*, OECD Publishing, Paris, *http://dx.doi.org/10.1787/empl_outlook-2006-en*.

OECD Employment and Labour Market Statistics (database), *http://dx.doi.org/ 10.1787/lfs-lms-data-en*.

Oreopoulos, P., T. Von Wachter and **A. Heisz** (2006), "The short- and long-term career effects of graduating in a recession: hysteresis and heterogeneity in the market for college graduates", *National Bureau of Economic Research Working Papers*, No. 12159.

Pissarides, C.A. (1992), "Loss of skill during unemployment and the persistence of employment shocks", *Quarterly Journal of Economics*, Vol. 107, No. 4.

Quintini, G. and **S. Martin** (2014), "Same but different: School-to-work transitions in emerging and advanced economies", *OECD Social, Employment and Migration Working Papers*, No. 154, OECD Publishing, Paris, *http://dx.doi.org/ 10.1787/5jzbb2t1rcwc-en*.

Quintini, G., J.P. Martin and **S. Martin** (2007), "The changing nature of the school-to-work: Transition process in OECD countries", *IZA Discussion Papers*, No. 2582.

Schmillen, A. and **M. Umkehrer** (2013), "The scars of youth: effects of early-career unemployment on future unemployment experience", *IAB Discussion Paper*, No. 6/2013, Institute for Employment Research, Nuremburg.

5

Policies towards integrating youth into the labour market

Ensuring that all youth leave the education system with the right skills and linking education systems more closely with the labour market (as discussed in Chapter 3) are crucial, but not enough to close the gap between the world of study and the world of work. This chapter discusses how labour market institutions and specific policies can ease youth's transition towards employment and help those who are not in employment, education or training to re-engage with education or find a job.

Youth can be considered successful in their school-to-work transitions if they are employed and on a path towards stable employment. Education and skills do not ensure a successful transition to the labour market as reflected by the relatively large share of youth neither in employement nor in education or training (NEET) having relatively high educational attainment and cognitive skills. However, better education systems and well-designed and progressive transitions from school to work that combine study and work help young people successfully integrate into the labour market (see Chapter 3). In addition, many other factors can help youth move towards stable employment. Favourable macroeconomic conditions and high labour demand ease school-to-work transitions. A combination of sound labour market and social institutions, as well as specific policies which target youth, is needed to ease school-to-work transitions but also to help those who belong to the NEET group to renew with job search or re-engage with education and training.

DEVELOPING A COMPREHENSIVE STRATEGY

A "whole-of-government" approach

Many countries have made substantial efforts to strengthen their labour market and social institutions, for example, by making the granting of social benefits and tax incentives conditional on obligations to look for work. Many countries have also improved the efficiency of public employment services by merging various institutions, and developing tools to better monitor job searches and assess the efficiency of programmes. More recently, some countries have started to reform their employment protection legislation (EPL) to limit labour market dualism that has emerged as a consequence of incomplete reforms in the past aiming to develop temporary employment.

However, these reforms have often been incomplete and policies to integrate youth into the labour market are not customised enough to individual needs, in the context of the skills required in the labour market. Easing school-to-work transitions and helping NEETs to integrate into the labour market requires a comprehensive approach with strong co-operation between all stakeholders and a strong focus on specific needs. In return, these policies have the potential to increase youth employment in the short term but also youth employability in the longer term and mitigate the risk of falling into unemployment later in life.

Reaching inactive NEETs requires strong co-operation between stakeholders and policies. For instance, introducing a national obligation to offer education or work placements to youth belonging to a certain age group – a policy which has been developed in some countries – encourages education, labour market and social institutions at both the national and local levels to co-operate with one another. Systems with a "single gateway" or "one stop" that give access to all benefits and employment services in the same place are convenient for job seekers and help reduce duplication of services, but do not guarantee strong co-operation (OECD, 2013a). However, if there are obligations on both young people and institutions to take actions towards employability, co-operation between institutions can grow.

In this context, OECD countries have agreed in 2013 to take a comprehensive range of measures as part of the OECD Action Plan for Youth (see Chapter 1). The objectives of this action plan are both to tackle the current situation of high youth unemployment and to improve outcomes for youth in the long term by equipping them with relevant skills and removing employment barriers. Following the launch of the plan, the OECD is working with countries to implement the comprehensive set of measures in their national and local contexts.

The European Youth Guarantee

In Europe, several countries have submitted plans or taken steps to implement the European Youth Guarantee, which can be seen as one way to implement part of the OECD Action Plan for Youth in the European context (OECD, 2013b). Drawing from the experience of Austria, Finland and Sweden, the main principles of the Youth Guarantee include developing an integrated strategy with strong co-operation between institutions; early intervention and activation; and mutual obligations (Box 5.1). In particular, countries have committed to ensuring that, within four months of leaving school or losing a job, people under the age of 25 should receive a good-quality offer of employment, further education, an apprenticeship or a traineeship. According to the Survey of Adult Skills, in 2012, 7% of youth were NEET, on average, and had not participated in education or training in at least 12 months, with this share as high as 15% in Italy and the Slovak Republic. This is an indication of the efforts countries will need to make to fulfil the Youth Guarantee requirements.

> ### Box 5.1 **Adopting a comprehensive strategy to facilitate school-to-work transitions: the example of the European Youth Guarantee**
>
> According to the European Council recommendation, the Youth Guarantee ensures that all young people under the age of 25 – whether registered with employment services or not – get a good-quality, concrete offer within four months of leaving formal education or becoming unemployed. The good-quality offer should be for a job, apprenticeship, traineeship, or continued education, and should be adapted to each individual need and situation.
>
> To be successful, the Youth Guarantee needs to fulfil a number of principles (European Commission, 2013a):
>
> - **An integrated strategy.** It should not be the sum of existing and often uncoordinated measures. It needs to entail a structural reform of the way in which the public, private and voluntary sectors engage and support young people to complete education and enter the labour market through a co-ordinated, holistic and individualised approach, which understands and meets the needs of each young person.
>
> - **Strong co-operation.** All key stakeholders including public authorities, employment services, career guidance providers, education and training institutions, youth support services, businesses, employers and trade unions should co-operate with each other. This is particularly important for reaching inactive young people who are not registered with the public employment services (PES).
>
> - **Early intervention and activation.** For instance, the OECD has recommended that the first phase of the Irish Youth Guarantee start after three months of unemployment (OECD, 2014a).
>
> - **Mutual obligation.** Youth should be provided with a good-quality offer of employment, continued education, apprenticeship or traineeship. The offer should be personalised and meet youth's individual needs to gain a strong foothold in the labour market. In turn, young people need to take individual responsibility for the opportunity that is offered.
>
> In 2014, EU countries developed National Implementation Plans of the Youth Guarantee. Countries considered to be facing the biggest challenges in terms of youth employment are eligible to EU funds. They include, among OECD countries, Belgium, the Czech Republic, France, Greece, Hungary, Italy, Poland, Portugal, Slovak Republic, Slovenia, Spain, Sweden and the United Kingdom.
>
> To monitor the implementation and impact of the Youth Guarantee schemes, the European Commission has developed an Indicator Framework (Employment Committee, 2014).
>
> **Sources:**
>
> Employment Committee (2014), "Indicator Framework for Monitoring the Youth Guarantee", INDIC/10/16092014/EN-rev, Employment Committee (EMCO), European Commission.
>
> European Commission (2013a), "Practical support for the design and implementation of Youth Guarantee schemes: Synthesis of key messages", Brussels.
>
> OECD (2014a), "OECD Youth Action Plan: Options for an Irish Youth Guarantee", *www.oecd.org/ireland/YouthActionPlan-IrishYouthGuarantee.pdf*.

The Youth Guarantee schemes are expected to improve youth employment through two main channels: i) they help young people to make more informed decisions about their transition to work through personal development plans and needs assessment; ii) they improve the speed of services provided to young people and their quality by giving incentives to the PES to focus on youth-specific characteristics. Rapid action is expected to prevent disengagement from setting in and scarring effects from appearing.

However, experiences from countries that have implemented a Youth Guarantee underline the importance of its design in ensuring its efficiency. An available empirical estimate of the Swedish Youth Guarantee found a small positive effect on employment in the short term and no significant effect in the long term (Carling and Larsson, 2002). The Swedish Youth Guarantee has increased participation in programmes, which in the short run has increased the number of youth finding employment, but in the long term has "locked" more youth into programmes and reduced their job search efforts. It is therefore crucial to address the trade-offs between the objective to cover all youth and the risk of deadweight losses, and, even worse, the risks of trapping some youth in programmes while they could have transitioned from school to work better themselves. One of the most challenging goals of the Youth Guarantee is to reach all youth, including those who are inactive NEETs. The Youth Guarantee cannot simply be an umbrella programme for all the pre-existing ones. Instead, it should be used as an opportunity to reform and reorient labour-market and social policies towards youth, with a clear focus on the activation of their skills.

Guidance, counselling and targeting systems based on skills assessment

The OECD Youth Action Plan, as well as the EU Youth Guarantee, and any system of active labour market policies (ALMPs) require a good assessment of the skills available and the skills in demand in the labour market, as well as an efficient guidance system to counsel and help individuals. Learning and career guidance is an integral part of several measures to support young people. It supports their progression through their learning and work experience and can thereby limit the number of dropouts (see Chapter 3). Guidance can help to tailor programmes to the particular needs and challenges faced by young people and generally help them to enhance their employability (Borbély-Pecze and Hutchinson, 2013).

In an ideal framework, skills have to be at the core of guidance and targeting systems. In the first place, it is important to distinguish between youth who are lacking skills and would benefit from enrolling in appropriate education programmes to acquire them, and those who have the skills and can be encouraged or helped to activate them (and possibly to develop them further) and get into employment relatively quickly. The Survey of Adult Skills shows that in all countries covered, young NEETs have lower cognitive skills than employed youth (Figure 5.1). On average per country, the gap in literacy and problem-solving skills is not excessively high (and close to 0 in Korea and Japan) although this hides some heterogeneity between individuals. The NEETs may also lack some other employability skills.

■ Figure 5.1 ■

Gap in literacy and problem-solving skills between young NEETs and employed youth

Percentage difference, 16-29 year-olds, 2012

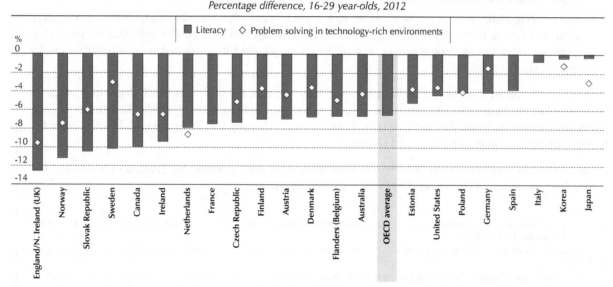

Notes: Employed youth are those who work and are not in education.

Source: OECD calculations based on the *Survey of Adult Skills (PIAAC) (2012)* (database).

StatLink ᴹˢᵖ http://dx.doi.org/10.1787/888933214773

Some countries already implement efficient guidance systems with early intervention, while others are trying to put these systems in place (Box 5.2). In these countries, a new scheme such as the Youth Guarantee could be introduced gradually by first targeting specific groups and then extending it to other groups, as planned by Ireland. Jobseeker profiling tools can help in this process, but experience from countries such as Australia, shows that when the tool is extensively and rather exclusively used, its adequacy is debatable (OECD, 2013a). This type of tool can be used to support or complement analysis by caseworkers. For instance in Finland, the profiling tool is used to generate a score showing the risk of long-term unemployment and the counsellor can use it, but is not obliged to, to separate jobseekers into categories. In 2010 in Norway, a tool was implemented with the aim of determining the "work capability" of job seekers.

Box 5.2 **Reaching all youth and developing early intervention as part of the Youth Guarantee: Country examples**

Countries have adopted various strategies to reach all youth and guide them within the Youth Guarantee scheme, according to their implementation plans.

Denmark has a long tradition of activation policies and already fulfils the criteria of the Youth Guarantee. Youth guidance centres are responsible for guiding youth and are required to closely follow youth aged 15-24 who have not completed upper secondary education. These centres are experienced at assessing the skills of youth in light of their readiness for further education or employment. The assessment of skills through interviews is used to classify youth into three categories depending on their distance to the labour market: youth without education, youth with education and youth without the preconditions to begin and complete ordinary education. Specific programmes are tailored to the three categories. Cash benefits and education grants are allocated to these categories under specific obligations for each group, but youth are not to receive social assistance without a counter-obligation.

Austria and Germany are also very close to full implementation of the Youth Guarantee: there are single-entry-point services to offer guidance for youth (the PES in Austria and "Team U25" in Germany). The first contact between youth and authorities starts with a guidance service, including a personal interview. In addition, Austria has developed guidance at the end of compulsory education to improve the quality of students' choices in terms of further education and limit drop-outs from university.

Italy was relatively far from implementing the framework of the Youth Guarantee but has taken a range of measures to move into this direction (Italian Ministry of Employment and Social Affairs, 2013). One challenge is to reach inactive NEETs who are not registered at the PES. Another one is to raise and harmonise the quality of services provided to the unemployed at the local level, in particular by improving the assessment system. There is a strong commitment of the government to develop individualised good quality and easily accessible policies to raise youth employability, including by developing the combination of work and study. However, lack of sufficient resources in PES and unclear incentives for inactive NEETs to participate in the scheme are challenges to overcome for a successful implementation of the scheme (European Commission, 2014a). The recently established e-Portal allows people to register directly on line and be connected to a national register, which facilitates automatic verification of fulfilment of requirements and transmission of offers.

In Spain, the Youth Guarantee targets all NEETs below the age of 25 who apply to the system, whether registered with the PES or not. Priority is given to youth with specific needs. As most NEETs are registered at the PES, it should be easier to reach them. The government has launched a large range of measures (100 measures) targeted to youth who have left school and are not integrated into the labour market (Spain Ministry of Employment and Social Security, 2013). The country aims to develop VET programmes with a work-based learning component. The number of VET centres involved in these has increased in 2014. However, lack of co-ordination between the central government and the autonomous regions can undermine the implementation of the Youth Guarantee (European Commission, 2014b). Furthermore, initial evidence points to a widespread use of short-term measures, such as non-wage recruitment subsidies and social security rebates for hiring young workers. The main challenge remains the development of high-quality education and training and labour market programmes and the allocation of the right support measure to the right individual.

In Ireland, the main challenges of the implementation of the Youth Guarantee are to intervene at an earlier stage of the unemployment or inactivity spell, to reach inactive NEETs and to improve the quality of programmes (European Commission, 2014c). The Youth Guarantee first focuses on youth under the age of 18 who have left school, and those who have been unemployed for at least four months. Then, it will be gradually extended to include all unemployed youth, starting with long-term unemployed youth (OECD, 2014a). The scheme starts when youth register for welfare or unemployment support at their local PES offices (Intreo). At registration, youth are profiled using the profiling system. A one-to-one interview takes place within two weeks for those identified at risk and after four or six months for those less at risk if they have not found jobs. A personal progression plan is agreed upon.

Sources:
European Commission (2014a), "Assessment of the 2014 National Reform Programme and Stability Programme for Italy", *Commission Staff Working Document*, No. 416.
European Commission (2014b), "Assessment of the 2014 National Reform Programme and Stability Programme for Spain", SWD(2014) 410 final.
European Commission (2014c), "Assessment of the 2014 National Reform Programme and Stability Programme for Ireland", *Commission Staff Working Document*, No. 408.
Italian Ministry of Employement and Social Affairs (2013), "Italy Youth Guarantee Implemantation Plan".
National Youth Guarantee Implementation Plans, *http://ec.europa.eu/social/main.jsp?catId=1090&langId=en*.
OECD (2014a), "OECD Youth Action Plan: Options for an Irish Youth Guarantee", *www.oecd.org/ireland/YouthActionPlan-IrishYouthGuarantee.pdf*.
Spain Ministry of Employment and Social Security (2013), "Spanish Youth Guarantee Implementation Plan", *www.empleo.gob.es/ficheros/ garantiajuvenil/documentos/plannacionalgarantiajuvenil_en.pdf*.

The role of local actors

At the local level, various initiatives have been developed to boost youth employment, especially for lower-skilled and disadvantaged youth (OECD, 2010; Box 5.3). Although developing co-operation between local stakeholders can be difficult, some initiatives have been successful (Froy, Giguère and Hofer, 2009). A particular challenge is to broaden these successful initiatives to reach a critical mass and to make them sustainable. For these reasons, a balance must be found in ensuring that local initiatives are co-ordinated across regions and not disconnected from national and mainstream institutions, while still being given the flexibility needed to adapt to local conditions (OECD, 2013c).

Box 5.3 Local actions to boost employment of low-skilled and disadvantaged youth: Local level examples

"New Inflow into New Jobs in the Harbour", Netherlands. In 2009, the Dutch government launched the three-year National Action Plan Combatting Youth Unemployment in the Netherlands. Through this plan, municipalities and other local authorities were charged with creating regional action plans to address school dropout and youth unemployment. Considerable flexibility was given to local authorities to develop education and apprenticeship programmes tailored to local conditions. The "New Inflow into New Jobs in the Harbour" project established before 2009 was a strong example of the type of programme supported by the regional action plan for the Rotterdam-Rijnmond region.

Rotterdam's port employs approximately 90 000 people, predominantly older workers. The Port of Rotterdam Authority, the Shipping and Transport College and DAAD (regional employers service desk) joined forces to revitalise the port's workforce while addressing high rates of youth unemployment through this programme. It offers a 40-week dual "study-work" programme (four days a week working, one day a week attending Shipping and Transport College) which trains young people to be operational assistants, after which they receive further, more specialised training. The programme also includes the development of social and emotional skills such as communication and listening, as well as reading, writing, simple mathematics and problem-solving skills. For four months, candidates receive an apprentice fee, after which they are offered a contract for at least 12 months. From a yearly intake of 100, 75% complete the course and of these, 80% proceed to a follow-up course and train as all-round operators.

"The Mayor's Apprenticeship Campaign" in London, United Kingdom. The London government has established the Mayor's Apprenticeship Campaign to boost apprenticeships through a joined-up approach that includes public sector leadership, the use of public procurement and business-to-business sales based on a clear business case. These efforts have required collaboration between stakeholders including: the London Development Agency, the Greater London Authority, London councils, a number of sector skills councils, the Young Person's Learning Agency, the Skills Funding Agency, National Apprenticeship Services and employers groups.

The campaign has resulted in a significant increase in the number of apprentices in London, doubling in one year alone: from 20 000 in 2009/10 to 40 000 in 2010/11. There is also evidence suggesting that quality has been maintained, if not improved: completion rates have risen from one in three to two in three, the fastest growth rate in England and the greatest rise has been in ISCED Level 3 (where evidence shows the greatest returns are) rather than ISCED Level 2. Additionally, the campaign has led to greater coverage of apprenticeship frameworks in "non-traditional" sectors, such as finance, which dominate London's economy.

"The Career Cluster Model" in the United States. Local and regional government agencies in the United States have increasingly adopted industry cluster approaches to economic development and a similar approach is surfacing in the workforce development field. As partnerships between workforce and economic development agencies become more common, the role of education and workforce agencies in mapping and building skill pipelines for key industries becomes more critical to economic development practitioners.

...

For example, the state of Maryland started working on career sectors/career clusters in 1995 under the School to Work Opportunities Act. Some 350 business executives in ten different sectors were brought together to inform education policy makers about their bottom line – how they made money and what they needed to be successful. The original project was funded with USD 25 million of Federal School to Work funds, and the approach was very bottom-up. Within each county there is a Cluster Advisory Board (CAB), focused on different industry clusters. In Montgomery County, for example, which is home to the third largest biotechnology cluster in the United States, there is a CAB focused on the Biosciences, Health Science and Medicine cluster. Administrators, counsellors and faculty members are using the career cluster system to develop programmes that extend from high school to two to four years in colleges/universities, graduate schools, apprenticeship programmes and the workplace. Although the cluster framework was originally developed for high schools and young people, it is now being adopted by workforce investment boards and other programmes serving adults.

The Flemish "Work Experience Programme for Young People" (WIJ) in Belgium. The programme aims to tackle youth unemployment and increase youth employability by supporting vulnerable young people into employment through real life work experience. It was introduced in 2013 by the Flemish PES and targets young people in large cities who have been unemployed for more than six months. The programme consists of an individualised approach with counselling and the provision of work experience. The number of participants has increased gradually but it is too early to assess the impact of the programme.

Sources:

Hamilton, V. (2012), "Career pathway and cluster skill development: Promising models from the United States", *OECD Local Economic and Employment Development (LEED) Working Papers*, No. 2012/14, OECD Publishing, Paris, *http://dx.doi.org/10.1787/5k94g1s6f7td-en*.

OECD (2013c), "Local strategies for youth employment", *www.oecd.org/employment/leed/Local%20Strategies%20for%20Youth%20Employment%20FINAL%20FINAL.pdf*.

SMOOTHING TRANSITIONS FROM SCHOOL TO WORK

Labour market conditions

As new entrants in the labour market and thus outsiders, youth are likely to be affected by institutional arrangements that aim to protect insiders, but structurally weaken labour demand. Conversely, employers are often more willing to hire youth when doing so implies fewer long-term obligations. But there are trade-offs, and policies to ease school-to-work transitions could put other groups at risk of losing their jobs, or increase inequalities. These trades-offs call for sound, but not excessively flexible, general framework conditions combined with well-designed, specific policies targeted at youth.

Employment protection legislation

Trial periods enable youth to demonstrate their skills with very few risks to employers since, during the trial period, severance pay generally does not apply. Some countries increased the trial period during the economic crisis: in 2013, the average trial period was five months compared to four before the crisis (Figure 5.2). However, since trial periods can be used in abusive ways by employers, there are limits to the extent to which the length of these periods can be increased.

As many youth enter the labour market on temporary contracts, an important issue is to ensure that these temporary jobs act as "stepping stones" into more stable employment and do not trap them in precarious situations with higher risks of becoming unemployed.

Exemptions from EPL for particular groups of workers, in order to encourage their employment, already exist in some countries (Venn, 2009). The most common type of exemption is for apprentices, workers undertaking training and participants in active labour market programmes (e.g. Australia, Canada, Italy, Norway, Poland and Spain). Countries with strict EPL on permanent contracts could consider relaxing it for youth facing labour market integration problems. Furthermore, last-in-first-out rules in case of collective dismissals and dismissal practices based on seniority rules are harmful to youth.

▪ Figure 5.2 ▪
Length of trial periods in OECD countries
Average of maximum trial periods for different workers or collective agreements, in months

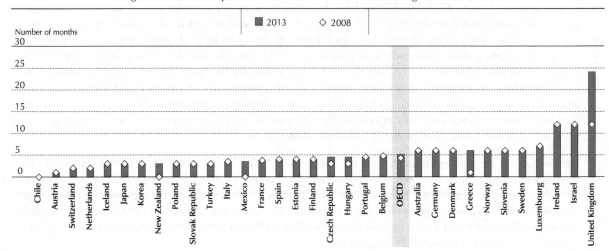

Source: OECD (2014b), "Employment Protection Legislation", *OECD Employment and Labour Market Statistics* (database), *http://dx.doi.org/10.1787/lfs-epl-data-en.*

StatLink ⬛ http://dx.doi.org/10.1787/888933214784

More generally, to address the risk of duality, the OECD recommends reducing the asymmetry between job protection provisions applying to permanent and temporary contracts that make it costly to firms to convert fixed-term contracts into permanent ones. Policy makers have become increasingly aware of the costs of this asymmetry (OECD, 2014a). Various policy options have been recently explored in OECD countries to reduce the asymmetry in EPL between temporary contracts and permanent ones. Several countries with a tradition of relatively high levels of protection have taken steps to make termination costs and obligations for different contracts, converging towards a uniform rate or procedure (Box 5.4). OECD countries are showing signs of a pause in these reforms but efforts are still needed in this area in several countries (OECD, 2015). As these reforms may also lead to greater dismissals of permanent workers, they should be coupled with the provision of adequate unemployment benefits made conditional on strictly enforced job-search requirements and integrated into well-designed activation packages.

Labour costs

High labour costs can also create barriers to hiring young people. Minimum wages have various effects on youth employment and education. They raise the minimum level of productivity required for employment and may thereby exclude those with the lowest skills, but provide incentives to inactive youth to supply their skills to the labour market. Minimum wages also provide incentives to low-educated youth to continue education to reach the skill threshold that is required for the labour market, but lead to narrow wage distribution, thereby lowering the return to higher education. Empirical evidence suggests that minimum wages that are set too high can have a negative impact on youth employment, especially if combined with high non-wage labour costs (Kramarz and Philippon, 2001; Neumark and Wascher, 2004; Neumark, Ian Salas and Wascher 2013) although some studies have failed to find employment effects. Around half of the OECD countries with statutory minimum wages have special provisions for youth. In countries where minimum wages are set by collective agreements (e.g. the Nordic countries), they are often differentiated by age.

Taxes and social contributions also add to labour costs. On average accross OECD countries, taxes and social contributions on labour accounted for more than 30% of the labour cost for low-paid jobs (67% of the average wage) in 2013. To limit the negative impact of high labour costs on low-skilled and youth employment, some countries have cut social contributions for low-paid jobs (e.g. Belgium, France and Sweden) or for youth (e.g. Belgium, Spain and Sweden). These cuts could also be made conditional to firms training their workers, or hiring apprentices or young long-term unemployed (OECD, 2014c). While empirical evidence suggests that these policies can boost employment of groups at the margin of the labour market, they are costly and countries with the highest youth unemployment rates are also those facing the largest constraints on their public finances. Overall, while there is room to make tax policies more skill-friendly, potential losses of tax revenues would have to be offset by increases in other taxes that are less detrimental to skills and growth.

> Box 5.4 **Moving towards sounder employment protection legislation: Country examples**
>
> One question is whether a reform, which makes temporary contracts more easily available, facilitates a quicker integration of workers into stable employment. One of the few studies investigating this question, based on the 1984 liberalisation of fixed-term contracts in Spain, suggests that facilitating labour market access through temporary contracts does not help youth's labour market prospects (Garcia-Perez, Marinescu and Vall-Castello, 2014; OECD, 2014d).
>
> In fact, the effect of regulations on fixed-term contracts on youth labour market outcomes cannot be seen in isolation, but it is conditional on the degree of stringency of employement protection legislation (EPL) for regular contracts (OECD, 2013d). Countries with highly protective regulations for permanent contracts could see the emergence of a "dual" labour market: in the presence of protected insiders, those under fixed-term contracts (often youth and other disadvantaged groups) will bear the main burden of employment adjustment (Saint-Paul, 1996).
>
> Several countries have taken actions recently to reduce the asymmetry in EPL between temporary and permanent contracts. The 2013 Slovenian reform has equalised the level of severance pay across contracts, while simultaneously significantly enlarging the definition of fair dismissal. In Greece, reforms in 2010 and 2012 significantly reduced notice periods and severance pay for permanent contracts (OECD, 2013a). In June 2012, Italy restricted the use of reinstatement clauses under permanent contracts and relaxed dismissal procedures. In France, the 2013 reform of the labour code relaxed the legislation for permanent contracts although the size of the effect is difficult to estimate at the moment. Portugal also introduced a set of reforms that have shortened notice periods while making them dependent on job tenure, reduced severance payments and eased the procedure for dismissals.
>
> Spain, a country in which labour market duality is prevalent has taken steps to reduce it. In 2011, a first reform increased severance pay for temporary contracts and extended the severance pay subsidy scheme to all employers and types of dismissal for permanent contracts signed after the date of approval of the reform. In 2012, a major reform gave priority to collective bargaining agreements at the firm level over those established at the sector or regional level for dismissals. The reform also reshaped the definition of fair economic dismissal, reduced monetary compensations for unfair dismissal, eliminated the requirement of administrative authorisation for collective redundancies, and a new permanent contract for full-time employees in small firms with an extended trial period of one year was introduced.
>
> **Sources:**
>
> Garcia-Perez, J.I., I. Marinescu and J. Vall-Castello (2014), "Can fixed-term contracts put low-skilled youth on a better career path?", paper presented at the Elsa Seminar Series, March 2014, OECD, Paris.
>
> OECD (2014d), *OECD Employment Outlook 2014*, OECD Publishing, Paris, *http://dx.doi.org/10.1787/empl_outlook-2014-en*.
>
> OECD (2013a), *OECD Employment Outlook 2013*, OECD Publishing, Paris, *http://dx.doi.org/10.1787/empl_outlook-2013-en*.
>
> Saint-Paul, G. (1996), *Dual Labor Markets*, MIT Press, Cambridge.
>
> OECD (2013d), *The 2012 Labour Market Reform in Spain: A Preliminary Assessment*, OECD Publishing, Paris, *http://dx.doi.org/10.1787/9789264213586-en*.

Work experience outside formal education

While there is growing consensus and evidence that exposure to the world of work, within an education programme, can ease transition from school to work, much less is known about the impact of internships undertaken after graduation. Internships are short work periods that can be undertaken as part of, and during the school year, or at the end of study, generally with learning content. These internships have become very common. According to a 2013 Eurobarometer survey (European Commission, 2013b), on average accross European countries, 33% of young people reported having completed one or several internships after graduation. The Survey of Adult Skills also shows that a significant share of students engage in work outside structured VET and apprenticeships in areas linked to their fields of study (Chapter 2).

Internships following education bring advantages to both employers and youth (Neumark, 2009), but there are risks of abuse in this model. On the side of employers, internships are typically weakly regulated, especially those not linked to education programmes, and thus give them an opportunity to assess the skills of workers with little labour market experience at a relatively low cost. Young people, for their part, are willing to undertake internships to gain experience and raise their employability, as employers increasingly put a premium on work experience. According to the Eurobarometer survey mentioned above, there is not always an internship agreement regulating the placement in terms of objectives, learning content terms and conditions, and when there is one, it is explicitly not an employment contract (European Commission, 2013b). In contrast to apprenticeships, internships are not always remunerated, or if they are, the remuneration can be much lower than the standard minimum wage (Table 5.1). This can exacerbate inequalities between youth as some may be unable to bear the cost, particularly if the internship requires relocation. Furthermore, social partner involvement is not as extensive as in other forms of work-based learning, and in some cases is non-existent.

■ Table 5.1 ■

The role of internships after education

Percentage, 2013

	Share of respondents who had internships after education:		Share of respondents who:		Share of respondents who:	
	one internship	more than one intership	received financial compensation for internship	could turn to a mentor who explained how to do the work	consider the training was or will be helpful for finding a regular job	were offered an employment contract at the end of the internship
Austria	18	21	64	93	66	22
Belgium	15	8	38	94	83	28
Czech Republic	21	4	70	86	71	18
Denmark	10	5	69	93	81	22
Estonia	7	4	62	95	75	40
Finland	10	7	70	90	80	33
France	9	10	42	89	66	27
Germany	18	20	39	95	65	25
Greece	34	8	38	80	78	25
Hungary	14	8	45	90	80	36
Ireland	44	9	75	93	85	33
Italy	35	7	53	89	70	25
Latvia	11	10	67	90	78	56
Luxembourg	14	7	44	92	80	28
Netherlands	5	7	32	91	77	32
Poland	31	5	30	88	55	25
Portugal	43	13	58	96	83	25
Slovak Republic	23	15	64	88	80	34
Slovenia	64	4	69	95	79	56
Spain	56	11	29	79	83	33
Sweden	17	10	61	94	73	33
United Kingdom	19	9	68	94	78	28
EU28	22	11	46	91	71	27

Source: European Commission (2013b), "The Experience of Traineeships in the EU", *Flash Eurobarometer*, No. 378.

StatLink ᴀᴍ͟sᴩ http://dx.doi.org/10.1787/888933214765

Nonetheless, the Eurobarometer survey shows that at least in European countries, most interns found this kind of work experience useful for finding jobs; they benefited from some form of mentoring during the internship and almost 30% of them were offered an employment contract at the end of the traineeship (Table 5.1). These results suggest that internships after graduation can ease school-to-job transitions, but they do need to be regulated to prevent them from becoming a low-cost way for replacing regular staff. France, for instance, has taken action to regulate the minimum pay, maximum length, and social security coverage of internships. However, some of these regulations, such as the maximum length, might prove difficult to enforce. Limiting the gaps in labour costs and employment protection legislation between internships and other types of work would lower the incentives for employers to exploit internships. In theory, these gaps should be justified by the cost for firms to develop and adapt youth skills to labour market needs.

Some students also work during their studies in jobs unrelated to their fields of study, generally because of financial constraints. These jobs can be an opportunity to develop certain skills, and to make contacts in firms. However, they can also have detrimental effects on education outcomes. Results in terms of education outcomes are not clear-cut, but some studies have found a negative impact of part-time work, at least for a certain number of hours worked (Montmarquette, Viennot-Briot and Dagenais, 2007; Beffy, Fougère and Maurel, 2009; Tyler, 2003). Another study found no significant impact (Buscha et al., 2008). Having contact with employers through summer jobs and internships in the final year of high school can ease labour market entry (Hensvik and Nordström Skans, 2013). However, when EPL or taxation encourages firms to hire students instead of other types of young workers, there can be some displacement effects, as has long been the case in Slovenia, for instance (OECD, 2011). Overall, these findings suggest that the combination of work and study should be encouraged when work experience is integrated into the education programme or involves a learning content.

HELPING NEETS TO (RE-)ENGAGE WITH EDUCATION OR THE LABOUR MARKET

The need for further education

Some youth leave education without the skills needed for the labour market or to continue further in education. Some of these youth could enter VET programmes and some countries, such as Sweden for instance, increased the number of places in VET programmes during the crisis. However, there are limits to this strategy. First, youth who have not been successful in the education system may fail again unless different approaches are taken. Second, lowering the requirements to enter VET or placing youth with low skills in these programmes tend to lower the attractiveness of VET to other students. Some countries, like Germany and recently Denmark, have introduced transition systems to help youth develop their skills to enter VET.

Another option is to develop specific schools or programmes for youth who need to strengthen their skills, but would better achieve this outside the formal education system. These programmes typically try to fill gaps in skills acquisition, especially for social and emotional skills, while providing work-based learning and job-search support. There are various examples of such programmes in countries and regions, with some of them appearing to work (Box 5.5). The main challenge is to assess the benefits and costs of these programmes, and to decide whether the benefit-to-cost ratio justifies continuing and extending them.

Adult learning programmes (not specifically targeted to youth) can also help youth upgrade their skills. There are two main issues concerning these programmes. First, adults with already high levels of cognitive skills participate the most, while those with lower levels of skills participate the least (OECD, 2013e). Second, the quality and efficiency of adult learning programmes has been mixed (OECD, 2005). Hence efforts should concentrate on ensuring that low-skilled adults participate in adult learning. The quality and efficiency of adult learning programmes can be improved through better monitoring and assessment of outcomes as well as streamlining of existing programmes.

Box 5.5. **Second-chance programmes: Country examples**

Second chance schools in the European Union

"Second chance" schools aim to provide labour market integration for young people aged 18-25 who lack the skills necessary to enter the job market or to re-engage in education (European Commission, 2001). The characteristics of these schools depend on local and national circumstances, but they share a number of features (Second Chance, 2012):

- strong co-operation between local authorities, social services, other institutions and the private sector;
- a teaching and counselling approach focused on the needs, wishes and abilities of individual pupils in order to stimulate their active learning;
- flexible teaching modules allowing combinations of basic skills development (numeracy, literacy, social skills, etc.) with practical training in and by enterprises;
- a central role for the acquisition of skills in and through ICT and new technologies.

Second Chance Schools in France

Second chance schools have developed in many EU countries, but particularly in France, where the number of students has been multiplied by ten since their introduction. French second chance schools have spread to 105 local areas. Although there are only few evaluations of French second chance schools and the long-term effect of these schools on youth employability is unknown, they are generally considered as promising. Over the last three years, 58% of youth left these schools with an educational or labour market option: 20% in training, 17% in regular jobs, 12% in apprenticeships and 9% in subsidised employment (Réseau E2C France, 2014). Some 22% dropped out before signing their individualised plans.

This relative success is attributed to the quality of education, with a highly individualised approach, combining the acquisition of literacy, numeracy and ICT skills, labour-market-specific skills and strong links with employers. Work experience takes place gradually with the skills needed for the job being taught in parallel. These schools have managed to build a good reputation, which attracts both students and employers. Furthermore, employers and schools benefit from French state funding of the apprenticeship system. First, firms that hire apprentices benefit from tax relief. Second, the schools can benefit from revenues from the apprenticeship tax if firms identify them as beneficiaries.

Youthreach programme in Ireland

In Ireland, one of the most prominent initiatives to provide education and training opportunities outside mainstream education settings for early school leavers is "Youthreach", a joint programme funded by the Department of Education and Skills and the Department of Jobs, Enterprise and Innovation. Youthreach seeks to provide early school leavers (aged 16-20) with the knowledge, skills and confidence required to participate fully in society and

...

progress to further education, training and employment (Irish Department of Education and Science, 2008). The programme is delivered through Youthreach centres and community training centres.

An internal evaluation study by the Irish Department of Education and Science found the programme to be relatively efficient and for the most part maximising output from the input available. This is particularly true in relation to the following input areas – learner supports, accommodation, national co-ordination and support, and programme support and development. The time and effort devoted by staff members in practically all of the centres evaluated to get to know the individual learners, their background, their parents and families, play a key role in the support offered to learners. The programme appears effective in addressing learners' needs for personal and social development and in recruiting its target group. Those learners who engaged fully with the programme that was on offer to them in their centres indicated positive learning experiences, improved self-esteem and self-worth and enhanced personal and social development. Some centres also successfully implemented targeted strategies to promote learners' attendance and punctuality.

However, efforts appear to be necessary to retain more of the learners to the end of the progression phase. There is also room for improvement in terms of the number of learners who obtain certification, as well as the levels at which they obtain certification, so that they can successfully progress from the centres to appropriate further education, training or employment. The centres also seem to have very limited links or communications with national agencies and relevant post-primary curricular support services. Communication is also lacking between some of the centres evaluated and their local post-primary schools and businesses. Last but not least, tracking systems to monitor the progression of learners after they leave the centres still need to be developed.

US Job Corps

Job Corps is a free education and training programme introduced in 1964 in the United States that helps disadvantaged youth learn about careers, earn high school diplomas, and find and keep jobs. The programme includes vocational education and training, academic education and a wide range of other services, including counselling, social skills training, and health education. Most participants reside at a centre while training.

The performance of the Job Corps programme has been evaluated regularly, including by using random assignment methods (Schochet, Burghardt and McConnell, 2008). The programme has positive effects on educational attainment and skills, and it reduces criminal activity. The impact on wages appears to be higher for the younger age groups than for the older ones.

BladeRunners Programme in Canada

"BladeRunners" is an example of a regional employment programme that helps youth (ages 15-30) with multiple barriers to employment build careers in construction and other industries throughout the province of British Columbia (Canada), (OECD, 2013c). The Ministry of Jobs, Tourism and Innovation is the lead sponsor of the programme, which is now run in 32 locations across the province by 19 different local service delivery organisations. The BladeRunners programme provides participating youth a three-week training course, including instruction in both cognitive and social and emotional skills, and then facilitates direct job placement for programme graduates. The programme also provides extensive support services for participants and graduates 24 hours a day, seven days a week for an undetermined period of time after placement. The ultimate goal of the programme is to develop skills and work experience that foster long-term attachment to the labour force and to support the social and community integration of young people. BladeRunners is regarded as an effective employment training model for young people with multiple barriers to employment. It advertises an overall 77% post-training job placement rate, has won several awards and recognitions for its achievements, and is funded by a diverse group of public and private supporters.

Sources:

European Commission (2001), "Second chance schools: Results of a European pilot project", Brussels.

Irish Department of Education and Science (2008), "Youthreach and Senior Traveller Training Centre Programmes funded by the Department for Education and Science: A Value for Money Review".

OECD (2013c), "Local strategies for youth employment", www.oecd.org/employment/leed/Local%20Strategies%20for%20Youth%20Employment%20FINAL%20FINAL.pdf.

Réseau E2C France (2014), "L'Activité en 2013", Châlons-en-Champagne.

Schochet, P.Z., J. Burghardt and S. McConnell (2008), "Does Job Corps work? Impact findings from the National Job Corps Study", *American Economic Review*, Vol. 98, No. 5.

Second Chance (2012), "Second chance schooling in Europe", 2nd Chance, London, www.2ndchancelondon.org.uk.

Active labour market policies

"Work-first" strategies in which the goal is to place participants in jobs as quickly as possible appear to have positive effects on employment (OECD, 2013a). These strategies typically include the agreement of an individualised "back to work" plan, job-search assistance and regular monitoring of job-search activities. For instance, countries like Norway and Switzerland, which have consistently enjoyed low unemployment rates, have a strong focus on job searching and the placement of jobseekers into unsubsidised jobs (OECD, 2013c). These countries spend relatively more on PES and administration and relatively less on other types of active labour market policies (ALMPs). The empirical literature shows similar results. Intensified job-search assistance and frequent meetings with caseworkers lower unemployment spells, and this positive effect is particularly marked for youth (Forslund and Nordström Skans, 2006; Behaghel, Crépon and Gurgand, 2012; Rosholm, Svarer and Vikström, 2013). In countries like Denmark and Sweden, where there are relatively strong obligations associated with participation in ALMPs, it has even been shown that, on average, the positive effect of ALMPs on labour market outcomes comes from the threat of entering the programme rather than from the programme itself (Forslund and Nordström Skans, 2006; Rosholm and Svarer, 2008).

Despite the advantages of a "work-first" strategy, many of the youth who are NEET are not looking for jobs (Figure 5.3). Furthermore, the Survey of Adult Skills shows that the share of the NEET group not looking for jobs is higher for youth with low literacy skills. This may be because they are trying instead to re-enter the education system. But this also suggests that countries have room to strengthen efforts by PES to both reach youth with the lowest skills and increase the incentives for youth to look for jobs. The Survey of Adult Skills also shows that unemployed youth are less likely to have had contact with PES in the month prior to the interview than older job seekers (Figure 5.4).

▪ Figure 5.3 ▪

Share of youth neither in employment nor in education or training looking for jobs, by level of proficiency in literacy

16-29 year-olds, 2012

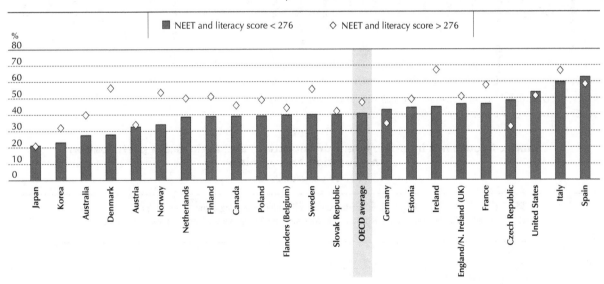

Notes: The figure shows the share of the NEETs who were looking for jobs in the four weeks prior to the interview.
Source: OECD calculations based the *Survey of Adult Skills (PIAAC) (2012)* (database).
StatLink ⬛▒🔗 http://dx.doi.org/10.1787/888933214790

Although a strong focus on activating youth skills can achieve good labour market outcomes, some youth need training and/or subsidised work experience to raise their employability. Many countries have been successful with programmes that target a specific group of unemployed. However, it has proved difficult to develop large-scale, cost-effective programmes, partly because of displacement effects. Furthermore, when participating in a programme, the unemployed generally do not look for jobs – the so-called "lock-in effects" – which can be particularly detrimental to youth who need to get jobs relatively quickly to prove their employability. For these reasons, some countries have moved to shorter programmes, such as short trainings or internships, which can limit "lock-in effects" but may not be enough to upgrade skills.

In times of high unemployment and low demand, unemployed youth face higher risks of remaining unemployed long term and seeing their skills erode. The market value for some skills can also depreciate substantially when severe business cycle downturns are associated with structural shifts (Forslund, Fredriksson and Vikström, 2011). Hence, well-targeted, short, vocational training, work trials and internships, combined with job-search requirements, can be developed during crises to help youth activate and link their skills better to the labour market. The Survey of Adult Skills shows that in some countries, a large share of youth were not in employment or education at the time of the survey and had not participated in education or training in the 12 months prior to the survey (Figure 5.5). This raises the issue of whether there was enough training for youth during the crisis, despite an increase in training places in several countries. Evidence from the Survey of Adult Skills on youth problem-solving skills in technology-rich environments also suggests that encouraging unemployed youth to develop these skills could increase their employability.

■ Figure 5.4 ■

Share of the unemployed who contacted public employment services in the four weeks prior to the survey, by age group

2012

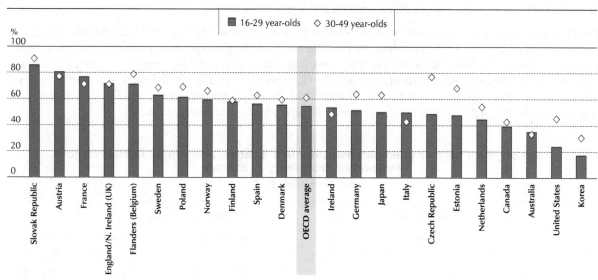

Source: OECD calculations based on the *Survey of Adult Skills (PIAAC) (2012)* (database).
StatLink http://dx.doi.org/10.1787/888933214806

■ Figure 5.5 ■

Share of youth not in employment or education, and their recent participation in education and training

16-29 year-olds, 2012

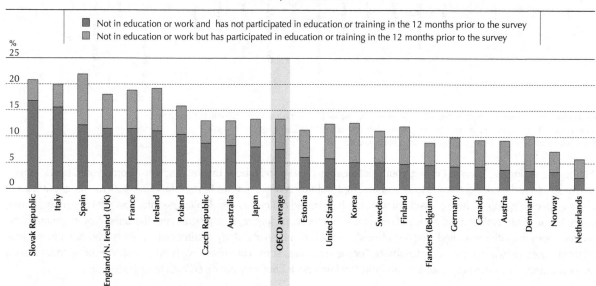

Source: OECD calculations based on the *Survey of Adult Skills (PIAAC) (2012)* (database).
StatLink http://dx.doi.org/10.1787/888933214816

Youth with immigrant backgrounds face specific challenges with regard to activating their skills. Whether they should benefit from specific activation policies depends on the factors driving these difficulties:

- Youth from disadvantaged backgrounds, such as native-born offspring of immigrants with low levels of education, face difficulties that stem from their low education levels. Policies to make the education system more inclusive, as discussed in Chapter 3, would help them increase their employability. Sound labour market framework conditions as well as efficient ALMPs would also contribute. Internships and other types of work experience can also help this group build contacts in the world of work.

- For foreign-born youth, particularly those who are highly educated, policies to formally recognise or raise awareness of their qualifications would help them find jobs and use their skills (see Chapter 7).

- To combat discrimination, many countries have introduced anti-discrimination laws. While these laws are crucial, at least to formally recognise discrimination as an issue, their effects have been limited so far as the number of cases brought to court has been relatively low. Policies to render hiring youth with immigrant backgrounds attractive to firms, e.g. through job subsidies, can help employer to overcome initial barriers.

- Finally, several countries have designed specific programmes to target youth with immigrant backgrounds who cumulate several challenges, such as low cognitive skills and low levels of education, language barriers and lack of confidence. One example of such a programme is The King Movement Foundation/Hi5 in the Netherlands. This programme seeks to transform inactivity and passivity of young migrants into positive aspirations and careers. It puts individual job seekers and organisations in contact with role models from their social environments and representatives from Dutch companies (Froy and Pyne, 2011).

Although improving the quality of education systems and combatting dropout rates are priorities in emerging economies, labour market policies can also support youth in their job searches. In several countries, these policies are under-developed (Quintini and Martin, 2014). This is the case of Brazil, for instance (OECD, 2014e). The PES lacks appeal and is only marginally used by youth to look for jobs. As a consequence, many job seekers find work through social networks and personal contacts, exacerbating inequalities of opportunities.

Social protection systems

Social protection systems can serve as springboards for youth, propelling them out of the poverty that can undermine their ability to activate their skills potential in the long term. NEETs are at greater risk of poverty than other youth (Carcillo et al., 2015). In OECD countries, about 50% of NEETs living without family or outside the family home do not receive any social benefits. Youth are less likely to be eligible for unemployment benefits given that in many countries, workers need to have contributed to unemployment insurance to benefit from it. If they do not have labour market experience, they would need to depend on social assistance, in countries where youth have access to it. Social assistance benefits tend to be low relative to the net earnings of an average worker, but since they are generally strongly mean-tested, the average effective tax rate associated with moving to low-paid jobs can be quite high (though there are large variations between countries), which may decrease incentives to work. In addition, these benefits often do not include education or labour market requirements. Finally, some social benefits, like social assistance, can have stigmatisation effects and weaken youth opportunities to find jobs.

A system of mutual obligations can help reconcile the objectives of limiting poverty risks among youth and ensuring that youth take up incentives to find work or take action to prepare for the labour market. To limit the risk of poverty, young NEETs with low income should be entitled to social benefits, but with some obligations attached to these benefits. Ideally, the obligations should depend on the distance of youth to the labour market. They can include looking for jobs, or renewing their skills with education, or undertaking actions to prepare for the labour market or education. On the side of institutions, there should be strong commitment and high-quality services to help youth renew their skills with education or to find jobs. There should also be strong co-operation between institutions to ensure that they all consistently enforce the system of mutual obligation, at both national and local levels. Overall, this mutual obligation system with strong co-operation between institutions would allow countries to reach and help a larger share of their inactive NEETs.

Moving to a system with a single social transfer for youth that would depend on their family situations, and on other factors with an obligation to register with PESs, would make incentives to take jobs clearer. However, in a system with several benefits, efforts can also be made to raise incentives for youth to integrate into the labour market, while providing financial support. Housing benefits, if associated with obligations to look for jobs in a larger area, can help youth activate their skills. Some countries have specific, often temporary, programmes delivered outside social assistance to the unemployed who are not eligible for unemployment benefits, possibly in combination with education or training. These programmes can be less mean-tested than social assistance and have lower stigmatisation effects, but they should include job-searching, education, or other types of obligations, depending on the distance of individuals to the labour market and the types of problems they face. Various countries have introduced in-work benefits with a view to encourage the transition from welfare to work. Regular monitoring and benefit sanctions can help offset the financial disincentives that otherwise result from the receipt of income support benefits.

KEY POINTS FOR POLICIES

Education and skills facilitate school-to-work transition but do not guarantee successful work trajectories. Ensuring successful transition and helping NEETs to integrate into the labour market require a consistent approach with strong co-operation between labour market, education and social institutions at national and local levels of government, as well as the participation of social partners.

Smoothing the transition from school to work

- Develop sound labour market institutions and skills-friendly tax policies to foster employment of low-skilled youth.

- Continue to lower the gap in employment protection legislation between temporary and permanent contracts.

- Encourage end-of-studies internships within a framework that combines flexibility and obligations to firms. Internships should include learning content and length, remuneration and other conditions should be regulated.

- Develop programmes targeting students at risk of facing difficulties in their school to work transitions, possibly at the local level, but carefully assess their effect.

Helping NEETs to (re-)engage with education or enter the labour market

- Introduce a system of mutual obligations between youth and institutions. Receiving social benefits should be backed with requirements to register with the public employment services, take actions and receive help in order to prepare for the labour market, including through further education.

- Adopt a work-first strategy that encourages employment through efficient job-search assistance and training, monitoring and financial incentives. Places in training programmes and job subsidies should be targeted to youth with low skills and those who face specific barriers in the labour market.

- Build comprehensive, high-quality guidance and counselling systems to help young people in their transitions to the labour market. Base these systems on an assessment of individuals' skills and skills in demand in the labour market.

References

Beffy, M., D. Fougère and A. Maurel (2009), "L'impact du travail salarié des étudiants sur la réussite et la poursuite des études universitaires", *Économie et Statistique*, No. 422, Paris.

Behaghel L., B. Crépon and M. Gurgand (2012), "Private and public provision of counselling to job-seekers: Evidence from a large controlled experiment", *IZA Discussion Papers*, No. 6518.

Borbély-Pecze, T.B. and J. Hutchinson (2013), "The youth guarantee and lifelong guidance", *European Lifelong Guidance Policy Network Concept Note*, No. 4.

Buscha F., A. Maurel, L. Page and S. Speckesser (2008), "The effect of high school employment on educational attainment: A conditional difference-in-differences approach", *IZA Discussion Papers*, N° 3696.

Carcillo, S., R. Fernandez, S. Königs and A. Minea (2015), "NEET Youth in the Aftermath of the Crisis: Challenges and Policies", *OECD Social, Employment and Migration Working Papers*, OECD Publishing, Paris, No. 164, http://dx.doi.org/10.1787/5js6363503f6-en.

Carling, K. and L. Larsson (2002), "Does early intervention help the unemployed youth?", *IFAU Working Paper*, No. 2002:10.

Employment Committee (2014), "Indicator Framework for Monitoring the Youth Guarantee", INDIC/10/16092014/EN-rev, Employment Committee (EMCO), European Commission

European Commission (2014a), "Assessment of the 2014 National Reform Programme and Stability Programme for Italy", *Commission Staff Working Document*, No. 416, Brussels.

European Commission (2014b), "Assessment of the 2014 National Reform Programme and Stability Programme for Spain", *Commission Staff Working Document*, SWD (2014) 410 final, Brussels.

European Commission (2014c), "Assessment of the 2014 National Reform Programme and Stability Programme for Ireland", *Commission Staff Working Document*, No. 408, Brussels.

European Commission (2013a), "Practical Support for the Design and Implementation of Youth Guarantee Schemes: Synthesis of Key Messages", Brussels.

European Commission (2013b), "The experience of traineeships in the EU", *Flash Eurobarometer*, No. 378, Brussels.

European Commission (2001), "Second chance schools: Results of a European pilot project", Brussels.

Forslund, A., P. Fredriksson and **J. Vikström** (2011), "What active labor market policy works in a recession?", *Nordic Economic Policy Review*, No. 1.

Forslund, A. and **O. Nordström Skans** (2006), "Swedish youth labour market policies revisited", *IFAU Working Paper*, No.6.

Froy, F. and **L. Pyne** (2011), "Ensuring labour market success for ethnic minority and immigrant youth", *OECD Local Economic and Employment Development (LEED) Working Papers*, No. 2011/09, OECD Publishing, Paris, *http://dx.doi.org/10.1787/5kg8g2l0547b-en*.

Froy, F., S. Giguère and **A. Hofer** (eds.) (2009), *Designing Local Skills Strategies*, Local Economic and Employment Development (LEED), OECD Publishing, Paris, *http://dx.doi.org/10.1787/9789264066649-en*.

Garcia-Perez, J.I., I. Marinescu and **J. Vall-Castello** (2014), "Can fixed-term contracts put low-skilled youth on a better career path?", paper presented at the Elsa Seminar Series, March 2014, OECD, Paris.

Hamilton, V. (2012), "Career pathway and cluster skill development: Promising models from the United States", *OECD Local Economic and Employment Development (LEED) Working Papers*, No. 2012/14, OECD Publishing, Paris, *http://dx.doi.org/10.1787/5k94g1s6f7td-en*.

Hensvik, L. and **O. Nordström Skans** (2013), "Networks and youth labor market entry", *IFAU Working Paper*, No. 23.

Irish Department of Education and Science (2008), "Youthreach and Senior Traveller Training Centre Programmes funded by the Department for Education and Science: Value for Money Review".

Italian Ministry of Employment and Social Affairs (2013), "Italy Youth Guarantee Implementation Plan", *www.garanziagiovani.gov.it/Documentazione/Documents/Italian-Youth-Guarantee-Implementation-Plan.pdf*.

Kramarz, F. and **T. Philippon** (2001), "The impact of differential payroll tax subsidies on minimum wage employment", *Journal of Public Economics*, Vol. 82.

Montmarquette, C., N. Viennot-Briot and **M. Dagenais** (2007), "Dropout, school performance, and working while in school", *The Review of Economics and Statistics*, Vol. 89, No. 4.

Neumark, D. (2009), "Alternative labor market policies to increase economic self-sufficiency: Mandating higher wages, subsidizing employment, and increasing productivity", *National Bureau of Economic Research Working Paper Series*, No. 14807, Cambridge.

Neumark, D. and **W. Wascher** (2004), "Minimum wages, labour market institutions, and youth employment: A cross-national analysis", *Industrial and Labour Relations Review*, Vol. 57, No. 2.

Neumark, D., J.M. Ian Salas and **W. Wascher** (2013), "Revisiting the minimum wage-employment debate: Throwing out the baby with the bathwater?", *National Bureau of Economic Research Working Paper Series*, No. 18681, Cambridge.

OECD (2015), *Economic Policy Reforms 2015: Going for Growth*, OECD Publishing, Paris, *http://dx.doi.org/10.1787/growth-2015-en*.

OECD (2014a), "OECD Youth Action Plan: Options for an Irish Youth Guarantee", *www.oecd.org/ireland/YouthActionPlan-IrishYouthGuarantee.pdf*.

OECD (2014b), "Employment Protection Legislation", *OECD Employment and Labour Market Statistics* (database), *http://dx.doi.org/10.1787/lfs-epl-data-en*.

OECD (2014c), "Designing skill-friendly tax policies", *OECD Skills Strategy Spotlight*, No. 6, *http://skills.oecd.org/developskills/documents/designing-skill-friendly-tax-policies.html*.

OECD (2014d), *OECD Employment Outlook 2014*, OECD Publishing, Paris, *http://dx.doi.org/10.1787/empl_outlook-2014-en*.

OECD (2014e), *Investing in Youth: Brazil*, OECD Publishing, Paris, *http://dx.doi.org/10.1787/9789264208988-en*.

OECD (2013a), *OECD Employment Outlook 2013*, OECD Publishing, Paris, *http://dx.doi.org/10.1787/empl_outlook-2013-en*.

OECD (2013b), "The OECD Action Plan for Youth: Giving Youth a Better Start in the Labour Market", *www.oecd.org/employment/Action-plan-youth.pdf* and *www.oecd.org/employment/action-plan-youth.htm*.

OECD (2013c), "Local strategies for youth employment", *www.oecd.org/employment/leed/Local%20Strategies%20for%20Youth%20Employment%20FINAL%20FINAL.pdf*.

OECD (2013d), *The 2012 Labour Market Reform in Spain: A Preliminary Assessment*, OECD Publishing, Paris, *http://dx.doi.org/10.1787/9789264213586-en*.

OECD (2013e), *OECD Skills Outlook 2013: First Results from the Survey of Adult Skills*, OECD Publishing, Paris, *http://dx.doi.org/10.1787/9789264204256-en*.

OECD (2012), *Closing the Gender Gap: Act Now*, OECD Publishing, Paris, *http://dx.doi.org/10.1787/9789264179370-en*.

OECD (2011), *OECD Economic Surveys: Slovenia 2011*, OECD Publishing, Paris, *http://dx.doi.org/10.1787/eco_surveys-svn-2011-en*.

OECD (2010), *Off to a Good Start? Jobs for Youth*, OECD Publishing, Paris, *http://dx.doi.org/10.1787/9789264096127-en*.

OECD (2005), *Promoting Adult Learning*, OECD Publishing, Paris, *http://dx.doi.org/10.1787/9789264010932-en*.

Quintini, G. and **S. Martin** (2014), "Same but different: School-to-work transitions in emerging and advanced economies", *OECD Social, Employment and Migration Working Papers*, No. 154, OECD Publishing, Paris, *http://dx.doi.org/ 10.1787/5jzbb2t1rcwc-en*.

Réseau E2C France (2014), « L'Activité en 2013 », Châlons-en-Champagne.

Rosholm, M. and **M. Svarer** (2008), "Estimating the threat effect of active labour market programmes", *Scandinavian Journal of Economics*, Vol. 110.

Rosholm, M, M. Svarer and **J. Vikström** (2013), "The effectiveness of active labor market policies: Evidence from a social experiment using non-parametric bounds", *Labour Economics*, Vol. 24.

Saint-Paul, G. (1996), *Dual Labor Markets*, MIT Press, Cambridge.

Schochet, P.Z., J. Burghardt and **S. McConnell** (2008), "Does Job Corps work? Impact findings from the National Job Corps Study", *American Economic Review*, Vol. 98, No. 5.

Second Chance (2012), "Second chance schooling in Europe", 2nd Chance, London, *www.2ndchancelondon.org.uk*.

Spain Ministry of Employment and Social Security (2013), "Spanish Youth Guarantee Implementation Plan", *www.empleo.gob.es/ficheros/garantiajuvenil/documentos/plannacionalgarantiajuvenil_en.pdf*.

Tyler, J.H. (2003), "Using state child labor laws to identify the effect of school-year work on high school achievement", *Journal of Labor Economics*, Vol. 21, No. 2.

Venn, D. (2009), "Legislation, collective bargaining and enforcement: Updating the OECD employment protection indicators", *OECD Social, Employment and Migration Working Papers*, No. 89, OECD Publishing, Paris, *http://dx.doi.org/10.1787/223334316804*.

6

Trends in using young people's skills at work

When they enter the world of work, young people need to use and enhance their skills to strengthen their employability. Many young people who have just left the education system are likely to have the most up-to-date skills in certain areas. At the same time, these skills may not be fully in line with employers' needs and making full use of them will take time. Some youth find that the skills they have acquired at school are simply not needed on the labour market. This chapter discusses how young people's skills are used at work.

HIGHLIGHTS

- According to the 2012 Survey of Adult Skills, young people use their skills less than prime-age workers, even in similar occupations. This concerns all types of skills including information and communication technology (ICT) skills. A substantial share of youth, ranging from 54% in Italy to 25% in Korea, has no computer experience at work.

- Low-skilled young workers use less frequently than their high-skilled peers a number of skills that can generally be developed on the job, such as problem solving and self-organising skills.

- While young workers tend to be more skilled than prime-age workers, the share of those who are in jobs involving routine tasks is similar to that of prime-age workers, ranging from nearly 35% for youth with low numeracy skills to less than 5% for those with high numeracy skills. Youth in jobs with routine tasks are twice less likely than other young workers to benefit from adult education and training.

- Compared with prime-age workers, youth are more likely to be over-qualified and over-skilled in literacy but the incidence of skills mismatch decreases with experience. There is evidence that mismatch has increased in some countries as a consequence of the crisis but limited evidence that the increase is structural.

- For some young people, entrepreneurship can offer opportunities to use their skills effectively. While many young people are interested in entrepreneurship and self-employment, self-employment rates for youth are low.

Youth have to use their skills to maintain and develop their employability. Young people who do not use their skills fully are likely to lose them over time, which can result in negative consequences for future employment and well-being. Furthermore, making good use of youth skills can foster productivity, innovation and economic growth.

There are various reasons why young people's skills may not be used efficiently. It can take time for employers to ascertain the types and levels of skills their employees have. It may also take time for young people to discover which jobs best match their skills. The lack of efficient use of skills will diminish with time as workers and employers learn about themselves. However, should it persist over time, it will lead to negative consequences for youth employability and the economy.

THE USE OF YOUNG PEOPLE'S SKILLS AT WORK

General trends

By using their skills, youth adapt them to concrete situations, develop them further and are more likely to have successful careers. At the same time, young people lacking work experience have greater difficulties finding jobs that perfectly match their skills and tend to be in jobs in which they under-use their skills. In addition, not fully using all skills at some point in time also means that youth will be able to add more value to their job in the future and to evolve in their careers. Having a reservoir of untapped skills can help an economy to innovate in the future. Overall, while it is important to make effective use of youth skills, making full use of all skills at any point in time may not be efficient.

The importance of using skills effectively and achieving a good match between workers' skills and jobs has gained prominence in the debate but measures available to apprehend these two features are still limited. The Survey of Adult Skills sheds some light on these issues. It measures on-the-job use of cognitive skills (reading, writing, numeracy, ICT and problem solving), some social and emotional skills (task discretion, influencing skills, co-operative and self-organisation skills) and some occupation-specific skills (learning at work, dexterity and gross physical skills) on the basis of self-reported assessments (OECD, 2013). It also provides an assessment of whether workers are well matched with jobs along a number of dimensions.

The Survey of Adult Skills shows that the intensity of skills use varies across skills domains and countries, but young workers use cognitive skills, on average, less at work than their prime-age peers (Figure 6.1). The result holds even when comparing young and prime-age workers with the same level of cognitive skills. The use of ICT at work is also lower among youth than among prime-age workers in participating countries. With respect to social and emotional and occupation-specific skills, the picture is more mixed: while young people use their task discretion, influencing and self-organisation skills less frequently than prime-age workers, they use their co-operative skills and learn new things from supervisors or co-workers, learn by doing, and keep up-to-date with new products and services more frequently (OECD, 2013).

■ Figure 6.1 ■

Use of cognitive skills at work, by age

Adjusted and unadjusted age difference in the mean use of skills,
in percentage of the average use of skills by prime-age workers, 2012

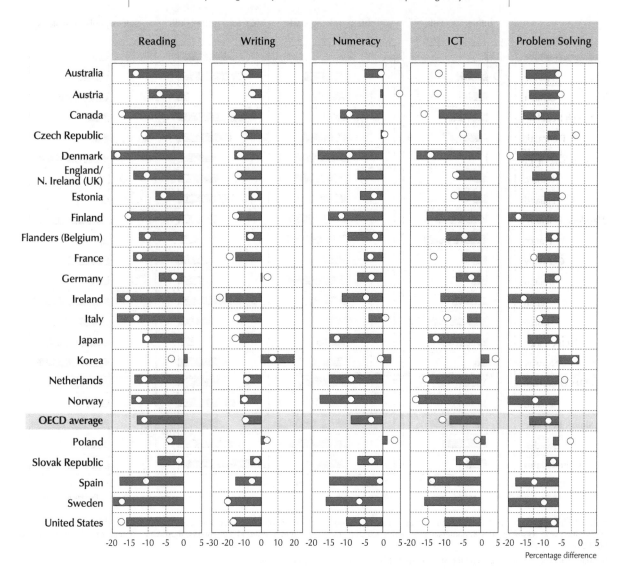

Notes: Results are adjusted for literacy and numeracy proficiency scores and contract type. Youth are 16-29 years old and prime-age workers are 30-54 years old.

Source: OECD calculations based on the *Survey of Adult Skills (PIAAC) (2012)* (database).

StatLink ᡂᡏᡅ http://dx.doi.org/10.1787/888933214829

When comparing among the youth group, it appears that youth with lower cognitive skills use less their skills than the high-skilled. High-skilled young workers are also more likely to use their problem-solving and self-organising skills as well as to influence decisions at work than middle-skilled youth (Figure 6.2). However, they are less likely to co-operate with other workers. These results suggest that even in their early careers, high-skilled youth have responsibilities and room of manoeuvre to use their skills while it is less the case for middle-skilled youth, which can undermine lower-skilled young workers' employability. There are however differences between countries that could partly be explained by differences in work organisation cultures and labour market institutions.

▪ Figure 6.2 ▪

Use of skills at work, by level of skills

16-29 year-olds, 2012

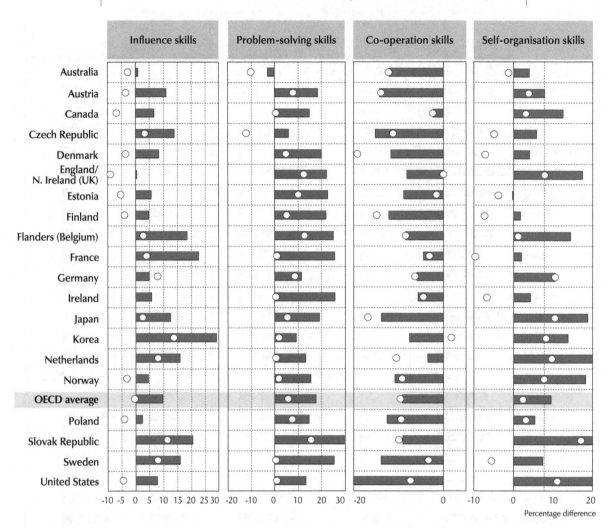

Notes: Adjusted estimates are based on ordinary least squares regressions including controls for education level, contract type and occupation dummies. High-skilled workers are those with numeracy proficiency scores at level 4 or 5 and middle-skilled workers, those with numeracy proficiency scores at level 2 or 3.

Source: OECD calculations based on the *Survey of Adult Skills (PIAAC) (2012)* (database).

StatLink ⧉ http://dx.doi.org/10.1787/888933214832

Youth start their careers in jobs that typically lead to a lower use of skills, such as temporary jobs. Young workers who are on temporary contracts use their skills less intensively than young workers on permanent contracts even if they have the same level of skills (see Chapter 4). However, the underuse of skills by youth is not fully explained by the high incidence of temporary contracts among them. When comparing the use of skills by youth and prime-age workers on the same type of contract, young people still tend to under-use their skills (OECD, 2013).

Digital skills

Most jobs today require some digital and ICT skills. New jobs and occupations have emerged or developed such as digital artists and designers, digital marketing, application development, and automation engineering. At the same time, existing jobs and occupations also increasingly require digital skills. Traditional cognitive skills such as problem-solving skills, as well as literacy and numeracy are used in combination with digital and ICT skills, making it important for workers to be able to make the most of the whole set of skills.

Digital skills are also required for job searching, collecting job-related information including training, education and job vacancies, and applying for jobs. Job matching and recruitment increasingly depend on digital methods. If youth do not have relevant digital skills, a smooth school-to-work transition will be challenging.

As youth generally perform better than the older generation in this skills domain (OECD, 2013), they are likely to be better matched to jobs with high ICT requirements. Yet, as with other skills, youth use less frequently their ICT skills at work than prime-age workers (see Figure 6.1), although they use them more at home. A substantial share of youth has no computer experience at work while the share of youth with no computer experience in everyday life is much lower (Figure 6.3). This share ranges from 54% in Italy to 25% in Korea.

■ Figure 6.3 ■
Youth with no computer experience
Percentage of working youth aged 16-29, 2012

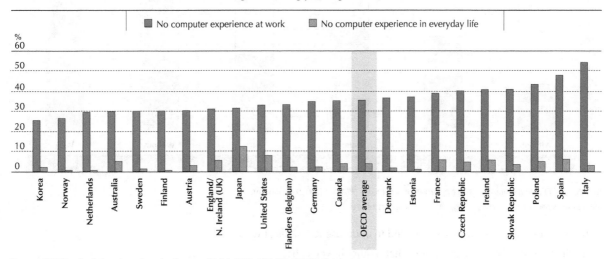

Source: OECD calculations based on the *Survey of Adult Skills (PIAAC) (2012)* (database).
StatLink ⚒ http://dx.doi.org/10.1787/888933214840

The small proportion of youth without digital skills is at a distinct disadvantage. Having ICT skills can be a signal to employers of youth's future potential, whether or not employers need those skills at present. On average, according to the Survey of Adult Skills, about 5% of youth consider that they lack the ICT skills necessary for work and 6% of youth consider that their lack of ICT skills affects their career (Figure 6.4).

■ Figure 6.4 ■
Self-reported ICT skills deficiency
Percentage of working youth aged 16-29, 2012

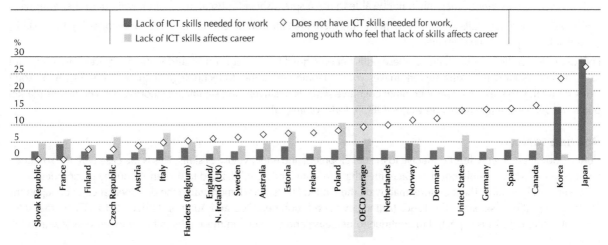

Source: OECD calculations based on the *Survey of Adult Skills (PIAAC) (2012)* (database).
StatLink ⚒ http://dx.doi.org/10.1787/888933214851

Having no computer experience at work is associated with other forms of low use of skills (Figure 6.5). Youth without computer experience at work are less likely to have a supervisory role (10%, compared to 24% of working youth who have computer experience at work). These youth often execute physical tasks for long hours (79%), and use their hands or fingers (72%), yet rarely engage in solving complex problems (84%).

■ Figure 6.5 ■

Use of skills at work, by computer experience at work

16-29 year-olds, 2012

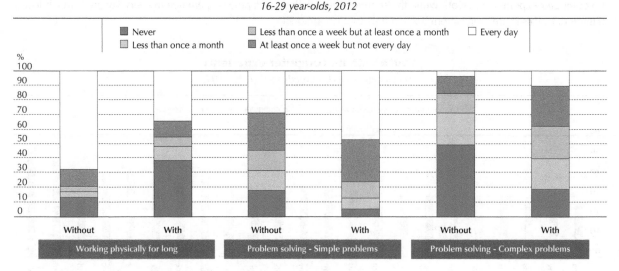

Source: OECD calculations based on the *Survey of Adult Skills (PIAAC) (2012)* (database).

StatLink ⌐🔳📈 http://dx.doi.org/10.1787/888933214861

Various factors can explain why youth tend to underuse ICT skills at work:

■ Youth are more likely to work in jobs that require lower skills.

■ Youth may not fully exploit the opportunities that the digital economy has brought. Many start-ups have been established in ICT-related sectors and new ICT enterprises have higher survival rates than their counterparts in manufacturing and services (ITU, 2014; OECD, 2014a). However, youth may not be able to fully exploit such opportunities – although the founders of start-ups in the ICT sector are becoming younger and the pace is faster – not because of lack of ICT skills but because of lack of entrepreneurship experience, business network and knowhow, finance management skills or funding opportunities (see below).

■ Youth may not be equipped with the specific ICT skills or relevant digital skills that are required at work. The set of ICT skills used at work may be different from those used at home and computer activities in which young adults engage at home are not the same as those required on the job (OECD, 2013). Although youth may use spreadsheets for tracking their own daily expenses, they might not be able to use a spreadsheet for fiscal accounting without further training.

■ ICT skills and digital skills are relatively new, thus there are still insufficient mechanisms for recognising these skills, especially in specialised domains.

Low use of ICT skills is problematic, as these skills become quickly obsolete and acquiring them requires retraining. Not using and developing ICT skills at work makes young people vulnerable to technological change. The Survey of Adult Skills shows that the use of ICT, as with other cognitive skills, is positively and significantly correlated with labour market outcomes such as employment and wages (OECD, forthcoming [a]).

Routine tasks

Certain jobs are by nature less conducive to the development and effective use of skills. This is the case with the so-called "routine jobs" which mainly consist of activities that are sufficiently well defined to be carried out by a computer or by a worker with low skills. The literature, mainly on the United States, has demonstrated the disappearance of occupations focused on routine tasks since the 1980s (Autor, Levy and Murnane, 2003 and Autor and Price, 2013). The demand for jobs with routine tasks is expected to continue to decrease and workers on these jobs to become more exposed to job losses.

The Survey of Adult Skills identifies workers who perform jobs in which they are unable to "change the sequence of tasks" or "how to do the work", which can be considered as a type of routine job. It also identifies jobs that "do not involve learning-by-doing from the tasks" or "keeping up to date with new products or services", which is another signal that the job may involve some routine and little or no learning-by-doing. The share of youth on these types of jobs varies widely across countries (Figure 6.6).

▪ Figure 6.6 ▪

Share of workers in jobs with routine tasks and little learning-by-doing

As a percentage of total employment in each age group, 2012

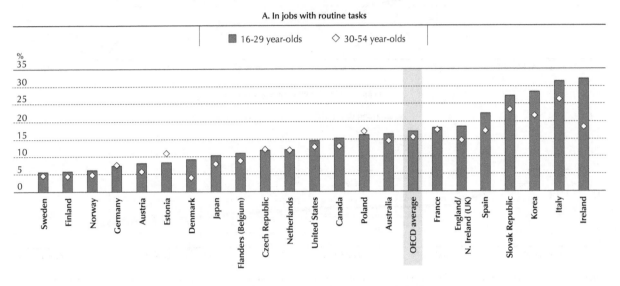

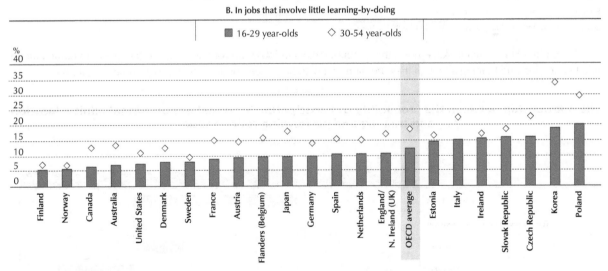

Notes: Workers who are considered in jobs with routine task are those who answered "not at all" or "very little" to the question "To what extent can you choose or change the sequence of your tasks?". Workers who are considered in jobs with little learning-by-doing are those who answered "never" or "less than once a month" to the question "How often does your job involve learning-by-doing from the tasks you perform?".

Source: OECD calculations based on the *Survey of Adult Skills (PIAAC) (2012)* (database).

StatLink ⟪⟫ http://dx.doi.org/10.1787/888933214878

Unsurprisingly, the share of workers in these types of jobs decreases along with higher-level skills (Figure 6.6). However while young workers tend to be more skilled than prime-age workers (see Chapter 1), the share of those who are in jobs involving routine tasks is higher than that of prime-age workers in certain countries (Figure 6.7, panel A). Young workers are less frequently in jobs where they do not learn, compared to prime-age workers, especially if they have low numeracy skills (Figure 6.7, panel B).

▪ Figure 6.7 ▪

Share of workers in jobs with routine tasks and little learning-by-doing, by level of numeracy skills

2012

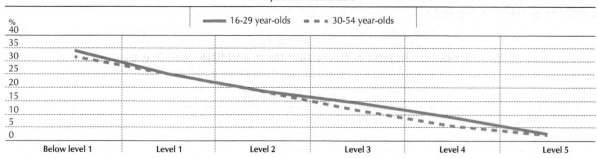

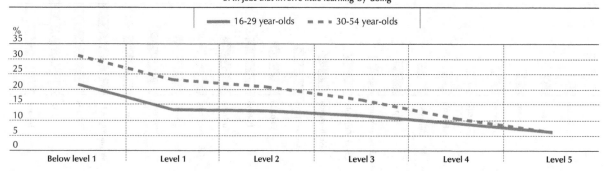

Notes: Workers who are considered in jobs with routine task are those who answered "not at all" or "very little" to the question "To what extent can you choose or change the sequence of your tasks?". Workers who are considered in jobs with little learning-by-doing are those who answered "never" or "less than once a month" to the question "How often does your job involve learning-by-doing from the tasks you perform?".

Source: OECD calculations based on the *Survey of Adult Skills (PIAAC) (2012)* (database).

StatLink ▬▬ http://dx.doi.org/10.1787/888933214883

In addition, the Survey Adult Skills shows that young workers in jobs with routine tasks are less likely to participate in adult education and training although they are more likely to be in need of up-skilling programmes (Figure 6.8).

▪ Figure 6.8 ▪

The relationship between the probability of participating in formal or non-formal adult education and training and performing routine tasks

16-29 year-olds, 2012

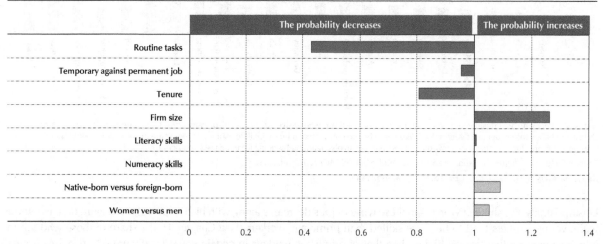

Notes: The figure shows the results of a logit regression on all countries. Statistically significant values are shown in darker tones.

Source: OECD calculations based on the *Survey of Adult Skills (PIAAC) (2012)* (database).

StatLink ▬▬ http://dx.doi.org/10.1787/888933214898

JOB MISMATCH

A sub-optimal allocation of young workers to jobs, the so-called "mismatch" issue, contributes to the less frequent use of their skills at work. As with the underuse of skills compared to prime-age workers, some form of mismatch is common at the beginning of careers. The skills acquired in schools are not exactly those required for a position. Therefore, the first few years may be viewed as a process of skills adjustment: youth may seem to be struggling in the labour market looking for a job and then working in a mismatched job. During this process, unused skills depreciate, useful skills appreciate, and new skills are acquired. A study by Imai, Stacey, and Warman (2011) confirms this skills adjustment process. This study examines the skills mismatch among Canadian immigrants and concludes that individuals' skills gradually converge to the optimal skills sets required by firms' technology, and over time skills mismatch tends to disappear. However, mismatch is problematic if it leads to persistent low use of skills, for instance if the skills developed in the education system lack relevancy for the labour market (see Chapter 3).

There are various dimensions to the mismatch issue. At least three types of mismatch can be identified (OECD, 2013 and 2014b):

- *Qualification mismatch* when the formal qualification a young person holds does not correspond to the requirements of the job.

- *Field-of-study mismatch* when individuals are employed in an area of specialisation other than the one they have studied. This form of mismatch can be problematic if it leads to over-qualification and when certain job-specific skills are not used. Then the person is likely to be penalised in terms of earnings and employment opportunities. However, some young people integrate very well into jobs outside their field of study; they are able to adapt to labour demand and new work situations easily.

- *Skills mismatch* when there is a gap between workers' skills and skills needed to cope with the job. Skills mismatch is complex to assess as a broad range of skills is needed for a job and workers might have some of them but lack others. The Survey of Adult Skills gives information on skills mismatch in numeracy, literacy and problem solving in technology-rich environments.

Qualification mismatch and skills mismatch are related, but they are not the same. People with the same qualification have different skills (OECD, 2013). Some of the people who do not have the level of formal qualification deemed necessary for the job do not actually lack the skills necessary to perform the job, and vice versa. For instance in the health sector, while there is relatively low qualification mismatch due to licensing, considerable skills heterogeneity exists among both medical doctors and nurses (OECD, forthcoming [b]).

Compared with prime-age workers, youth are more likely to be over-qualified and over-skilled in literacy (Figure 6.9). They are also more likely to encounter field-of-study mismatch that is a source of over-qualification. On the other hand, youth are less likely to work in an area outside their field of study, but for which their qualification level is appropriate. Empirical evidences also show that the incidence of skills mismatch decreases with experience and the returns to skills increase with experience (OECD, 2014b). When these three dimensions of mismatch are combined, the analysis suggests that the incidence of mismatch varies little by age group (OECD, 2014b).

■ Figure 6.9 ■

Mismatch, by type of mismatch and age group

As a percentage of total employment in each age group, 2012

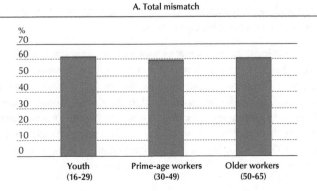

■ Figure 6.9 (continued) ■

Mismatch, by type of mismatch and age group

As a percentage of total employment in each age group, 2012

B. Selected components

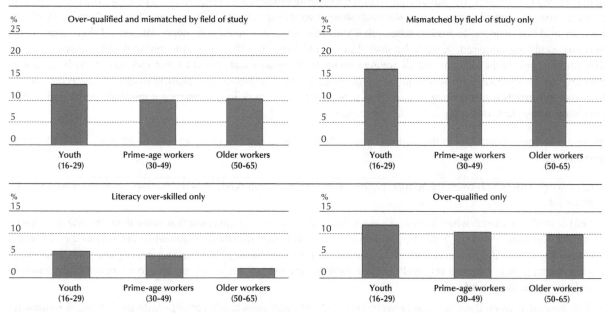

Notes: Workers are classified as mismatched "by qualification" if they have higher or lower qualifications than required by their jobs. Workers are classified as mismatched in terms of "literacy skills" if they have literacy proficiency exceeding or below that required in their jobs. Workers are classified as mismatched by "field of study" if they are working in an occupation that is not related to their field of study.

Source: OECD (2014b), *OECD Employment Outlook 2014*, OECD Publishing, Paris, http://dx.doi.org/ 10.1787/empl_outlook-2014-en.

StatLink http://dx.doi.org/10.1787/888933214904

The questions of whether mismatch has increased recently and if so, whether the increase is a temporary or persistent phenomenon have gained prominence. However, there is little evidence on this issue, partly due to the lack of data on job mismatch over time. With low labour demand, youth may have opted for jobs below their level of education or skills, which can lead to a temporary increase in the number of over-qualified or over-skilled young workers. In addition, the economic crisis has triggered structural changes, which might have exacerbated structural mismatches (Arpaia, Kiss and Turrini, 2014; CEDEFOP, 2014; ILO, 2013). For instance, the construction sector has shrunk in several countries as a consequence of the burst of housing bubbles. Moreover, weak external demand has led countries to change their export patterns. In particular, firms have externalised activities based on routine tasks, exacerbating the historical decline in routine occupations (Jaimovich and Siu, 2012). These changes may have enhanced skills mismatch if education systems have not been responsive enough. Young people who have gained experience in these sectors now find themselves in a situation in which these skills are not needed anymore.

Looking forward, mismatch of different types will gradually decrease over time provided education systems adapt to changing needs, institutions equip workers with transferable skills to integrate into labour markets, and governments and firms retrain workers. Changes in industrial structures are expected to be smaller in the next decades than over the last 20 years in main OECD countries and some emerging economies (Braconier, Nicoletti and Westmore, 2014). Yet, they are expected to be large in Japan and main emerging economies.

Limited geographical mobility from one local labour market to another may force young people to accept jobs below their skill levels or in sectors outside their fields of study. This is another cause for a structural mismatch. The wide variations of youth unemployment across regions in a country illustrate the issue (Figure 6.10). These variations arise from geographical or sector-specific shocks and the history of production specialisation. As a result, some regions are characterised by low value-added production, populated with employers operating in low-cost competitive markets. In such regions, a "skills surplus" situation can arise, where well-trained young people cannot find adequate jobs and so accept less demanding ones, or remain unemployed (see OECD 2014c). Where geographical mobility is high, young people from such regions can migrate to find better quality jobs commensurate with their skills in another region.

■ Figure 6.10 ■

Regional variation in the youth unemployment rate

2013

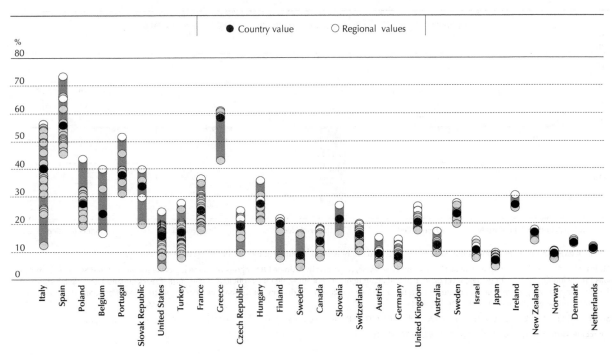

Notes: The youth unemployment rate is the ratio between unemployed persons aged 15-24 and the labour force in the same age class. Each point represents a TL2 region.

Source: OECD *Regional Statistics and Indicators* (database).

StatLink ᴀᵢˢᴾ http://dx.doi.org/10.1787/888933214910

THE CONSEQUENCES OF UNDERUSING SKILLS AND JOB MISMATCH

Overall, these results show that young workers underuse their skills or are mismatched because of both transitory and structural factors. By moving from a temporary job to a permanent one, young workers are expected to improve the use of their skills. Likewise, it can take time for employers to ascertain the level and types of skills their employees have and make full use of them, and for employees to find the job that matches their skills. Moreover, in some countries, the nature of occupational hierarchies implies that it can also take time for young employees to move into positions of greater responsibility in which they fully use their skills. High-skilled youth may not immediately use their skills in a relatively low-tech economy, but the availability of a highly skilled workforce offers the potential for businesses to upgrade their production processes. However, the underuse of skills can be pervasive or lasting if young workers are trapped into temporary jobs or in jobs with large gaps between the skills they have and those skills that are needed for the job.

Mismatch and the underuse of skills, if they come from structural issues and are lasting can have negative consequences on both individuals and society. If persistent, not making full use of skills is not only a waste of investment in initial education, but a missed opportunity to reap the returns on the investment. Beyond the immediate private and public fiscal costs, skills under-utilisation can have longer term consequences: young people who do not use their skills fully are likely to lose them over time, which can result in negative consequences for future employment and well-being, as well as lower participation in further training.

Skills and qualification mismatch can also impact wages (Figure 6.11). Over-qualified young workers earn less than their well-matched counterparts. The effect of over-skilling on wages is small and often not statistically significant, particularly for youth.[1] Field-of-study mismatch alone does not seem to imply a wage penalty for young people compared to their well-matched counterparts (OECD, 2014b). However, this is often accompanied by over-qualification, which leads to a wage penalty.

• Figure 6.11 •

Wages and mismatch, by type of mismatch and age group

Percentage change in wages[1] due to mismatch, 2012

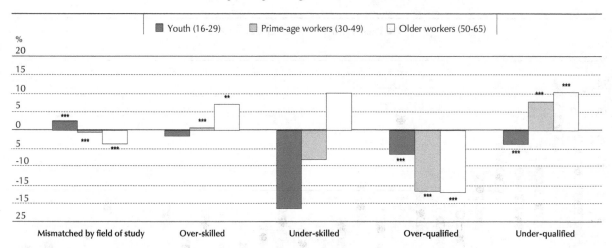

1. Log of gross hourly earnings including bonuses for wage and salary earners, trimmed at the 1st and 99th centile, by country.

Notes: ***, **, *: Statistically significant at 1%, 5% and 10% levels, respectively. A single OLS regression of the log of wages on the three types of mismatch was run including controls for gender, level of educational attainment, field of study, literacy proficiency score, firm size, occupation at 1-digit, industry at 1-digit, contract type, sector (public, private, non-profit), a dummy for students, a dummy for full-time work and country fixed effects. Standard errors are corrected for measurement error and sampling design.

Source: OECD (2014b), *OECD Employment Outlook 2014*, OECD Publishing, Paris , *http://dx.doi.org/10.1787/empl_outlook-2014-en*.

StatLink ⟨᠊᠊᠍᠍⟩ http://dx.doi.org/10.1787/888933214920

Mismatch also has negative consequences on individuals' job satisfaction. Empirical evidence reveals that being over-qualified reduces job satisfaction, and being under-qualified increases it, compared with well-matched workers with the same level of qualification, even when individual characteristics are accounted for. Over-skilling also significantly reduces the likelihood of being satisfied with one's job (OECD, 2011a).

Because of its negative effect on wages and job satisfaction, mismatch can spur job turnover. Both over-skilled and over-qualified workers appear to be more likely to engage in on-the-job search, even when socio-demographic characteristics, job attributes and monthly pay were accounted for, with the effect of over-skilling being much larger than that of over-qualification (OECD, 2011a). This is true whether workers are compared with their well-matched counterparts with similar qualifications or with their well-matched peers in the same job.

Taken together, all these negative consequences for individuals negatively impact employers too. A poor match leading to on-the-job search and high turnover increases recruitment costs and lowers productivity. Likewise, if people are unsatisfied with their jobs, this has negative consequences on their motivation and their willingness to engage at work. Workers who are under-skilled for the job probably have to exert extra effort at work, given their levels of skills, and are likely to be less productive than workers whose skills fully match the requirements of the job. These effects of sub-optimal skills use may have negative implications for the productivity of an economy as a whole.

ENTREPRENEURSHIP

Entrepreneurship, i.e. starting one's own business, can offer an alternative option for young people to use their skills and for the economy and society to benefit from new talent. However, businesses run by young entrepreneurs have lower survival rates than those of older entrepreneurs. Yet, those start-ups run by young people that do survive have more growth potential than those of older entrepreneurs, on average. Among businesses that survived three years, those run by people under 30 years old had an average value-added growth rate of 206% – nearly double the growth rate of businesses run by those over 40 (114%) (Van Praag, 2003; OECD/European Union, 2012).

Entrepreneurship can also make contributions to the economy overall. Empirical evidence shows that entrepreneurship can add to employment growth (Haltiwanger, Jarmin, Miranda, 2010). Moreover, youth entrepreneurship can spur innovation and productivity growth by channelling new ideas into the market. It can also help the economy to restructure towards new demands: an increasing number of young people's start-ups, for example, operate in the area of social entrepreneurship and green enterprises as well as innovative forms of resource sharing (OECD, 2011b). Finally, at the individual level, the job satisfaction of the self-employed tends to be higher than that of the average employee (OECD, 2001).

Many young people are indeed interested in entrepreneurship and self-employment. The European Commission's Eurobarometer shows that overall, in the European Union, young people have stronger preferences for self-employment and are more likely to consider it feasible, compared to the average adult (Figure 6.12).[2] Attitudes to the feasibility of self-employment in the European Union drop off with age: the two youngest age cohorts appear to have the highest level of interest for self-employment, responding that self-employment in the next five years was either "very feasible" or "quite feasible", much higher than the figures for adults aged 40-54, and even more so than those for adults aged over 55 (Figure 6.13). However, the actual self-employment rates for youth are, on average, much lower than for working age adults (Figure 6.14). It seems they face greater barriers to starting a business than more experienced adults do.

■ Figure 6.12 ■
Young people's opinions on self-employment in European countries
2012

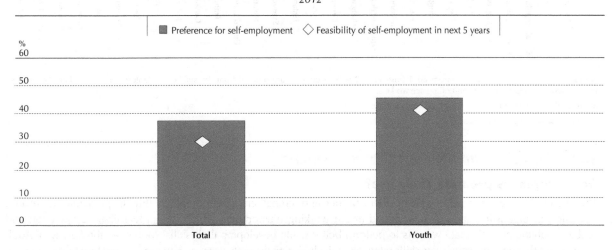

Notes: Data show positive answers to questions i) "If you could choose between different kinds of jobs, would you prefer to be self-employed?" and ii) "Regardless of whether or not you want to become self-employed, would it be feasible for you to be self-employed within the next 5 years?".

Source: European Commission (2012), "Entrepreneurship in the EU and beyond", *Flash Eurobarometer*, No. 354.

StatLink ᵃᵇᵍ http://dx.doi.org/10.1787/888933214939

■ Figure 6.13 ■
Share of individuals interested in entrepreneurship, European countries
2012

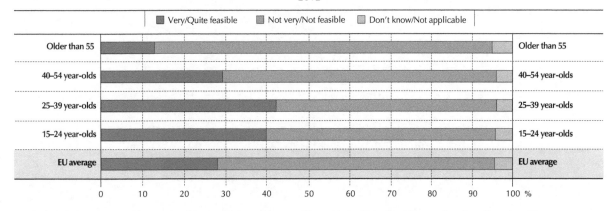

Notes: Data show answers to the question "If you could choose between different kinds of jobs, would you prefer to be self-employed?".

Source: OECD/European Union (2012), *Policy Brief on Youth Entrepreneurship: Entrepreneurial Activities in Europe*, Publications Office of the European Union, Luxembourg.

StatLink ᵃᵇᵍ http://dx.doi.org/10.1787/888933214943

▪ Figure 6.14 ▪

Self-employment rates for youth and prime-age workers

As a share of total employment in each age group, 2013

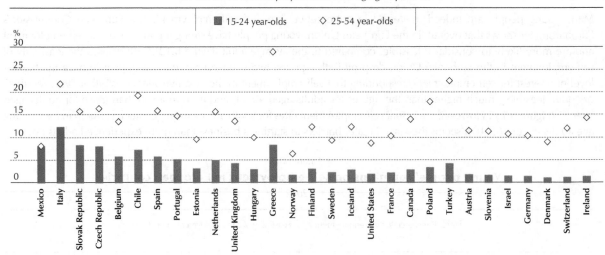

Notes: Data for Chile and Israel are from 2011 (instead of 2013). Countries are ordered from the smallest to largest percentage difference in self-employment rates between youth and prime-age workers.

Source: OECD calculations based on Labour Force Surveys.

StatLink ▄▄▄ http://dx.doi.org/10.1787/888933214959

SKILLS SCOREBOARD ON YOUTH EMPLOYABILITY

Do workplaces promote skills use?

The use of skills at work helps develop them further and strengthens youth employability. In particular, more task discretion in organising one's own workload and a working environment which fosters learning, co-operation and problem solving can stimulate workers to perform better while developing their skills. Moreover, the Survey of Adult Skills shows that people accumulate skills relatively quickly during the early years of their careers and lose them relatively slowly during the later years. The effective use and development of youth's skills become even more important so. To measure this concept, the Skills Scoreboard uses four indicators of the share of young employed people who use these skills at work (Table 6.1).

■ Table 6.1 ■

Skills Scoreboard on youth employability: Do workplaces promote skills use?

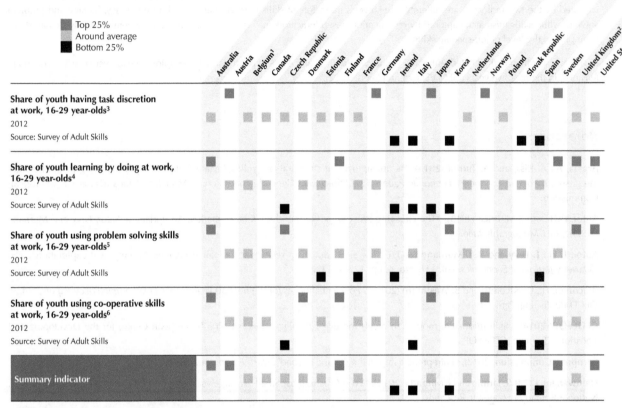

Top 25%
Around average
Bottom 25%

1. All indicators from the Survey of Adult Skills for Belgium refer to Flanders.

2. All indicators from the Survey of Adult Skills for the United Kingdom refer to England and Northern Ireland.

3. The indicator is based on the questions D_Q11a and D_Q11b (To what extent can you choose or change i) the sequence of your tasks? and ii) how you do your work?). It shows the share of young workers who have answered both questions with "To some extent", "To a high extent" or "To a very high extent".

4. The indicator is based on the questions D_Q13b and D_Q13c (How often does your job involve i) learning-by-doing from the tasks you perform and ii) keeping up to date with new products or services?). It shows the share of young workers who have answered the questions with "Less than once a week but at least once a month", "At least once a week but not every day" or "Every day".

5. The indicator is based on the question F_Q05b (How often are you usually confronted with more complex problems that take at least 30 minutes to find a good solution?). It shows the share of young workers who have answered the questions with "Less than once a week but at least once a month", "At least once a week but not every day" or "Every day".

6. The indicator is based on the question F_Q01b (In your job what proportion of your time do you usually spend in co-operation or collaboration with co-workers?). It shows the share of young workers who have answered the question with "Up to a quarter of the time", "Up to half of the time", "More than half of the time" or "All the time".

Notes: All indicators have been normalised in a way which implies that a higher value and being among the "top 25%" reflect better performance. The summary indicator is calculated as a simple average of the four indicators.

Source: OECD calculations based on the *Survey of Adult Skills (PIAAC) (2012)* (database).

Notes

1. Qualification mismatch and skills mismatch may both have distinct effects on wages, even after accountig for both qualification level and proficiency scores, because jobs with similar qualification requirements may have different skill requirements. This may happen because employers can evaluate qualifications, but they cannot measure skills directly. In addition, the kinds of mismatch in skills captured by the two indicators are different: the survey's indicators of skills mismatch are based on numeracy, literacy and problem solving, while skills mismatch captured by qualification-based indicators may be interpreted as more general and may be based, for example, on the level of job-specific skills.

2. This is lower than in the United States and China, where 36 % and 49 % of people saw self-employment as "very feasible" or "quite feasible" in the next five years (OECD/European Union, 2012).

References

Arpaia, A., A. Kiss, and **A. Turrini** (2014), "Is unemployment structural or cyclical? Main features of job matching in the EU after the crisis", *European Economy - Economic Papers 527*, Directorate General Economic and Monetary Affairs (DG ECFIN), European Commission.

Autor, D.H. and **B.M. Price** (2013), "The changing task composition of the US labor market: An update of Autor, Levy and Murnane (2003)", *MIT Monograph, June*.

Autor, D.H., F. Levy and **R. J. Murnane** (2003), "The skill content of recent technological change: An empirical exploration", *The Quarterly Journal of Economics*, Vol. 118, No. 4, pp. 1279-1333.

Braconier, H., G. Nicoletti and **B. Westmore** (2014), "Policy challenges for the next 50 years", *OECD Economic Policy Papers*, No. 9, OECD Publishing, Paris, *http://dx.doi.org/10.1787/5jz18gs5fckf-en.*

CEDEFOP (2014), "Skill mismatch: more than meets the eye", *Briefing Notes No. 9087*, European Centre for the Development of Vocational Training (CEDEFOP).

European Commission (2012), "Entrepreneurship in the EU and beyond", *Flash Eurobarometer*, No. 354.

Haltiwanger, J.C. R.S. Jarmin and **J. Miranda** (2010), "Who Creates Jobs? Small vs. Large vs. Young," *NBER Working Papers,* No. 16300, National Bureau of Economic Research.

ILO (2013), *Global Employment Trends 2013: Recovering from a Second Jobs Dip*, International Labour Organization.

Imai, S., D. Stacey and **C. Warman** (2011), "From Engineer to Taxi Driver? Occupational Skills and the Economic Outcomes of Immigrants", *Working Papers 1275*, Queen's University, Department of Economics.

ITU (2014) *Digital opportunities: Innovative ICT solutions for youth employment.* International Telecommunication Union.

Jaimovich, N. and **H.E. Siu** (2012), "The trend is the cycle: Job polarization and jobless recoveries", *NBER Working Paper*, No. 18334. National Bureau of Economic Research.

OECD (forthcoming [a]), *Adults, Computers and Problem Solving: What's the Problem?*, OECD Publishing, Paris.

OECD (forthcoming [b]), *Health Workforce Policies in OECD Countries* (preliminary title), OECD Publishing, Paris.

OECD. (2014a), *Measuring the Digital Economy: A New Perspective*, OECD Publishing, Paris, *http://dx.doi.org/10.1787/9789264221796-en.*

OECD (2014b), *OECD Employment Outlook 2014*, OECD Publishing, Paris, *http://dx.doi.org/ 10.1787/empl_outlook-2014-en.*

OECD (2014c), *Job Creation and Local Economic Development*, OECD Publishing, Paris, *http://dx.doi.org/10.1787/9789264215009-en.*

OECD (2013), *OECD Skills Outlook 2013: First Results from the Survey of Adult Skills*, OECD Publishing, Paris, *http://dx.doi. org/10.1787/9789264204256-en.*

OECD (2011a), *OECD Employment Outlook 2011*, OECD Publishing, Paris, *http://dx.doi.org/10.1787/empl_outlook-2011-en.*

OECD (2011b), *Entrepreneurship at a Glance 2011*, OECD Publishing, Paris, *http://dx.doi.org/10.1787/9789264097711-en.*

OECD (2001), *Putting the Young in Business: Policy Challenges for Youth Entrepreneurship*, OECD Publishing, Paris, *http://dx.doi. org/10.1787/9789264188648-en.*

OECD/European Union (2012), *Policy Brief on Youth Entrepreneurship: Entrepreneurial Activities in Europe*, Publications Office of the European Union, Luxembourg.

Van Praag, M. (2003), "Business survival and success of young small business owners: An empirical analysis", *Small Business Economics*, Vol. 21, pp. 1–17.

7

Policies towards using young people's skills at work

This chapter discusses policies to improve the match between skills and jobs, to encourage youth to make better use of their skills on the job and to remove barriers to entrepreneurship, which can be an alternative for youth to use their skills. Many different policies influence the use of skills and the matching process both on the side of employees and employers, and therefore, efforts should be on many fronts: removing barriers to geographical mobility, designing consistent national and international qualification frameworks but also promoting effective work organisations and removing barriers to youth entrepreneurship.

Various efforts and policies would contribute to more effective use of youth skills. Linking more prominently the education system to the labour market and better preparing youth for the world of work, would avoid the build-up of large imbalances between skills supply and demand. However, solving those imbalances takes time as doing so requires major structural adjustments, which can take the form of aligning education and training systems better with the needs of the labour market or altering the structure of the economy towards higher value-added production.

Labour market rigidities also make it difficult for youth who have no experience to enter jobs that would allow them to use their skills fully. Sound labour market institutions increase the ability of employers to identify and reward youth skills. They also raise the likelihood for employers to learn about workers' skills over time (OECD, 2014a). As discussed in Chapter 4, youth are more likely to be hired on temporary contracts, and these contracts lead to lower utilisation of skills than permanent contracts. Sound employment protection legislations ease transition from temporary to permanent employment, which is associated with a more effective use of skills. Flexible wage setting arrangements make it easier to adjust wages to the effective skills of workers and thereby to mitigate the potential negative impact of mismatch on job satisfaction.

In addition, there is a need for specific policies that would help youth find a job which matches their skills, allows them to develop skills at work in order to adapt to future changing needs and overall make the best use of their skills. While developing young people's skills and activating them are clear public policy objectives, there is less assessment of whether skills are used effectively at work, and less consensus on the role of policy in addressing the issue.

LIMITING SKILLS MISMATCH AND MAKING BETTER USE OF YOUNG PEOPLE'S SKILLS

The impact of new technologies

New technologies have changed the way employers recruit staff and job seekers look for jobs. The Internet now plays a central role as social media such as LinkedIn, Facebook, and Google, and new tools such as applicant tracking systems, mobile recruiting, jobs boards and career pages are increasingly used by employers and job seekers. These new channels for recruitment have opened up opportunities for companies to inform a much wider pool of potential candidates about job opportunities and careers and for employees to make more informed decisions on finding or changing jobs.

Firms are increasingly using social media to recruit workers. Certain tools (Recruiter) allow employers and job seekers to conduct sophisticated search queries for candidates and jobs. The search functionality allows recruiters to sift through members (mainly of LinkedIn) based on a variety of characteristics: years of experience, job title, current or past employer, or the size of the company at which someone has worked. A study on Belgium shows that employers use both LinkedIn and Facebook to increase the volume of information about candidates available for a selection interview, however only a minority use these networks/tools to actually select the first round of candidates (Caers and Castelyns, 2011). According to this study, employers claim that they do not attribute a lot of weight to Facebook profiles although they admit they review all publicly available information on Facebook. This is consistent with another study according to which, while approximately 60% of companies used or planned to use social media as a hiring tool in 2013, less than 30% believed the data are useful in determining the candidates' fit, while only 11% believed it is critical to hiring decisions (Society for Human Resource Management, 2013). Employers mainly look at information on career history and education but they also check candidate pictures and stated interests, which can include participation in certain communities or religious groups.

There is evidence that Internet has improved labour market matching. A study on the US market shows that unemployed persons who look for work online are re-employed about 25% faster than those who do not search online (Kuhn and Mansour, 2014). However, the overall impact of the Internet on labour market outcomes remains to be fully understood.

Young people are more likely than older workers to use the Internet and more specifically social media to look for a job. They are particularly exposed to the impact these new technologies have on their chances of finding a job and on the efficiency of the matching process. There are however both positive and negative impacts:

- The Internet lowers transaction costs when looking for jobs and hiring workers and can render a more effective matching process. It makes it easier for workers to apply to new jobs and interact with their future employers. Moreover it facilitates employers' search for potential candidates, allowing them to advertise for the job online and ask for referrals; the Internet is a one-stop job market.

- Young people benefit from increased and more accessible information concerning job offers and the company itself, which in turn leads to a more accurate perception of the job. This can ease the match between young people's skills and job requirements.

- The use of new technologies means that information is now available on a large geographic scale which in turn lowers geographical mismatch.

- The use of new technologies during the hiring process can exacerbate inequities between young workers, as highly educated workers are more likely to job search online than other less qualified workers. Candidates are increasingly requested to have mobile access and often a part of the recruitment process is carried out through mobile devices, especially in emerging economies (Society for Human Resource Management, 2013). Young people with little access to computer or smart phones are in a less favourable situation.

- There is an increased risk of poaching as employers have access to an abundance of information when searching for candidates. Moreover, new technologies mean that passive job seekers are also better informed concerning job opportunities and are more visible to competing organisations. In addition, these practices may make it more difficult for those who do not have a job history that fully fits the job to be selected.

- By accessing personal information through social media, employers can more easily discriminate between candidates. According to a study, 50% of respondents to the survey indicated that recruiters and hiring managers are allowed to review candidate data from social media sites (Society for Human Resource Management, 2013). While only 20% are allowed to use this data to make hiring decisions, the line between accessing this information and using it when making recruitment decisions is difficult to draw.

These concerns suggest several directions for policies. In schools, job centres and other types of institutions, young people could be advised on the use of social media and how to make the most of the information they deliver through their LinkedIn and Facebook profiles. Parents also have a role to play on alerting children about the unintended consequences of making certain information public. Many countries have specific laws governing how such information should be used during employee selection.

The information gained from online tools needs to be interpreted and applied which may require support from independent professional advisors to reduce unwanted negative effects on equity by excluding potential workers with limited access to the Internet or with low levels of digital literacy (see Chapter 3). Public employment services can improve the efficiency of the matching process by facilitating the exchange of information between employers and potential employees through these technologies (see Chapter 5).

Skills and diplomas

Despite an easier access to candidate profiles through new technologies, recruitment processes remain complicated when qualifications are not fully understood by employers. In contrast to nationally recognised qualifications and standards, a plethora of credentials at local or institutional level, typically mean that employers do not know which skills they can expect a young person with a given credential to have. The Survey of Adult Skills has shown that people holding the same formal qualifications have different levels of cognitive skills (OECD, 2013a). For older adults, this might have a lot to do with skills either gained through work experience or lost due to lack of use. For recent graduates, this is likely to reflect heterogeneity in the quality of education provision, with graduates holding the same formal qualification but leaving education with very different skills sets.

It is important that a qualification signals the composition and level of skills. Competency-based standards and qualifications developed in close collaboration with social partners and updated according to the changing needs of the labour market can: i) help young people understand which skills are required for which jobs; and ii) provide reliable information to employers about the kind of skills they can expect a graduate with a given qualification to have, regardless of which education pathway the individual has chosen to attain the qualification (OECD, 2010a). Some initiatives have been developed either to directly assess the skills of young graduates or to develop education programmes that exactly match the skills requested by the labour market (Box 7.1).

Box 7.1 **Initiatives to match young people's skills with labour market needs:**
Country examples

Aspiring Minds is an Indian company founded in 2007 with the goal to "help talent meet opportunity". The starting point was a company assessment that almost half of Indian graduates were unemployable in any sector because of their insufficient English language knowledge and low cognitive skills. Aspiring Minds works closely with students, job seekers and educational institutions in helping them evaluate their employability and connecting them with job opportunities.

Concretely, the company has developed a multi-dimensional evaluation of the employability of young university graduates. The assessment (Aspiring Minds Computer Adaptive Test or AMCAT) covers a wide range of skills: English language proficiency, logical and analytical abilities, quantitative skills (numeracy), managerial skills, social and emotional skills (the "Big Five"), technical skills in a number of domains such as engineering, banking, finance and accounting, and more recently, computer programming skills.

To ensure that the test is relevant to employers' needs, it is carried out on employees at an industry level and correlated with on-the-job performance to predict what kind of test results a person needs to have in order to be successful in the job. The test is delivered in colleges but can also be taken online. It has become by far the largest employability assessment in the country with 50 000 assessments every month.

Another goal of the initiative is to provide a level playing field for candidates. Where the recruitment process is based on the direct measure of skills, which means how these skills have been acquired (at a specific education institution or through massive open online courses) does not hold importance anymore, all candidates have equal opportunities to find a job.

The company has influenced the matching process between skills and jobs in many ways:

- To firms, Aspiring Minds provides a platform for hiring from a pre-assessed pool of candidates across the country. The multi-dimensional aspect of the assessment enables employers to identify candidates who are more likely to have or easily develop the skills needed for the job if they are trained.

- To students, the test, especially if taken at the beginning of college, provides information on their performance relative to national averages, their strengths and weaknesses, their employability in specific sectors, and how they can develop skills to fulfil their aspirations. The test also gives information on social and emotional skills. This information is transmitted to the person by an individualised diagnostic report.

- To educational institutions, Aspiring Minds provides a diagnostic report based on the outcomes of their students' test results. The report discusses the employability of students and suggests areas for action. It can therefore act as a powerful tool for institutions to increase the quality of education. The company also awards institutions that have students in the last year of education with the highest skills, which can also motivate institutions to improve quality.

- Finally, the company publishes yearly National Employability Reports that are extensively discussed in the media and can be used by governments to make informed decisions.

So far, there has been no independent assessment of the impact of the initiative on the quality of the matching process between skills and jobs. However, increasing demand from firms, educational institutions and candidates suggests that they all benefit from the initiative. One challenge Aspiring Minds is facing is to extend its coverage, especially to rural areas, while maintaining quality. Labour market candidates in rural areas may face a double penalty coming from lower quality educational institutions coupled with lack of access to or knowledge of Aspiring Minds. Another issue could be that the initiative may place too much weight on the development of skills that are currently needed on the labour market and less on future needs. It would therefore benefit from being backed by efforts to anticipate future skills needs.

Ecole 42 is a French school that was created to address the gap between supply and demand of computer programming skills. The starting point of the initiative which was launched and personally financed by a French entrepreneur in the telecommunications and technology industry, was the lack of young graduates with good-quality programming skills. The school aims to develop these skills through an innovative pedagogical approach.

...

The school is open to anyone aged between 18 and 30. With no previous degree required, students are selected on the basis of an in depth selection process assessing their motivation, skills and potential to become excellent programmers. Particular emphasis is placed on the one-month long immersion phase known as the "Swimming Pool" during which candidates have to carry out a few information technology projects. Teaching methods aim to develop students' creativity and innovative skills as well as technical skills that are highly demanded on the labour market. The school has no lectures or teachers, instead a pedagogical team is in place. Student learning is based on a "peer-to-peer" review approach including group projects and team problem solving.

The programme is free but as the school does not offer a diploma recognised by the government, students do not have access to grants to pay for their living costs. There is no available assessment of the labour market outcomes of the school's graduates but according to the school and media, students receive several job offers even before graduating

Sources:

Aspiring Minds, *www.aspiringminds.in/*.

Wharton University (2014), "Assessing employability is disrupting India's higher education model", *http://knowledge.wharton.upenn.edu/article/assessing-employability-disrupting-indias-higher-education-model/*.

Ecole 42, *www.42.fr/*.

Qualifications also have to be portable, at least nationally if not internationally. A multitude of regional or institution-based qualifications makes it difficult for employers and young people to signal skills, and qualifications risk becoming meaningless as a recruitment tool if they are not based on nationally recognised standards. Several countries have introduced or streamlined their national qualification systems in the recent past (e.g. Hungary, Ireland, Spain and the United Kingdom). The European Qualifications Framework (EQF) has encouraged many European countries to establish national frameworks consistent with the EU-wide framework. The EQF provides a grid of eight levels, each described in terms of the associated skills, knowledge and competencies, and all European countries are required to sort their national qualifications into the appropriate level. This renders qualifications comparable within and between countries, thus allowing mobility beyond national borders (OECD, 2010a). The process of sorting national qualifications into qualification frameworks has been difficult in some countries, particularly with regard to establishing the status of vocationally-oriented qualifications, compared to the academically-oriented ones in the qualification hierarchy.

Recognising skills acquired informally or in another country

Young people lacking formal qualifications may have the right skills to execute more demanding jobs, but encounter much greater difficulties obtaining them. Under-qualified individuals also earn less than better-qualified workers in the same occupation, even once skills proficiency and job characteristics are taken into consideration. While some employers might rely primarily on experience and personal encounters as a recruitment strategy, others are very focused on formal qualifications, putting an under-qualified, albeit well-skilled candidate at a disadvantage. A formal recognition of skills acquired through non-formal or informal learning (RNFIL) and raising employer awareness of these systems can help youth market their skills better.

Migrants are particularly likely to be in the over-qualified category, with related penalties in the labour market (see Chapter 4). Highly educated immigrants experience greater rates of over-qualification than the native-born in virtually all countries. This is somewhat less pronounced for the medium-qualified (OECD, 2014b). Over-qualification occurs either because immigrants' qualifications are not recognised in the host country or because the education they received in their country of origin was of poorer quality and their qualifications do not come with the necessary skills for the job requirements. Estimates suggest that between one-third and one-half of the observed higher over-qualification of immigrants with foreign qualifications vis-à-vis the native-born, is associated with lower skills levels at given qualification levels (Bonfanti and Xenogiani 2014; OECD, 2008a and 2007a).

Some immigrants have the required job-specific and cognitive skills, but lack the language proficiency or professional networks necessary to find adequate jobs: more than one out of five immigrants report that language difficulties are a main obstacle for finding suitable jobs, and immigrants with lower education levels are over-represented among this group (OECD,2014b). Furthermore, immigrants, including native-born children of immigrants, are at an obvious disadvantage with respect to knowledge of the host country labour market and hiring practices, as well as employer contacts, direct or indirect. Targeted initiatives for the validation of skills and the recognition of foreign qualifications in concert with language training and guidance to navigate a foreign labour market might help decrease the incidence of qualification mismatch for migrant workers (Box 7.2).

> ### Box 7.2 Recognising skills and foreign qualifications: Country examples
>
> OECD work demonstrates the potential benefits of recognition of non-formal and informal learning (RNFIL) for both workers and employers. In the context of under-qualification, recognition can provide greater visibility and therefore add value to the skills of people in the labour market. It can also facilitate structural adjustment by enabling the skills of displaced workers to be recognised and used in other parts of the labour market. Although many OECD countries have established RNFIL systems, recognition processes are often small-scale and complex, which reduces their value to employers (OECD, 2011a). One area in which some countries have made progress is to recognise skills acquired abroad.
>
> In Australia, some states have established programmes to overcome the problem of over-qualification among skilled migrants. In Victoria, for example, the Overseas Qualified Professionals Programme established in 1996 provides recently arrived professionals, who acquired their skills abroad, with work-experience placements to enhance their opportunities for employment in their fields of study. The participants must be either unemployed or employed in low-skilled jobs. The programme consists of an initial six-week training period to develop job-search skills, followed by a four- to six-week work-experience placement in the participant's field or in a closely related occupation. The work-placement component is generally not remunerated. The programme includes mentoring elements and industry-specific networking sessions with employers and professional associations to provide further orientation and networking opportunities. Six months after completing the programme, more than 60% of participants were in paid employment in a field corresponding to their qualifications and experience.
>
> Taking a different approach, in 2004, Denmark established regional knowledge centres for the assessment of the skills and qualifications of immigrants – a joint project by the Ministry of Employment and the social partners. The assessment is generally done in workplace situations at companies and participants obtain "competence cards" relating immigrants' skills to labour market needs. The centres also assist in finding employment that matches the immigrants' skills (OECD, 2007b).
>
> In other countries, programmes have focused on over-qualification in specific occupations. In Portugal, two non-governmental organisations (the Gulbenkian Foundation and the Jesuit Refugee Service) developed, jointly with universities and various ministries (Health, Interior and Foreign Affairs), a programme for foreign-trained doctors who were found to be working in low-skilled occupations such as in construction or cleaning. The programme provided for the translation of documents, bridging courses at medical faculties, as well as comprehensive preparation material, internships in teaching hospitals, and vocation-specific language training. Participants had to pass a final assessment examination. At the end of the pilot project, about 90% of the participants were employed as doctors. Participants were followed for one year after completion of the programme to ensure a lasting integration. The programme has now been mainstreamed. In Sweden, the government has assigned a number of universities and colleges to arrange supplementary courses for immigrants with a foreign university degree in law, education, health and public administration. The programme was introduced to provide an opportunity to adjust foreign credentials to the Swedish labour market, thereby helping highly skilled immigrants obtain employment in their fields of study.
>
> One group that is particularly affected by skill under-utilisation is that of refugees who might be well-skilled but whose primary objective for migration is not employment. To address this issue, the Netherlands, for example, has set up several specific training programmes for highly qualified refugees (OECD, 2008a).
>
> **Sources:**
>
> OECD (2007b), *Jobs for Immigrants (Vol. 1): Labour Market Integration in Australia, Denmark, Germany and Sweden,* OECD Publishing, Paris, *http://dx.doi.org/10.1787/9789264033603-en.*
>
> OECD (2008a), *Jobs for Immigrants (Vol. 2): Labour Market Integration in Belgium, France, the Netherlands and Portugal,* OECD Publishing, Paris, *http://dx.doi.org/10.1787/9789264055605-en.*
>
> OECD (2011a), *OECD Employment Outlook 2011,* OECD Publishing, Paris, *http://dx.doi.org/10.1787/empl_outlook-2011-en.*

Geographical mismatch

There is evidence that unemployment can be reduced by reallocating job seekers to areas with better job opportunities, at least in the United States (Şahin, Song, Topa, and Violante, 2012; Manning and Petrongolo, 2011). Policies can facilitate mobility from one local labour market to another to maximise the matching of skills and jobs. They can, for instance, provide public transport to connect inner-city jobs to affordable housing in the outskirts or connect rural areas with urban centres or industrial hubs (OECD, 2014c); removing housing policies that impede residential mobility can also have a significant impact on labour mobility and the allocation of skills and jobs in local labour markets (Caldera Sánchez and Andrews, 2011).

However, further promotion of geographic mobility can have significant trade-offs, especially for rural regions that could suffer from "brain drain" and remain in a situation of low productivity/low-skilled employment for many years (Froy, Giguère and Meghnagi, 2012; OECD,2014d). Hence, policies to ease geographical mobility of skills have to be accompanied by other policies to gradually upgrade regional activities to render them more productive and in demand.

The effect of non-compete clauses

Non-compete clauses if they are widely or even abusively used can hinder workers' mobility and the matching process between jobs and skills. They are clauses under which an employee agrees not to work for a competitive firm for a period of time after resigning or after their contract is terminated. These agreements aim at protecting firm-specific knowledge and are generally thought to be used for a small range of workers, typically those with technical and high skills. However, although no comprehensive international assessment exists, there is some evidence that non-compete clauses are sometimes used abusively even for young low-skilled workers to restrict competition or simply to reinforce employers' power on their workforce. The goal of non-compete clauses is to separate workers from the use of their skills: employers deny workers the opportunity to apply firm-specific skills outside the firm as they cannot be separated from their skills (Becker, 1964). Hence, they can bind employees to their employers (Bishara, Martin and Thomas, 2015), which can be a barrier to the matching process and lead to an ineffective use of skills. Studies have found that employers can also generate "brain drain" from enforcing states or regions to non-enforcing ones and thereby contribute to geographical skills mismatch (Marx and Fleming 2012). They can also force employees to involuntary leave their technical field to avoid potential lawsuit, leading to so-called "career detours".

There is only limited assessment of the scope of the use of these rules due to lack of data availability. A study on a large sample of publically available chief executive officers' contracts in the United States found that 80% of them had non-compete clauses (Bishara, Martin and Thomas, 2015). Another study in the United States using a smaller sample but including young skilled workers, found that around 40% of them were subject to non-compete clauses (Marx, 2011). Recently, the media[1] have argued that the use of non-compete clauses has spread to many professions (such as hair stylists, summer camp counsellors and yoga instructors). Danish employer and employee confederations have raised attention to cases of student jobs which contain clauses preventing them from seeking employment afterwards in the same sector, or with the company's clients.

Usually governments have no direct way to intervene on these clauses: they are set by employers and their consequences depend on how courts implement them. However, governments can raise awareness of the potential negative impact of these clauses especially for young workers. Young people and low-skilled workers may not even realise they are agreeing to such conditions as they may be less well informed than high-skilled workers. Furthermore, they may typically accept entry-level jobs precisely because these jobs give them the experience they need to move on to a more rewarding job.

Governments and employer and employee organisations can carry out assessments of the trends in these clauses and try to agree on good practices. For instance, the requirement to sign a non-compete agreement can be made more transparent at an early stage of the recruitment process rather than being disclosed after the employee has accepted the job offer. The duration of non-compete clauses can also be shorter (it is often one year and more). Better information on these issues would also help courts in their decisions. The implementation of non-compete clauses by courts evolves with time. In the United States for instance, these clauses were relatively easy to enforce by employers in the 1990s, as the courts were able to modify the terms of an overbroad employee non-compete agreement to render the agreement enforceable (Garrison and Wendt, 2008). Since 2000, many US courts have limited the reach of these clauses to foster employee mobility and competition between firms.

Work organisation and management policies

Work organisation and management practices can foster the use of youth skills in an effective way. According to the Survey of Adult Skills, young people use task discretion, influencing and self-organisation skills less frequently than prime-age workers, but use their co-operative skills and learn new things from supervisors or co-workers, learn by doing, and keep up-to-date with new products and services more frequently than prime-age workers (see Chapter 6). In the European Working Conditions Survey (Eurofound, 2013), young people also report having limited levels of autonomy at work compared to their prime-age peers, that is to say, less opportunity to determine job tasks, work methods and processes, pace at work, or working time. These findings are not surprising as young workers are more likely to be learning on the job, rather than deciding on tasks. However, it is important that youth specific skills such as knowledge of recent techniques, curiosity, and creative skills are fully used, even if youth do not have a lot of responsibilities in the beginning of their careers.

Employers have a range of policies to make better use of their employees' skills. These policies may not be specific to young workers but youth may be particularly affected as they often lack experience. Effective recruitment and management methods, often called high performance work practices, are those that evaluate, assign, and continuously develop employees' skills to match job tasks and create room for initiative, innovation and personal development and involve employees in the work process (Ichniowski and Shaw, 2009). They include skills audits and job redesign to match skills profiles, job rotation and active encouragement of knowledge transfer, as well as employee autonomy and participation. These types of organisations can help workers make better use of their skills, thereby improving the company's performance (Ichniowski, Prennushi and Shaw, 1997). They have been found to improve the use of skills and employee job satisfaction and motivation (Skills Australia, 2012; OECD, 2014a). This is especially the case when the introduction of these policies is perceived as a way to improve quality or employee wellbeing, but it is not the case if they are perceived as a way to cut costs or increase control over employees (Nishii, Lepak, and Schneider, 2008).

The European Working Conditions Survey sheds some light on the development of working organisation practices at the country level (Figure 7.1). Countries have unevenly developed working organisations that can be conducive to an effective use of skills. Furthermore, in some countries (Denmark, Norway and Sweden), young people are more likely than prime-age workers to consider facing work organisation practices that are not fully conducive to the use and development of their skills.

■ Figure 7.1 ■

Young workers' perception of work organisation practices in European countries

Share of individuals answering positively to the statements below, 2010

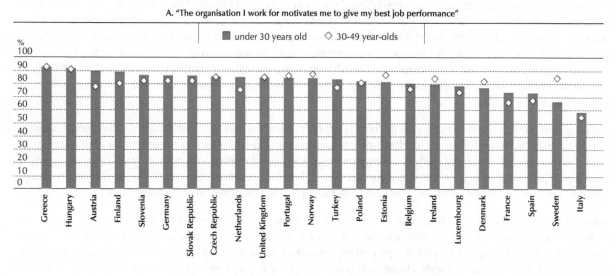

A. "The organisation I work for motivates me to give my best job performance"

B. "I work in a group or team that has common tasks and can plan its work"

■ Figure 7.1 (continued) ■

Young workers' perception of work organisation practices in European countries

Share of individuals answering positively to the statements below, 2010

C. "In general, your immediate manager / supervisor provides you with feedback on your work"

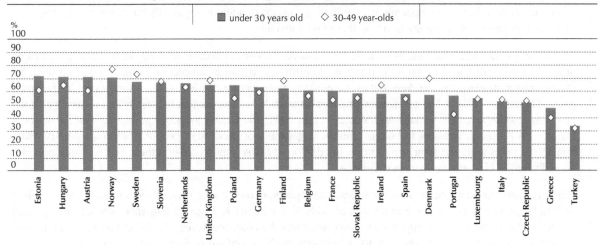

D. "In general, your immediate manager / supervisor encourages you to participate in important decisions"

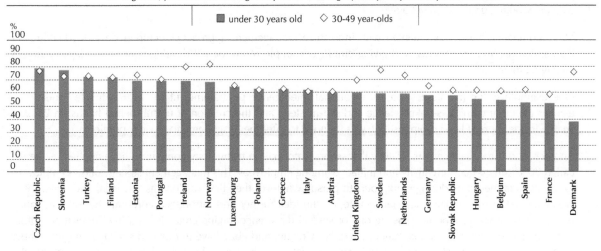

Source: Fifth European Working Conditions Survey.

StatLink ⎯⎯ http://dx.doi.org/10.1787/888933214968

Various factors can inhibit the development of high performance work practices (Cox, Rickard and Tamkin, 2012). They include lack of competition, reluctance to change, reluctance of middle managers to delegate responsibilities and of employees to take on responsibilities, and lack of skills amongst managers to put in place these practices. The financial cost (in terms of training) can be another obstacle. Furthermore, some of these practices might be easier to implement in big firms with large internal labour markets. Large firms generally have lower incidence of skills mismatch, most likely because they have greater capacities to engage in training to adjust the skills match of their employees and because bigger internal labour markets allow them to move employees around without having to resort to lay-offs and new recruitment (OECD, 2013a).

One specific issue related to youth is how to make the most of their innovative skills, knowledge of modern technologies and curiosity while they are in jobs with relatively low levels of responsibility. Some firms have developed innovative management approaches to make better use of such talent (Box 7.3). These approaches put their focus on the quality of human relationships at work, personal development and self-awareness, aiming to increase employee satisfaction and motivation as well as employer outcomes, such as improvements to innovation, productivity, profitability, staff retention and safety at work.

Box 7.3 **Working organisation practices for an effective use of youth skills: Country and firm examples**

Helping the development of effective working organisation practices has been less a focus for public policies than other goals such as boosting employment or improving working conditions. Especially for young people, the main concern of governments generally is to help them find a first job.

Yet, in many countries, governments try to foster the development of effective working organisation practices by providing information to firms on these practices. In Australia, as part of various measures to boost productivity for the benefit of enterprises, workers and the community, the government tries to raise awareness of the potential gains of better use of skills. The government provides research-based information to identify and disseminate good practices to other employers (Skills Australia, 2012). In 1991, the United Kingdom government established the Investors in People programme to help organisations get the most from their people. The programme provides human resources tools and standards to firms. In addition, it helps firms to develop these practices and provides accreditation of high management performance.

France has introduced a specific programme (so-called "generation contracts") that subsidises young people paired with older people to ensure the transmission of skills. This contract is a way to influence working organisation practices. The young person is supposed to work alongside the older employee who in turn acts as a trainer and mentor. For companies with fewer than 300 employees, the financial aid is given – for a three-year period – for young people aged 26 and less who are hired on indefinite contracts, and for senior employees aged 57 and over who are working until retirement age.

Many companies have experimented with innovative management approaches centring on individuals rather than structures and procedures, and giving employees ample room for self-development and independence in managing their work.

One example is the mindfulness-based, emotional intelligence programme, titled "Search Inside Yourself". It teaches attention training, self-knowledge and self-mastery, and the creation of useful mental habits. In 2012, a Search Inside Yourself Leadership Institute was founded to offer the programme to a wider public.

Another innovative management strategy that several information technology companies have applied, is the so-called 20% Rule to boost creativity and initiative among employees. This management strategy allows employees to use 20% of their time during work hours to pursue whatever they like - as long as it is legal and ethical. The Australian software company Atlassian developed the idea further and introduced corporate hackathons, open events for software development lasting one or several days, encouraging creativity and free innovation. Other companies like Twitter, Facebook, Yahoo, LinkedIn, Google, and eBay have introduced similar strategies. Under LinkedIn's InCubator, creators of top experiments can get up to three months to develop their ideas (Tate, 2012).

Several institutions have been created to undertake research on, evaluate, further develop and teach similar innovative management approaches. The method developed at the Institute for Mindful Leadership in Oakland, New Jersey, is based on results from neuroscience research demonstrating that training in mindfulness and self-awareness enhances mental health and increases performance in creativity, strategic thinking and error reduction. The training for managers and employees focuses on four central themes: train the mind's innate capability to focus, see with clarity, cultivate creativity and embody compassion. Leaders from diverse organisations like the US Army and Air Force, the Red Cross, Intel and the Mayo Clinic have attended the training or hosted customised programmes at their organisations.

Another centre for the development of innovative management approaches is the Society for Organizational Learning, a global community of corporations, researchers, and consultants dedicated to the "interdependent development of people and their institutions." It originated from the Center for Organizational Learning founded and run in the 1990s by Peter Senge at the Massachusetts Institute for Technology. The work of these institutions builds on Senge's main oeuvre 'The Fifth Discipline', a theory and method for group problem solving aiming to transform companies into "learning organisations" and enhancing the ability of employees to work

...

productively towards common goals. According to this approach, understanding the perceptions and assumptions that shape actions, developing capabilities for reflective conversation, team learning and complex system thinking are the cornerstones of successful co-operation at work.

Sources:

Government of Australia, www.awpa.gov.au/our-work/better-use-of-skills/Pages/Skills-Utilisation.aspx.

Institute for Mindful Leadership, *http://instituteformindfulleadership.org/*.

Society for Organizational Learning, *www.solonline.org/?home*.

Tate, R. (2012), *The 20% Doctrine: How Tinkering, Goofing Off, and Breaking the Rules at Work Drive Success in Business*, HarperCollins, New York.

Tan, C.M. (2012), *Search Inside Yourself: The Unexpected Path to Achieving Success, Happiness (and World Peace)*, HarperCollins, New York.

There are various ways in which public policies can support employers in their efforts to make better use of young people's skills (Box 7.3). Governments can promote good human resource and management practices directly by offering skills brokerage services or by contributing to covering their costs. These measures could target small and medium-sized enterprises (SMEs), for instance by helping them engage in local clusters to achieve economies of scale, as in the case of shared training arrangements (see Chapter 3). Public employers can introduce innovative management practices to make the best use of their young employees. In some cases, government regulation can act as a trigger for improvement to skills utilisation by ensuring that quality standards are enforced. This can be the case with health and safety regulations that can lead to a better use of skills. Performance standards on products can also lead firms to improve work organisation to fulfil requirements (Sung, Ashton and Raddon, 2009). More generally, sound product market regulations that lead to healthy competition between firms can also foster the development of work organisation practices that lead to better use of skills.

Finally, the effect of work organisation practices depends on the reward system while governments have influence on wage setting systems. A reward system that encourages team work can increase the effect of work organisation practices with similar goals but group-based pay systems need to be recognised as a way to give recognition for accomplishment and not as management tools for controlling one's effort (Cox, Rickard Tamkin, 2012; OECD, 2010b). A minimum wage that is too high limits room for firms to develop this type of reward system. Likewise, in the public sector, it is also important to have wage setting systems that reward accomplishment.

REMOVING BARRIERS TO ENTREPRENEURSHIP

Entrepreneurship and education

Being entrepreneurial, creative and adaptive are qualities that are of general value in today's labour markets, especially in jobs that favour initiative and leave room for innovation. However, in many countries, young people lack the skills to become successful entrepreneurs (OECD/ECLAC, 2012).

Entrepreneurship education has three dimensions: first, to raise awareness that business creation and self-employment are viable career options, and to develop the right attitudes towards this possibility through role models and information services; second, to teach the legal, managerial, financial and technical knowledge and skills necessary to set up and run a successful business; third, to provide concrete practical support, often in the form of mentoring and other services in the business creation and establishment phase. Beyond entrepreneurship education aimed at skilling youth to create their own businesses, entrepreneurial skills and attitudes are also useful for youth looking to work in established companies, as such skills and attitudes are often valued by employers.

Developing entrepreneurship programmes

In primary education, the goals of entrepreneurship education are mainly to incite curiosity, create a basic awareness of entrepreneurship as an option for adult life, and to build the foundations for the knowledge, skills, and attitudes that are conducive to entrepreneurial behaviour. Often, this is done by inviting local entrepreneurs to visit classrooms to speak to students about running businesses. Other programmes take students to local businesses to spend the day watching and learning about the day-to-day operation of small businesses (OECD/European Union, 2012). In secondary school, entrepreneurship education focuses more on the delivery of specific technical skills using activities entailing active learning and real-life situations (European Commission, 2005; Box 7.4). For example, school students can learn about business planning and access to start-up financing through the setting up of simulation of real business enterprises (OECD/ European Union, 2012). Familiarising students early on with real business and innovative technologies can also help to widen their horizons and channel their interests into subject areas that are not traditionally part of school curricula.

Box 7.4 **Integrating entrepreneurship education at all levels of education: Country examples**

In Germany, the Students' Institute for Technology and Applied ICT (*Schüler-Institut für Technik und angewandte Informatik, SITI*), founded in 1999, is a pioneer in the field of entrepreneurship education and in the promotion of innovation and technology skills among young students, mainly from secondary schools (aged 10-18). SITI's primary aim is to support the skills development of young people in technology-oriented fields, in order to develop opportunities for a career, particularly self-employment, in innovative sectors of the economy.

SITI offers a large variety of extra-curricular learning-by-doing projects in the areas of manufacturing technology, applied ICT, natural sciences and entrepreneurship which follow a systematic and long-term oriented approach. In a so-called "ideas conference", students and coaches jointly decide on the projects to be worked upon in the next school year. Basic regular training courses in ICT, multimedia, robotics, computer-integrated manufacturing, physics and astronomy lay the foundations for the comprehensive, theme-specific project work. Each year, SITI-students work on three to four challenging research and development (R&D) projects on behalf of technology-oriented companies and universities, and on six "Young researchers" projects, as part of a national R&D-competition. In addition, students also participate in several other public competitions in the fields of R&D and entrepreneurship. SITI maintains regular and close network relations with more than 30 institutions, among them schools, universities, innovative companies, technology and start-up centres, business associations and ministries.

A SITI survey carried out among its alumni in 2013 found that approximately 75% of them had chosen career paths in technology, ICT and entrepreneurship-related fields. The alumni almost consistently point out that SITI has been strongly decisive in detecting, shaping and promoting their talents and career choices.

The University of Strathclyde in Scotland is a technological university based in Glasgow. It pioneered in entrepreneurship education by engaging alumni and opened one of the United Kingdom's first university business incubators in the 1990s as part of its vision to create a "place of useful learning". It has since become a recognised leader in entrepreneurship education, research and knowledge exchange. By engaging with alumni, many of whom are in leading influential positions in business and industry, the university maintains a lifelong relationship with mutual benefits. At "Enterprise Partners", selected alumni help the university deliver start-up services to students and other alumni at relatively low cost, and help keep entrepreneurship education relevant and inspiring.

For several decades, the university has relied on alumni as guest speakers and role models in teaching entrepreneurship, with case studies on alumni written and taught by faculty and sometimes by the alumni themselves. The Strathclyde Entrepreneurship Initiative, a teaching unit providing elective courses in entrepreneurship education across all faculties, was renamed Hunter Centre for Entrepreneurship in 2000 following a GBP 5 million endowment for the unit from Sir Tom Hunter, alumnus, entrepreneur and philanthropist. The Strathclyde University Incubator offers innovative services involving alumni, including the Upstarts programme that links researchers developing technologies with commercial potential with alumni who have relevant business experience, as well as an angel investment arm (Gabriel Investments).

In 2003, Strathclyde 100 (S100) was launched, an exclusive, invitation-only network of successful alumni and friends of the university. It meets three to four times per year to listen to students, staff and alumni pitch their new business ideas and to give feedback and advice. S100 is led by the Alumni and Development Office and supported by the Technology Transfer Office and Hunter Centre staff. The management board of S100 is chaired by the principal of the university. Currently, 45 S100 members serve as voluntary Enterprise Partners to mentor other Strathclyde early-stage entrepreneurs in their own time. Being alumni of the same university creates a unique sense of trust and altruism and many S100 members have invested in, or joined the board, of ventures presented at S100.

Entrepreneurship education can also be developed through businesses or charities than can more easily involve employers. In the United Kingdom, Young Enterprise is a large business and entrepreneurship education charity developed in the United Kingdom in the 1960s, based on the American Junior Achievement programme and now present in several EU countries. It aims to equip young people to learn and succeed through enterprise. The guiding principle is learning-by-doing and developing aptitudes and attitudes that cannot be learned from a textbook or traditional curriculum.

...

In the United Kingdom, Young Enterprise offers a number of programmes from primary school to university (age 4-25). Every year they help about 250 000 young people to learn about business and working life under the guidance of about 5 000 volunteers from 3 500 different companies. Young Enterprise does not focus solely on building entrepreneurship skills, but also on other skills such as teamwork, practical thinking, innovative and business-like behaviour in order to support students' employability.

In the Company Programme targeted at secondary and vocational education, students set up and run a real firm for a year under the guidance of a business volunteer. The Entrepreneurship Masterclass is a half-day seminar that challenges students to think about starting their own business as a career by exposing them to the vision, experiences and achievements of real entrepreneurs; in presentations, activities and discussions around the theme of entrepreneurship students get an overview of the personal qualities needed to run a business. The Industry Masterclass gives students an insight into the workings of a particular type of business and the skills needed to build a career in it, what jobs are available and how to go about starting up a business in that sector. All the programmes include interactive workshop sessions to encourage students to think about and rehearse responses they would make to obstacles that come up and to ask questions and seek advice from the teachers and practitioners.

Sources:

OECD (2003), *Entrepreneurship and Local Economic Development: Programme and Policy Recommendations*, Local Economic and Employment Development (LEED), OECD Publishing, Paris, *http://dx.doi.org/10.1787/9789264199798-en*.

Young Enterprise, *www.young-enterprise.org.uk*.

Students' Institute for Technology, *www.siti.de/*.

Higher education is increasingly engaging in entrepreneurship education programmes (Box 7.4). Traditional approaches at this level have been to create entrepreneurship schools at universities or to integrate entrepreneurship within traditional subject teaching. It has become evident that entrepreneurship is best supported by developing implementation skills rather than solely theoretical knowledge. Universities are therefore reaching out to external assistance to fill their own competence and resource gaps, establish interdisciplinary programmes or partner with real-life businesses and facilitate the encounter of would-be entrepreneurs with experienced professionals and potential funding sources (OECD, 2008b).

Entrepreneurship training is also being developed within vocational education and training (VET). However, current entrepreneurship education in VET seems to emphasise mainly on training in the development of business plans for new enterprises (OECD/European Union, 2012). While this is important, the focus should also be on actual business creation and on ensuring that students get real-world experience in the workplace and with mature businesses in their fields. An integration of entrepreneurship education into VET programmes can be expanded at all levels, from a revision of the curricula, teacher training, to new forms of assessment and accreditation and – most importantly – more effective engagement with entrepreneurs.

Entrepreneurship skills and attitudes can also be developed outside the formal education system and in the context of career guidance and active labour market policies for young people. Governments can partner with community and business organisations to promote entrepreneurship. These programmes typically provide young people with a first-hand look at the day-to-day operation of small firms. Alternatively, entrepreneurship mentorship programmes such as the "Erasmus for Young Entrepreneurs" programme, in the European Union, or the "Young Enterprise Company", in the United Kingdom, and "Young Achievement" programmes in Australia, help new entrepreneurs acquire the skills for running a small business through interaction with other entrepreneurs (OECD/European Union, 2012). Evidence shows that these programmes have developed entrepreneurship skills in young people and increased the chances of success of their start-ups (CSES, 2011; Athayde, 2009; Peterman and Kennedy, 2003).

A decision to become an entrepreneur can also be influenced by family tradition and social background. Whether society and potential employers consider an unsuccessful attempt to create a business as a failure, or values it can be instrumental in encouraging or deterring a young person from venturing down the entrepreneurship path. Role models of both women and men as successful entrepreneurs are often pivotal in supporting entrepreneurial intentions (Van Auken, Fry and Stephens, 2006) and are integral to developing and sustaining new start-ups (Bosma et al., 2012). Examples of entrepreneurial role models that have successfully created pathways out of economic disadvantage can be important to particular communities and individuals where entrepreneurship is under-represented. For example, young people with low educational attainment are less likely to have role models, which may discourage their attempts to develop and sustain their new businesses (Bosma et al., 2012). Some educational institutions have managed to make very effective use of their own alumni network to serve as role models and entrepreneurship mentors for students (Box 7.5).

Box 7.5 **Specific support to youth entrepreneurship: Country examples**

Countries have developed various types of targeted support to youth entrepreneurship in various areas (OECD/ European Union, 2014).

Financial support

Start-up support grants typically have strong selection criteria to determine who is eligible for support. They are often awarded through a competition, where applicants are judged by their business plans. The EXIST Business Start-up Grant in Germany, for example, supports university graduates and students in developing their business ideas into business plans and advancing into products and services. To cover their living expenses, the entrepreneurs receive a grant of EUR 800 – 2 500 per month for a maximum of 12 months. In addition, they may receive materials and equipment grants (worth EUR 10 000 for solo starts and EUR 17 000 for team starts), funding for coaching (EUR 5 000) and, if necessary, child benefit of EUR 100 per month and per child. The university can also offer them access to infrastructure.

There are relatively few micro-finance schemes that target youth specifically, but one example is "The Plan for Self-Employment" in Belgium that provides low-interest loans for young people under the age of 30. The French government in partnership with regional Directorates for Youth, Sports and Social Cohesion has also set up a micro-finance scheme, *DEFi jeunes* for young people aged 18-30. Financed through a combination of national funding and private sector sponsors, the programme selects young people through regional and national competitions and supports them with up to EUR 6 000 for a period of two years.

Private and public entrepreneurship centres

For many years, the city of Shawinigan (Québec, Canada) was an industrial town built around its large electric power facility and heavy industry. The city was strongly affected, however, by structural changes in the global economy with many employers shutting down their operations. The city is now pursuing an approach that seeks to develop a community of entrepreneurs and small business operations as a sustainable economic base. In collaboration with the school commission, Shawinigan opened the Entrepreneurship Centre in 2013. The Entrepreneurship Centre offers skills development programmes along with other support measures that will allow for the growth of a critical mass of entrepreneurs. Future entrepreneurs will be supported over a five-year period: the first 18 months will be focused on training and start-up; the second 18 months will be dedicated to management and operations within space provided in the centre; the final two years will be given to consolidating the operations of the new enterprise and its relocation into the community. A textile factory will rent commercial and office space at market rates to established businesses as a way to generate revenue for the centre (OECD, 2014e).

Impact Hubs in the United Kingdom have similar aims and strategies, except that they are based on private, rather than government, initiative. They are physical spaces for co-operation and co-creation where young people can rent an office or room for a low fee to develop their business ideas into start-up companies. The first Impact Hub opened in central London in early 2005. Today, Global Impact Hubs are a rapidly expanding network of currently over 7 000 members in 54 locations around the world. Impact Hubs consist of three distinct elements. First, it is a community of entrepreneurial people who share an underlying intention to bring about positive change and act as peers to cross-fertilise and develop their ventures. Second, it can act as a source of inspiration and learning through events, innovation labs, learning spaces, incubation, programmes and facilitated conversations. Third, an Impact Hub is a physical space that offers a flexible infrastructure to work, meet and learn.

Many universities have incubators for their students and graduates. An example of linking students into existing facilities is the Technology Centre and Business Incubator in the city of Brandenburg in Germany, currently housing 45 companies and organisations, where business start-ups can make use of a "start-up package" that includes services such as tax consulting, advertising, banking services and office equipment. Students of the nearby Brandenburg University of Applied Sciences are assisted with access through the Studenten im TGZ (Students in TGZ) programme, which exempts them from paying rent in the incubator for 6-12 months. The students are selected through a business plan competition.

...

Integrated approach

The programme *IkStartSmart* ("I Start Smart") in the Netherlands is an integrated support programme for people in the province of Gelderland who wish to start a business or develop an existing business that is less than five years old. Businesses in this province have lower than average survival rates and there are few policy instruments that aim to support new start-ups. The programme aims to increase business creation in Gelderland and to support young businesses in their development.

The *IkStartSmart* initiative uses an eight-step scheme to train and support new business owners. First, potential participants attend information meetings that screen their interest and suitability for the support. Following this, participants take a test to identify their strengths and weaknesses and the results are discussed with a business advisor from the Chamber of Commerce. In this meeting the advisor designs a personal training plan. Coaches are then assigned and their role is defined in collaboration with the participant. The aim of the coach is to support personal development. The business advice stage provides access to more specialised business support and relies on experts to provide more technical support than the coaches. This is complemented with training according to the personal plan and networking workshops. The final stage supports access to microcredit, which are offered by partner organisations. Participants pay a fee of EUR 250 for this support.

An evaluation shows that the IkStartSmart programme achieved all of its stated objectives (OECD, 2014d) even though the programme has wide eligibility criteria, namely all those individuals who have had their own company for a maximum of five years, regardless of gender, age or background. A significant proportion of entrepreneurs were women and immigrants.

Sources:

OECD/European Union (2014), *The Missing Entrepreneurs 2014: Policies for Inclusive Entrepreneurship in Europe*, OECD Publishing, Paris, *http:// dx.doi.org/10.1787/9789264213593-en*.

OECD/European Union (2012), *Policy Brief on Youth Entrepreneurship: Entrepreneurial Activities in Europe*, Publications Office of the European Union, Luxembourg.

OECD (2014e), *Employment and Skills Strategies in Canada*, OECD Reviews on Local Job Creation, OECD Publishing, Paris, *http://dx.doi. org/10.1787/9789264209374-en*.

The effectiveness of entrepreneurship education

Available research on school programmes suggests that students' interest increased after they were introduced to entrepreneurship (ILO, 2006; Lepoutre et al., 2010). Furthermore, surveys show that participants in entrepreneurship education are at least 20% more likely than other groups to engage in entrepreneurship in the early part of their careers, though the study does not specify whether the participants and non-participants shared the same characteristics or whether the engagement with entrepreneurship was driven by the same factors (such as motivation and interest or a parent entrepreneur) as participation in the education programme in the first place (Danish Foundation for Entrepreneurship, 2010).

There are also some contrasting results, however: students who participated in the Dutch Association *Jong Ondernemen* (part of the Junior Achievement programme) were more likely to form negative intentions towards entrepreneurship and have lower self-assessed enterprise skills (Oosterbeek, van Praag and Ijsselstein, 2010), which may simply highlight that entrepreneurship is not for everybody and that some students realised this during the programme (OECD/European Union, 2012).

At university level, there is evidence that some programmes are effective and could usefully be adopted more broadly. For example, French and UK engineering and science university students who had taken part in enterprise education had increased entrepreneurial intentions (Souitaris, Zerbinati and Al-Laham, 2007), while for one programme in the United States, entrepreneurship students were three times more likely to start a business than business students and their start-ups had more sales and employees compared to a matched sample of non-entrepreneurship business graduates from the same school (Charney and Libecap, 2000). Key elements of that programme included its adaptability and incorporation into mainstream education, new venture classes, links with the local business community, and consulting projects for undergraduate and graduate students.

Barriers to creating enterprises

Entrepreneurs face various challenges, due to the small size of their business, imperfections in labour, product and financial markets, and the higher (real or perceived) risks of this type of employment. Young people typically have even greater difficulties starting and growing their own businesses since they lack experience, networks and a history of successful ventures to attract funding. They need integrated support beyond entrepreneurship education to get their businesses off the ground and running.

Start-up support

Cost-effective entrepreneurship support for young people is selective. Several of the most successful programmes measured in terms of business growth and survival have operated strong selection criteria, which ensure that support goes to those young people with the most promising projects and human capital resources (OECD/European Union, 2012).

In addition, some groups of young people could benefit from specific support to entrepreneurship. The promotion of business creation by young people who face multiple disadvantages and are under-represented in entrepreneurship and self-employment is seen as a way for governments to address problems of social exclusion (OECD/European Commission, 2013). Such groups include ethnic minorities, those living in deprived areas, those from low-income families and those with low education levels.

The long-term unemployed (including unemployed youth) might be willing to become self-employed as an alternative to unemployment. However, their abilities to operate successful businesses and to access funding can decline as skills erode and scarring effects appear with time spent in unemployment. There is also evidence that businesses created by the unemployed generate fewer jobs than those established by the employed (OECD, 2003). A good policy example that addresses this challenge is the UK programme "Outset" which fosters entrepreneurship among the long-term unemployed. It includes a strong filter because it acknowledges that not all individuals have the risk-prone behaviour or skills to be successful entrepreneurs. After filtering, offering support and follow-ups, this programme has been relatively successful in activating the long-term unemployed (including under-25 year-olds) and providing them with a sustainable source of income.

Migrants are found to have a higher entrepreneurial spirit, even after controlling for individual observed characteristics (OECD, 2010c). At the same time, they might have greater difficulties navigating the legal and financial landscapes of the host country, and may need targeted assistance that might differ somewhat from assistance offered to the native youth (OECD, 2010c and 2013b). To effectively reach these marginalised groups, efforts should be made to target entrepreneurship support and training to their needs, and make such support and training both visible and accessible.

Framework conditions and specific funding programmes

The lack of initial capital and difficulty in obtaining finance from private lenders is often identified as the most significant barrier to business start-up for entrepreneurs, especially for youth (European Commission, 2009). Bankers and other lenders or investors might not have sufficient trust in the capabilities of young people to succeed in building and running their businesses if they lack proof of credit history, past business performance and collateral (OECD, 2001 and 2003). Young entrepreneurs from disadvantaged backgrounds, in particular, often find it difficult to borrow from banks, as they can offer neither collateral nor a track record of successful repayments. In response, governments have developed various finance programmes designed to support young entrepreneurs.

One commonly used tool is to provide grants to young entrepreneurs to develop their business ideas into business plans. Another option is to provide micro-financing which requires the young entrepreneurs to repay the loan at a lower than market value interest rate or to deliver micro-financing through financial institutions by offering loan guarantees. In these schemes, the government assumes some risk on behalf of the financial institution by covering a significant portion of defaulted loans (Box 7.5).

In addition, many countries have also been proactive in stimulating equity financing (Canada, Chile, Denmark, Finland, France, Italy, the Netherlands, New Zealand, Sweden and the United Kingdom). A growing number of countries, the Netherlands, New Zealand, the United Kingdom for example, have measures in place to support angel and venture capital investment, including through the creation of public-private co-investment funds to leverage private investment (OECD, 2011b).

Policies aimed at improving framework conditions have also been common. France has introduced the legal status of the auto-entrepreneur in 2009, a form of self-employment benefiting from a favourable tax regime. Special pro tempore fiscal measures for new firms (e.g. tax exemptions and tax deferments) have been tested in France, Italy, New Zealand and Sweden (OECD, 2012). These reforms are not specifically targeted at youth, but like regulations governing, the registration process of new businesses, for instance, concern all entrepreneurs alike.

There is limited evidence on the impact of financial support programmes and results are often mixed (OECD/European Union, 2012). Moreover, difficulties in gaining access to finance do not necessarily constitute evidence of market failure but can constitute rather a healthy market mechanism ensuring the birth of more viable enterprises. Three lessons nevertheless seem to emerge from the evaluation evidence of financial measures to support youth entrepreneurship. First, using selection criteria to identify participants who are most likely to succeed will increase success in terms of business start-up, growth and survival rates, although addressing the barriers of the most disadvantaged youth is a harder challenge that may call for different benchmarks. Second, support needs to be limited in time to avoid the risk of assisting unsustainable projects. Third, financing programmes work better when they are complemented by other start-up support measures, including advice, coaching and mentoring; integrated approaches are effective because financial and non-financial support reinforce each other (OECD, 2003, Walsh et al., 2001; Meager, Bates and Cowling, 2003).

Social security systems

Social security systems can exert a negative influence on entrepreneurship because relative to employees, self-employed people may pay more for the same benefits (e.g. paying for both the employer's and employee's contributions), receive fewer benefits for the same costs (e.g. lower pension benefits) or be ineligible for certain benefits (e.g. unemployment insurance). Individual entrepreneurs might have difficulty working with complex systems which the employer would normally deal with. Becoming an entrepreneur might entail losing existing benefits or facing requirements to contribute to the system for longer before being eligible for benefits (OECD/European Commission, 2013).

There are several ways to improve the design of social security systems to support young entrepreneurs. Welfare bridges allow claimants to continue receiving benefits in some form while they are establishing their own businesses. This eases the financial transition from welfare to self-employment and in some cases allows them to have a certain amount of start-up capital. Cuts in social contribution and taxes can ease the financial strain of starting a new business. However, they need to include carry-over provision or cash refund mechanisms to benefit young entrepreneurs who lose money in the early stage. Regulatory impact analyses should be undertaken when making amendments to social security systems, and they should include the impacts on entrepreneurship in general, and inclusive entrepreneurship in particular (OECD/European Commission, 2013).

Networks, shared labs and workshops

A common problem facing new entrepreneurs is a situation of isolation in the start-up phase (OECD/European Union, 2012). Business networks are important for young entrepreneurs because they provide opportunities to make contacts and represent interests (Chigunta, 2002; OECD, 2001, OECD/European Commission, 2013). Another tool that has frequently shown success is the business incubator. In addition to start-up financing, business incubators provide a physical work location where start-up entrepreneurs group together and, in most cases, supply complementary support, including coaching, mentoring, legal advice and access to an experienced network of experts. Some of the most successful public and private entrepreneurship centres (Box 7.5) are designed on such a model where the shared space of collaboration and co-creation plays an essential role. Finally, many young entrepreneurs state that they need more managerial skills and help to run a business and develop it beyond the initial start-up phase. However, continued assistance beyond the first year of operation is rare (OECD, 2001) or not well-targeted at their needs. Some countries or regions have managed, though, to extend their entrepreneurship services to include support for the first few years beyond business creation (Box 7.5).

KEY POINTS FOR POLICY

Not making full use of young people skills can be a waste of investment in education and a missed opportunity for individuals, employers and the society to reap the returns on the investment necessary to build these skills. Several policies can help to make better use of youth skills.

Limit skills mismatch and make better use of skills

- Remove barriers to geographical mobility to allow for local matching of jobs and skills. Housing policies and infrastructure policies can be designed in a more efficient way to remove some of the barriers to geographical mobility.
- Take stock of the spread of non-compete clauses and of their impact. Governments and employer and employee organisations can work together to assess the spread of clauses that restrict the use of skills of employees after resigning or after their contract is terminated.
- Develop national and international qualification frameworks to facilitate recruitment processes and ensure that young people enter jobs that match their skills.
- Develop formal recognition of skills acquired through non-formal and informal learning to better signal skills to employers. These systems can help migrants signal their skills and reduce the prevalence of over-qualification and over-skilling among them.
- Promote more effective work organisation and human resource management strategies.
- Develop high-quality systems and tools for assessing and anticipating skills needs.

Remove barriers to entrepreneurship

- Integrate high-quality entrepreneurship education more prominently at all levels of education, and in partnership with successful entrepreneurs. To ensure quality, these programmes need to be assessed carefully.
- Make sure that framework conditions are conducive to the creation of dynamic firms. Sound framework labour and product-market conditions, high-quality tertiary education programmes and infrastructure, as well as business-friendly environments can attract venture capital and facilitate start-up creation.
- Carefully design support to entrepreneurship needs and limit measures in time. They can target two groups: those who are selected for having the most promising projects, and those who face extra barriers.
- Encourage the development of various forms of public and private co-operation in the form of networks or shared facilities. Strengthen co-operation between universities and employers.

Note

1. Articles have been published on cases in the United States in the *New York Times* (*www.nytimes.com/2014/06/09/business/noncompete-clauses-increasingly-pop-up-in-array-of-jobs.html?_r=1*; *http://www.nytimes.com/2014/10/15/upshot/when-the-guy-making-your-sandwich-has-a-noncompete-clause.html?_r=0*); and in Denmark in *Politiken* (*www.euractiv.com/sections/social-europe-jobs/clauses-danish-student-contracts-inhibit-future-employment-301388*).

References

Athayde, R. (2009), "Measuring enterprise potential in young people", *Entrepreneurship Theory and Practice*, Vol. 33, pp. 481–500.

Becker, G. (1964), *Human Capital: A Theoretical and Empirical Analysis, with Special Reference to Education*, University of Chicago Press, Chicago.

Bishara, N., K Martin, and R. Thomas (2015), "An empirical analysis of CEO noncompetition clauses and other restrictive post-employment covenants", *Vanderbilt Law Review*, Vol. 68, No. 1.

Bonfanti, S. and T. Xenogiani (2014), "Migrants' skills: Use, mismatch and labour market outcomes – A first exploration of the International Survey of Adult Skills (PIAAC)", in OECD and European Union, *Matching Economic Migration with Labour Market Needs*, OECD Publishing, Paris, *http://dx.doi.org/10.1787/9789264216501-11-en*.

Bosma, N. et al. (2012), "Entrepreneurship and role models", *Journal of Economic Psychology*, Vol. 33/2, pp. 410-424.

Caers, R. and V. Castelyns (2011), "LinkedIn and Facebook in Belgium: The Influences and Biases of Social Network Sites in Recruitment and Selection Procedures", *http://ssc.sagepub.com/content/29/4/437.full.pdf+html*.

Caldera Sánchez, A. and D. Andrews (2011), "Residential mobility and public policy in OECD countries", *OECD Journal: Economic Studies*, Vol. 2011/1, *http://dx.doi.org/10.1787/eco_studies-2011-5kg0vswqt240*.

Charney, A. and G.D. Libecap (2000), "The impact of entrepreneurship education: An evaluation of the Berger Entrepreneurship Program at the University of Arizona 1985–1999", paper submitted to the Kauffman Centre for Entrepreneurial Leadership.

Chigunta, F. (2002), *Youth Entrepreneurship: Meeting the Key Policy Challenges*, Oxford University, Oxford.

Cox, A., C. Rickard and P. Tamkin (2012), "Work organisation and innovation",European Foundation for the Improvement of Living and Working Conditions.

CSES (2011), "Interim evaluation of the 'Erasmus for Young Entrepreneurs' pilot project/preparatory action", Centre for Strategy and Evaluation Services.

Danish Foundation for Entrepreneurship (2010), "Impact of entrepreneurship education in Denmark", *http://archive.ja-ye.org/ Download/impact_of_entrepreneurship_education_in_dk.pdf* (accessed 8 August 2014).

Eurofound (2013), "Working conditions of young entrants to the labour market", European Foundation for the Improvement of Living and Working Conditions.

European Commission (2009), "Entrepreneurship in the EU and beyond – A survey in the EU, EFTA countries, Croatia, Turkey, the US, Japan, South Korea and China", *Flash Eurobarometer*, No. 283.

European Commission (2005), "Mini-companies in secondary education", Best Procedure Project: Final Report of the Expert Group.

Froy, F., S. Giguère and M. Meghnagi (2012), "Skills for Competitiveness: A Synthesis Report", *OECD Local Economic and Employment Development (LEED) Working Papers*, 2012/09, OECD Publishing, Paris, *http://dx.doi.org/10.1787/5k98xwskmvr6-en*.

Garrison, M. J. and J. T. Wendt (2008), "The Evolving Law of Employee Noncompete Agreements: Recent Trends and an Alternative Policy Approach", Ethics and Business Law Faculty Publications, Paper 15, *http://ir.stthomas.edu/ocbeblpub/15*.

ILO (2006), "Stimulating Youth Entrepreneurship: Barriers and incentives to enterprise start-ups by young people", *Series on Youth and Entrepreneurship, SEED Working Paper* No 76, International Labour Organization.

Ichniowski, C, G. Prennushi, and K. Shaw (1997), "The effects of human resource management practices on productivity", *American Economic Review*, Vol. 86.

Ichniowski, C. and K. Shaw (2009), "Insider econometrics: empirical studies of how management matters", *National Bureau of Economic Research Working Papers*, No. 15618.

Kuhn, P. and H. Mansour, (2014), "Is Internet Job Search Still Ineffective?", *The Economic Journal*, Vol. 124.

Lepoutre, J., et al. (2010), "A new approach to testing the effects of entrepreneurship education among secondary school pupils", *Vlerick Leuven Gent Working Paper Series* 2010/01.

Manning, A. and B. Petrongolo (2011), "How Local Are Labor Markets? Evidence from a Spatial Job Search Model", *IZA Discussion Papers*, No. 6178, Institute for the Study of Labor (IZA).

Marx M. (2011), "The Firm Strikes Back Non-compete Agreements and the Mobility of Technical Professionals", *American Sociological Review*, No. 76, Vol. 5.

Marx, M. and L. Fleming (2012), "Non-compete Agreements: Barriers to Entry…and Exit?" in Innovation Policy and the Economy, Vol. 12, National Bureau of Economic Research.

Meager N., P. Bates and M. Cowling (2003), "An evaluation of business start-up support for young people", *National Institute Economic Review*, No. 183, October.

Nishii, L.H., D.P. Lepak, and B.Schneider (2008), "Employee attributions of the 'why' of HR practices: Their effects on employee attitudes and behaviors, and customer satisfaction", *Personnel Psychology*, Vol. 61, No. 3.

OECD (2014a), *OECD Employment Outlook 2014*, OECD Publishing, Paris, *http://dx.doi.org/10.1787/empl_outlook-2014-en*.

OECD (2014b), "Labour market integration of immigrants and their children: Developing, activating and using skills", in OECD, *International Migration Outlook 2014*, OECD Publishing, Paris, *http://dx.doi.org/10.1787/migr_outlook-2014-5-en*.

OECD (2014c), « Vers une croissance plus inclusive de la métropole Aix-Marseille: Une perspective internationale », *www.oecd.org/ regional/regional-policy/Aix-Marseille.pdf*.

OECD (2014d), *Job Creation and Local Economic Development*, OECD Publishing, Paris, *http://dx.doi.org/10.1787/9789264215009-en*.

OECD (2014e), *Employment and Skills Strategies in Canada*, OECD Reviews on Local Job Creation, OECD Publishing, Paris, *http://dx.doi.org/10.1787/9789264209374-en*.

OECD (2013a), *OECD Skills Outlook 2013: First Results from the Survey of Adult Skills*, OECD Publishing, Paris, *http://dx.doi.org/10.1787/9789264204256-en*.

OECD (2013b), *Entrepreneurship at a Glance 2013*, OECD Publishing, Paris, *http://dx.doi.org/10.1787/entrepreneur_aag-2013-en*.

OECD (2012), *Financing SMEs and Entrepreneurs 2012: An OECD Scoreboard*, OECD Publishing, Paris, *http://dx.doi.org/10.1787/9789264166769-en*.

OECD (2011a), *OECD Employment Outlook 2011*, OECD Publishing, Paris, *http://dx.doi.org/10.1787/empl_outlook-2011-en*.

OECD (2011b), *Financing High-Growth Firms: The Role of Angel Investors*, OECD Publishing, Paris, *http://dx.doi.org/10.1787/9789264118782-en*.

OECD (2010a), *Learning for Jobs*, The OECD Reviews of Vocational Education and Training, OECD Publishing, Paris, *http://dx.doi.org/10.1787/9789264087460-en*.

OECD (2010b), *Innovative Workplaces: Making Better Use of the Skills within Organisations*, OECD Publishing, Paris, *www.oecd-ilibrary.org/content/book/9789264095687-en*.

OECD (2010c), *Open for Business: Migrant Entrepreneurship in OECD Countries*, OECD Publishing, Paris, *http://dx.doi.org/10.1787/9789264095830-en*.

OECD (2008a), *Jobs for Immigrants (Vol. 2): Labour Market Integration in Belgium, France, the Netherlands and Portugal*, OECD Publishing, Paris, *http://dx.doi.org/10.1787/9789264055605-en*.

OECD (2008b), *Entrepreneurship and Higher Education*, Local Economic and Employment Development (LEED), OECD Publishing, Paris, *http://dx.doi.org/10.1787/9789264044104-en*.

OECD (2007a), "Matching educational background and employment: A challenge for immigrants in host countries", *in International Migration Outlook 2007*, OECD Publishing, Paris, *http://dx.doi.org/10.1787/migr_outlook-2007-4-en*.

OECD (2007b), *Jobs for Immigrants (Vol. 1): Labour Market Integration in Australia, Denmark, Germany and Sweden*, OECD Publishing, Paris, *http://dx.doi.org/10.1787/9789264033603-en*.

OECD (2003), *Entrepreneurship and Local Economic Development: Programme and Policy Recommendations*, Local Economic and Employment Development (LEED), OECD Publishing, Paris, *http://dx.doi.org/10.1787/9789264199798-en*.

OECD (2001), *Putting the Young in Business: Policy Challenges for Youth Entrepreneurship*, OECD Publishing, Paris, *http://dx.doi.org/10.1787/9789264188648-en*.

OECD/ECLAC (2012), *Latin American Economic Outlook 2013: SME Policies for Structural Change*, OECD Publishing, Paris, *http://dx.doi.org/10.1787/leo-2013-en*.

OECD/European Commission (2013), *The Missing Entrepreneurs: Policies for Inclusive Entrepreneurship in Europe*, OECD Publishing, Paris, *http://dx.doi.org/10.1787/9789264188167-en*.

OECD/European Union (2014), *The Missing Entrepreneurs 2014: Policies for Inclusive Entrepreneurship in Europe*, OECD Publishing, Paris, *http://dx.doi.org (manquant sur mail)*.

OECD/European Union (2012), *Policy Brief on Youth Entrepreneurship: Entrepreneurial Activities in Europe*, Publications Office of the European Union, Luxembourg.

Oosterbeek, H., M. van Praag and A. Ijsselstein (2010), "The impact of entrepreneurship education on entrepreneurship skills and motivation", *European Economic Review*, Vol. 54, pp. 442–454.

Peterman, N.E. and J. Kennedy (2003), "Enterprise education: Influencing students' perceptions of entrepreneurship", *Entrepreneurship Theory and Practice*, Vol. 28, pp. 129–144.

Şahin, A., J. Song, G. Topa, and G. L. Violante (2012), "Mismatch Unemployment", *NBER Working Paper*, No. 18265.

Skills Australia (2012), "Better use of skills, better outcomes: A research report on skills utilisation in Australia", Department of Education, Employment and Workplace Relations, Canberra.

Society for Human Resource Management (2013), "SHRM Survey Findings: Social Networking Websites and Recruiting/Selection", *http://www.shrm.org/research/surveyfindings/articles/pages/shrm-social-networking-websites-recruiting-job-candidates.aspx*.

Souitaris, V., S. Zerbinati and A. Al-Laham (2007), "Do entrepreneurship programmes raise entrepreneurial intention of science and engineering students? The effect of learning, inspiration and resources", *Journal of Business Venturing*, Vol. 22, pp. 566–591.

Sung, J., D. Ashton and A. Raddon (2009), *Product Market Strategies and Workforce Skills*, Futureskills Scotland, The Scottish Government, Edinburgh.

Tan, C.-M. (2012) *Search Inside yourself: The Unexpected Path to Achieving Success, Happiness (and World Peace)*, HarperCollins, New York.

Tate, R. (2012), *The 20% Doctrine: How Tinkering, Goofing Off, and Breaking the Rules at Work Drive Success in Business*, HarperCollins, New York.

Van Auken, H., F.L. Fry, and P. Stephens (2006), "The influence of role models on entrepreneurial intentions", *Journal of Developmental Entrepreneurship*, Vol. 11/2, pp. 157–167.

Walsh, K., et al. (2001), "Evaluation of the net impact of the active labour market programme in Bulgaria", Ministry of Labour and Social Policy of Bulgaria, Rotterdam.

Wharton University (2014), "Assessing employability is disrupting India's higher education model", *http://knowledge.wharton.upenn. edu/article/assessing-employability-disrupting-indias-higher-education-model/*.

ORGANISATION FOR ECONOMIC CO-OPERATION AND DEVELOPMENT

The OECD is a unique forum where governments work together to address the economic, social and environmental challenges of globalisation. The OECD is also at the forefront of efforts to understand and to help governments respond to new developments and concerns, such as corporate governance, the information economy and the challenges of an ageing population. The Organisation provides a setting where governments can compare policy experiences, seek answers to common problems, identify good practice and work to co-ordinate domestic and international policies.

The OECD member countries are: Australia, Austria, Belgium, Canada, Chile, the Czech Republic, Denmark, Estonia, Finland, France, Germany, Greece, Hungary, Iceland, Ireland, Israel, Italy, Japan, Korea, Luxembourg, Mexico, the Netherlands, New Zealand, Norway, Poland, Portugal, the Slovak Republic, Slovenia, Spain, Sweden, Switzerland, Turkey, the United Kingdom and the United States. The European Union takes part in the work of the OECD.

OECD Publishing disseminates widely the results of the Organisation's statistics gathering and research on economic, social and environmental issues, as well as the conventions, guidelines and standards agreed by its members.

OECD PUBLISHING, 2, rue André-Pascal, 75775 PARIS CEDEX 16
(87 2014 01 1P) ISBN 978-92-64-21087-5 – 2015-17